P9-DXE-529

Praise for *The Formula*

"If you are a parent or plan to be, read this book. You'll learn what you can do—and there is a lot you can do—to help your child succeed in the fullest sense of the word. Beautifully written, impeccably crafted. I loved it."

—Angela Duckworth, author of *Grit: The Power of Passion and Perseverance*

"This highly engaging and important book reveals the vital roles parents can play in supporting a growth mindset. *The Formula*'s fascinating real-world case studies provide much-needed guidelines for developing fully realized human beings."

—Carol S. Dweck, PhD, author of *Mindset: The New Psychology of Success* and professor at Stanford University

"I have known from the very beginning of my career that parenting really matters. In many ways it's the most important asset a child has in reaching his or her full potential. I am convinced that it is the major contributor to the academic and social differences between poor and middle-class children. Knowing that and understanding why and what we should do about it has remained a difficult challenge. Now we have the answers in *The Formula*. This book is the most thoughtful, analytical, and comprehensive study to date on parenting. It is a must-read for all parents and those of us who care about closing the achievement gap for poor children. It is well written, thoroughly researched, interesting, and compelling. It is a must-read!"

—Geoffrey Canada, founder and president of Harlem Children's Zone

"*The Formula* is for all parents who want to be powerful advocates and strategic partners for their kids. Refreshingly practical, it unpacks what parents of high-achieving adults did to help their children be successful and happy."

—Bridget Terry Long, PhD, dean of the Harvard Graduate School of Education

"With over forty years of education experience, I have learned that a child's success isn't solely dependent on grades or standardized tests. Success starts first and foremost at home, with parents that support an intrinsic motivation for their children to reach their fullest potential. However, just as children have different learning styles, parents, as well, have different parenting styles. *The Formula* masterfully combines the latest research with compelling, real-life stories and introduces us to different parenting styles and provides a formula for teaching, motivating, and empowering successful children."

—John D. Couch, Apple's first VP of Education and coauthor of *Rewiring Education*

"*The Formula* pursues an important question that social scientists, preoccupied with explaining the problematic outcomes of childhood, seldom address: the role parents play in developing children—regardless of their race, class, or national origin—who become extraordinarily successful in life. Ferguson and Robertson's compelling analysis of data collected on the life stories of interesting people who change the world is a must-read."

—William Julius Wilson, Lewis P. and Linda L. Geyser University Professor at Harvard University and author of *More than Just Race*

THE FORMULA

THE FORMULA

UNLOCKING THE SECRETS TO RAISING HIGHLY SUCCESSFUL CHILDREN

Ronald F. Ferguson and Tatsha Robertson

BenBella Books, Inc.
Dallas, TX

BenBella Books, Inc.
10440 N. Central Expressway, Suite 800
Dallas, TX 75231
www.benbellabooks.com
Send feedback to feedback@benbellabooks.com

Printed in the United States of America
10 9 8 7 6 5 4 3 2 1

Library of Congress Cataloging-in-Publication Data
Names: Ferguson, Ronald F., author. | Robertson, Tatsha, author.
Title: The formula : unlocking the secrets to raising highly successful children / Ronald F. Ferguson and Tatsha Robertson.
Description: Dallas, TX : BenBella Books, Inc., 2019. | Includes bibliographical references and index.
Identifiers: LCCN 2018033945 (print) | LCCN 2018050421 (ebook) | ISBN 9781946885616 (electronic) | ISBN 9781946885067 (trade cloth : alk. paper)
Subjects: LCSH: Child rearing. | Parenting. | Parent and child.
Classification: LCC HQ769 (ebook) | LCC HQ769 .F36 2019 (print) | DDC 306.874—dc23
LC record available at https://lccn.loc.gov/2018033945

Editing by Leah Wilson
Copyediting by James Fraleigh
Proofreading by Michael Fedison and Lisa Story
Indexing by Debra Bowman
Text design by Publishers' Design and Production Services, Inc.
Text composition by PerfecType, Nashville, TN
Cover design by Faceout Studio, Lindy Martin
Cover photo © iStock / Viperfzk
Printed by Lake Book Manufacturing

Distributed to the trade by Two Rivers Distribution, an Ingram brand
www.tworiversdistribution.com

To all the people who made us who we are

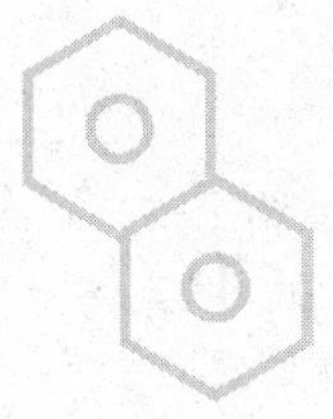

CONTENTS

CHAPTER 4
The Strategists 49

CHAPTER 5
The Early-Learning Partner (Role #1) 61

CHAPTER 6
The Flight Engineer (Role #2) 85

CHAPTER 7
Siblings 103

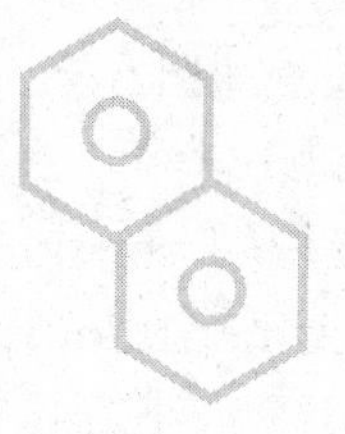

INTRODUCTION

ORIGIN STORIES OF EXTRAORDINARY PEOPLE

Primary night, 2015. Ryan Quarles, a handsome farmer with prematurely gray-speckled hair, paced a hotel suite floor. The night was going to be the best of the young man's life—or one of his biggest failures. At thirty-two years old, Quarles was running for agriculture commissioner for the entire state of Kentucky. He had arrived earlier feeling confident because he had campaigned hard, but now the numbers were looking ominous. It was becoming clearer that his lack of name recognition around the state made his chance of winning slim. Still, he was a ninth-generation farmer who knew situations could change in a flash.

He would win that night by a single percentage point. Weeks later, in the general election, he was victorious by twenty points over his Democratic opponent and became the youngest elected state official in the United States. But it was not his first big campaign win. Six years earlier, at the age of twenty-six, he beat out a fourteen-year incumbent for a state legislative seat, becoming the first Republican since the Civil War to hold it.

Becoming the Kentucky agriculture commissioner gave Ryan "a great sense of accomplishment," he said. "A sense that a kid from a farm, who grew up in a tobacco patch, could succeed."

Ryan started on his path to success as a tiny preschool boy on the farm, performing his job counting seedlings. That meticulous task helped him develop numeracy and patience that gave him a great advantage over other children when he entered the classroom. By age nine, his diligence and excellent grades had earned him entry into the world of politics when he became a page in the statehouse. Four years after enrolling at the University of Kentucky, Ryan graduated with a triple major, summa cum laude with high honors. What's even more impressive is that he completed all of that coursework during his first two years of college. During the final two years of what should have been undergraduate coursework, he finished one master's degree in international trade and development and another in agricultural economics. His schooling was financed partly by a Truman Scholarship, a prestigious national award he secured during his junior year. By the time he was elected agriculture commissioner, he had also earned a law degree and a master's degree in education, the latter from an Ivy League university and fully funded by another prestigious scholarship. He currently is helping to lead a national movement to legalize hemp as an agricultural commodity and remove it from a list of controlled substances, in hopes of it becoming an alternative crop for tobacco farmers as that industry declines, and still had time, in 2018, to complete his seventh degree, a doctorate of education at Vanderbilt University.

Sangu Delle, the son of a rural African doctor, hailed from the suburbs of Accra, Ghana. When Sangu was only fourteen years old, *Time* magazine named him one of Africa's twenty-five future leaders.

Like Ryan, Sangu finished multiple degrees in his twenties—a bachelor of arts degree with highest honors, a juris doctorate, and a master's in business administration, all from Harvard University.

As a Harvard undergraduate, Sangu was asked during a research project interview to rate how happy he was on a scale of one to five, with one being unhappy and five being very happy. "I'd say four," he decided. "I'm very blessed." But he wouldn't say five because, he explained, "there's so much more to do in life." When asked what he wanted to accomplish by the age of forty, Sangu said he wanted to make money first, probably in banking or investing, though he much preferred the latter. Then he'd use his funds to back social entrepreneurs in Africa.

In 2014, Sangu appeared on a *Forbes* list of the "Most Promising Young African Entrepreneurs." From the article, it was clear that most of the items from his do-by-forty list had been scratched off. Sangu had made money as an investor at Morgan Stanley and Goldman Sachs. But he also had his own holding company, launched with funds raised from Harvard classmates, that invested in African entrepreneurs. Along the way, he'd also created a nonprofit that made water accessible to 160 villages in Ghana. Sangu, at that time, was still in his twenties.

Since then, he's made water available to 200 villages, raised millions of dollars for African entrepreneurs, and given more than 100 speeches and talks encouraging companies to invest in Africa, including two popular TED Talks with millions of views.

Maggie Young,[1] a twentysomething virtuoso violinist and graduate student, won a Juilliard School competition that earned her a

[1] Name has been changed for privacy.

solo onstage at Carnegie Hall with Alan Gilbert, former music director of the New York Philharmonic and the Philharmonic Orchestra.

On the day of her debut, Maggie's brunette hair was pinned up in an elegant do, her cherubic face uncharacteristically made up. She had envisioned this moment, imagined the sound of her heels clicking across the stage, but nothing could prepare her for the feel of the Avery Fisher Stradivarius violin under her hands and the full orchestra and famous conductor standing at wait.

The review of the concert in the *New York Times* the next day was all about Maggie. It described her performance as sensuous and mature, and jump-started a career of traveling the United States and Mexico and collecting more rave reviews.

From the time Maggie was in middle school, she had spent her weekends along with her fellow string-musician siblings studying her craft at a famous performing arts center in New York City. But Maggie's path to that pivotal moment on the big stage was an almost-straight line stretching even further back: to when, as a two-year-old, she began learning the violin, and the importance of discipline, from her mother.

DIFFERENT STORIES, SAME PLOT

What made each of these adults extraordinary began with their parents. Maggie's earliest memory is from when she was three or four standing in the living room of her family's Long Island home with her little violin tucked under her chin, her mother holding a cup of tea and watching closely as the toddler tried to stand still within a foot chart, as directed, in order to play.

Asking a small child to stand still, as Maggie's mother did, may seem extreme. But is it that different from teaching a very young child to hold a baseball bat, to build a house of cards, or to read words? Maggie's mother made it a fun part of the child's day. And that habit planted the seeds of Maggie's greatness.

"It's not really a problem if you wiggle when you're three, but if you're standing in front of an orchestra playing Tchaikovsky you can't produce enough sound to be heard over a hundred-person orchestra if you're wiggling around. It's physics," Maggie said.

Ryan Quarles's academic accomplishments and leadership as Kentucky's agriculture commissioner link directly back to growing up in a make-it-or-break-it farm lifestyle, where even as a small child he had important chores to do, and to his father, who modeled high standards. Sangu's successes can be tracked to the lessons he learned from his mother, who taught him to read at age two, and to the deep, philosophical early-morning conversations he had as a pre-kindergarten child with his father. Some of these mornings were after late nights, when, having dressed himself in a little suit, he would sit around listening to Liberian or Sierra Leonean war refugees who had come to their home to talk with his father and tell their stories.

In fact, digging into the lives of high-achieving individuals like Ryan, Sangu, Maggie, and many others we will soon meet reveals something extraordinary: the same basic story arc, shaped by the same parenting principles, over and over again. The specifics differ from one family to the next; the parents exhibit no external parallels and their children differ in behaviors, interests, and the skills they conquered. And still, the expeditions toward realization and success on which each child was piloted were extraordinarily similar.

Class doesn't seem to matter.

Race doesn't seem to matter.

The successful parenting philosophy of a father who worked at a fast food restaurant was very similar to that of a mother who was a well-respected judge. A Caribbean mother and father whose Ivy League–educated son grew up to be a video game guru and Twitter star unknowingly followed the same effective parenting strategies that Albert Einstein's mother used to raise him a century ago. A struggling immigrant in Los Angeles who rode the bus to clean homes in Hollywood Hills used the same parenting style as a former president of the United States.

What did these parents do differently? Were they just a step ahead of everyone else? Were these parents following, consciously or not, a sort of parenting blueprint that better prepared their children for life? If so, can it be passed along to other parents? Is there a *formula* for parenting, one that reliably produces successful children and extraordinary, fulfilled adults?

CHAPTER 1

The Mystery of Success

THE BLACK BOX

We all know someone who was talented as a child but who nonetheless ended up leading an ordinary life. So when we encounter people who have experienced extraordinary success, people like Ryan, Sangu, and Maggie, while we admire their triumphs, we can't help but wonder: How did they do it? Was it just natural talent?

What transformed their natural-born abilities into extraordinary adult success? And could we, too, have been as successful, if only we, or our parents, had done something differently?

Plenty of books attempt to answer these questions, but few, if any, go beyond observing the children themselves. Most fail to investigate the connections between a child's achievement and their parents' own backstories and motivations. And seldom do they address the full span of the child's journey from birth through early adulthood.

Meanwhile, social science research is preoccupied with the things that go wrong in childhood and how parents can prevent or fix problems—not what they can do to create a high achiever. It's unusual to investigate the influence of the parents' approach on an achiever's remarkable success, and even rarer to try to understand the details of *why* that approach helped the child excel.

From long-established work on the differences and similarities between twins separated at birth, to more recent studies that show how early differences in children's language-processing abilities arise in the first few years of life, science has provided us with a plethora of studies that establish just how profoundly parenting matters. Yet when we read about outstanding adults, we have no way of knowing *how* they got to be so spectacular. How did the parents of successful people contribute to their lauded achievements, and how can we glean actionable insights about their childrearing?

This information is metaphorically hidden from view—as though inside a proverbial black box. In science, computing, and engineering, a "black box" is an object or system in which things go in one side (the input) and come out changed from the other (the output), but you have no idea what happens in between. We know certain childhoods result in outstanding adults, but we don't know why, because we were not there to see inside the "box," or the home, where the parenting happened. All we see is the output: the outstanding adult.

In medicine, a black box experiment is one that includes both a control group, which doesn't receive treatment, and another group, which receives the treatment being tested. Such experiments are considered the gold standard for determining if the treatment works, but they have a common shortcoming: we don't find out *how* or *why* the treatment works, which makes it hard to improve it based on what's been learned. Many treatments have been proven to cure illnesses, but often the scientists who produce the proof still don't understand what the medicine does inside a patient's body to result in a cure.

Similarly, when it comes to successful parenting, we don't know the details of what the parents did that guided their children to become so outstanding. Think of the lessons to be learned if we could take a close look into the homes where the world's most successful people grew up. What would we find out about success? What could *parents* learn about how to help their own children reach their full potential?

We now know that brain development for life success begins years before a child sets foot in a preschool. The science is clear that, starting at birth or even before, parental decisions can have a profound influence on how successful a child becomes, all the way into adulthood. And it's not just the things we do that are extremely important to a child's future; the things we *don't* do at home can cause kids' potential to go unharvested.

This book opens up the black box to find out what the parents of high achievers do. Over the course of fifteen years, we interviewed 200 high-achieving adults and some of their parents. In those interviews, a clear pattern emerged: the approaches that parents of high achievers adopted, beginning in the earliest years of life, bore real and striking similarities, despite those parents' widely divergent backgrounds and life circumstances.

We've given this pattern a name: "the Formula."

AN INVESTIGATION INTO SUCCESS

The research that would eventually yield the Formula began in two very different places.

For Tatsha Robertson, it started in 2003 in a newsroom at the *Boston Globe*, where she was a national correspondent whose job was to travel across the country. She'd begun to notice that the very smart and special people she came across during her reporting had parents with similar traits. She called Ron Ferguson at Harvard University, with whom she had spoken numerous times when she needed an expert perspective for a story.

"Could strategic parenting be taught?" she asked. He said it could and described an emerging movement among researchers who were starting to discuss how to do just that.

Ultimately Tatsha began to wonder if these parents of extraordinary people were following a discernible set of parental guidelines, a formula. Over the next ten years she interviewed sixty people about how they were raised, looking for similarities in their stories. Sometimes they were colleagues; other times they were new people she met while traveling for work. Although she mostly did the interviews on her own, sometimes she investigated the parenting of the people she interviewed for the *Globe* and other publications, including President Barack Obama.

For Ron, the search began during an advising session in his office at Harvard University in 2009. Kyoung Lee, a master's degree student, was selecting fall-term courses at the Kennedy School of Government, where Ron has taught and conducted research for over thirty years. The two found themselves talking about South Korean culture, academic standards, and parenting. Ron told Kyoung about South Korean students of his who had insisted it was unacceptable in Korea to score lower than the top 5 percent of students nationally in their age group. That struck Ron as unreasonable: Even if an achiever performs at the 90th percentile of their peers, they fail? Because of the way Ron had been raised, this simply did not compute—but it did for Kyoung, whose parents were born and raised in Korea. She observed, "If I got 99 percent on a test, my mom wanted to know where the other point was, even if nobody else got more than a 90."

Kyoung and Ron wondered together whether other Harvard students had been pressed to find that missing point. How prevalent, they wanted to know, were racial, ethnic, socioeconomic, and national differences in how her peers across the university were parented? After all, her classmates' parents had all raised children who, like Kyoung, had risen to the top of the extremely selective Harvard admissions process. Had their children been parented in similar ways?

Their conversations led to the How I Was Parented Project at Harvard: 120 interviews with Harvard undergraduates and graduate students, from which at least half the people in this book are drawn, including Sangu Delle. To launch that project in 2009, Ron and his student volunteers sent emails to hundreds of students at the university, inviting them to be interviewed around the question, "What roles did your parents play in your success?"

Over the next two years, student volunteers actively sought out these stories, drawing on Harvard students from virtually all walks of life and backgrounds—black and white, Asian and Latino American; Baptists, Catholics, Jews, Buddhists, and atheists. Some of the students came from very wealthy families, but many did not. For every student raised by doctors or lawyers, engineers or professors, another was raised by a cashier, a bus driver, or a cook. Some were born in Korea, China, or India, while others came from villages in Africa, cities in Mexico, or towns in the Dominican Republic, Jamaica, and Bulgaria. But most were Americans, hailing from points as varied as the cornfields of Oklahoma and the inner city of Detroit.

As the volunteers conducted one long interview after another, they asked the same scripted questions designed to delve into the subjects' recollections of childhood and the roles their parents played.

The recordings grew into a massive narrative catalogue of students' earliest memories and their journeys to high academic achievement. At the heart of these memories were their parents—their first and most lasting teachers and guides.

Ron and his research assistants began coding the data and looking for patterns, but it quickly became clear that the complexity involved would require someone who could single-mindedly focus on the interviews for an extended period of time, so the project was put on the back burner. When Tatsha called Ron again in 2014 to tell him about a book she wanted to write, on whether there was a parenting formula that successful parents were following, Ron said he believed so, but did not yet know what it was—and asked if they should write the book together, drawing in part from the How I Was Parented Project data. Rather than design social science tests of hypotheses about the nature of effective parenting, we set out to perform an investigation, more journalistic in nature, that would delve deep into the lives of achievers—and then, as our investigation began to suggest that strong commitment to purposeful parenting was grounded in a parent's personal narrative, into the lives of their parents, as well.

Tatsha spent months listening to and analyzing anonymous audio. She and Ron then compared the parenting of the Harvard achievers to that of the non-Harvard achievers Tatsha had interviewed over the years. A formula began to emerge.

Knowing that, in past research, people of different socioeconomic backgrounds exhibited different parenting styles, we had expected to see a culture-specific tapestry revealing a diverse range of parenting theories, values, and strategies that differed systematically by family background. But that's not what happened. There was, for example, no identifiably superior "Asian" or "American" way to do it. Rather, across race, socioeconomic status, education level, religion, and nationality, there were surprisingly strong, common parenting threads that helped produce future successes.

The initial recorded interviews by students were a good start but merely scratched the surface of the parenting patterns we saw emerging. Together, we re-interviewed achievers drawn from the Harvard project, who had since graduated, as well as non-Harvard achievers who we met through other means. (At the time of the interviews, all the achievers were in their twenties, thirties, or forties, apart from a set of twins who had just turned fifty.) And like so many rivers and streams that flow to the sea, the accounts they shared led us to return to the source and interview the parents themselves.

MASTERS OF THE FORMULA

We call the parents we meet and hear about in this book "master parents"—not because they started out knowing all the answers, but because they were masterful at figuring out how to unlock their child's full potential.

In most cases, the parents had not studied at the greatest schools. A few hadn't even finished high school. But what was unique, if not genius, about them was their ability to do whatever was needed to raise thoughtful, very smart, ambitious, and purposeful children.

Both the most and least educated among these parents had taught their child simple numerical concepts and how to read basic words well before the age of five, and they had talked to the child as an equal, respecting their intellect and answering their questions after careful thought. Regardless of material resources, these parents exhibited intense commitment and vision. Parents at every socioeconomic level were relentless in finding the time and resources needed to help launch and sustain their child as a high academic performer. They were motivated by their own backstories, which gave them insight into the types of qualities they hoped their child would grow up to have. But, crucially, they never tried to mold their child based on their own dreams—on what the parents themselves had once wished to be but failed to become.

This is the core of the Formula: strategic choices that help a child reach their greatest potential and well-being. Built on eight parenting principles, or "roles" the parents play in the child's life, the Formula inspires the development of both academic and non-academic skills in a way that sets the child up for future success.

But there are no superhumans here. The Formula can be learned and cultivated. And while every child may not become a virtuoso musician, a Harvard graduate, or a wealthy and famous business-woman, parents equipped with the Formula can still enhance their child's academic and life success no matter what the child's base level of potential might be.

Before we get to the Formula itself, however, let's take a closer look at the kind of people the Formula produces.

CHAPTER 2

What We Mean by Success

EUDAIMONIC FLOURISHING

Skeptical, but interested in the possibility that there's a parenting formula that can produce successful, academically and socially outstanding young people, listeners lean in close. Eyes half-squinted, heads cocked slightly to one side, they often pose several questions: What exactly is so special about these people—these products of the Formula? Why are they, and the parenting that cultivated them, worth emulating? How do you define "success"?

Success, simply put, is the attainment of a goal. But what goal or goals are the Formula-raised children achieving? What *kind* of success are we talking about?

There are two dominant but contrasting philosophies on the topic of success. One, often labeled *hedonism*, is the idea made famous by the ancient Greek philosopher Epicurus, who believed the purpose of life is to experience the greatest possible pleasure while avoiding pain. Imagine opulent parties, with the finest foods and flowing champagne inside a ridiculously large mansion. In this definition, the goal of success is satisfying one's material and carnal desires.

The other idea derives from the Greek word *eudaimonia*, translated as *human flourishing*, and was a central concept in Aristotle's philosophy. The goal in this kind of success is self-realization. It's the high you feel and the growth you achieve as you pursue a challenging goal—the idea that you can experience your best self by striving toward mastery. Picture American gymnast Simone Biles, flipping and twirling in space, practicing for years in order to compete in the Olympics, or a young Albert Einstein in 1905, his "miracle year," sitting at his desk fine-tuning the fourth in a series of papers that would revolutionize science.

Modern-day research agrees that pursuing this definition of success fosters well-being, while preoccupation with hedonistic goals often adds little to life satisfaction and can even detract from it. That doesn't mean a eudaimonic approach to achievement lacks financial or material payoffs, however. Several of the people you'll meet in the coming chapters have attained great wealth. Most of our master parents would have been happy for their child to grow up to be able to purchase a luxury car, live in a beautiful home, or travel to exotic locations. But these same master parents understood that material possessions are merely desirable trappings of achievement, distinct from the deeper and more lasting kind of success the Formula produces.

When we say the Formula produces successful adults, what we mean is that it produces adults who are *fully realized.*

PURPOSE + AGENCY + SMARTS = FULLY REALIZED

If there is one term that describes the men and women in this book, it's "fully realized."

Their stories paint a vivid picture of what this means; they include an American diplomat, a CNN television anchor, and three sisters whom pundits have called "the most powerful women in the world." What they, and the rest of the 200 achievers we looked at, all have in common is the way they have each pushed their potential to the limit and are still continuing to grow.

Raising fully realized adults was the goal of each master parent in the book, whether they knew the term or not. And they did this through fostering three key qualities: a sense of *purpose*, a sense of *agency*, and *smarts*.

Think of *purpose* here as a lofty goal or aim—something deeply meaningful that provides clear direction in life. Fully embracing it frequently requires years of persistence through periods of often difficult personal growth, but in pursuit of big accomplishments important enough to justify the effort.

It takes extraordinary initiative to get started on a journey toward such an ambitious destination. That initiative is called *agency*. Someone with a strong sense of agency thinks, "Let's do this!" and then follows through with actions and behaviors.

Which brings us to the third element in the equation: *smarts*.

What We Mean by "Smart"

Psychologists call ideas like "smart" *folk concepts*: most of us have a basic idea what they mean, even while the people who actually study them can't agree. In everyday life, we talk about many different types of smart. The most common relate to what we're taught in school: science smart, math smart, reading smart, writing smart. There's also social intelligence, for dealing with other people, and emotional intelligence, for managing our feelings.

Psychologist W. Joel Schneider, who specializes in the assessment of cognitive abilities, offers a broader definition: "We use the word . . . to describe people who are able to acquire useful knowledge, and who can solve consequential problems using some combination of logic, intuition, creativity, experience, and wisdom." Though he admits his own definition is "as vague as the thing I am trying to define."

For this book, we offer a two-pronged, commonsense definition of smart: the ability to perform cognitively challenging tasks, like figuring out difficult academic assignments; and the ability to take in information from one's environment, make sense of it, and then use it to make strategic decisions in the course of one's journey.

All the successful people we interviewed were very clearly, from a very young age, academically astute. However, they also had something much more. They achieved at very high levels, but they also just loved learning. While many of their interests were academic in nature, they often had other things they felt passionate about that they were in the process of mastering: the violin, activism, public speaking. (Though it's worth noting that the skills they developed in pursuing these interests did also help them achieve high grades.)

Doing well in school was important to them as children, but these were not the type of young people who only cared about a teacher's assessment; their personal standards were often higher than their teachers'. But that didn't mean grades were irrelevant; in high school or college, when several received their first C grade, they were knocked off balance—but only briefly, before assessing what went wrong and figuring how not to do it again. This response had nothing to do with parental pressure or the need for approval, and everything to do with how they saw themselves: as smart.

But what was really striking about these special achievers is how self-assured they seemed to be at such a young age, as if they knew the secrets to winning. Even the way they spoke to adults, as children, was impressive: they came off as sincerely thoughtful and wise about the world and themselves. They had the ability to use what they learned to generate their own questions, think through the implications of those questions, and form their own opinions, then communicate those opinions in a manner that genuinely interested their conversation partners. In other words, they came across as *smart.*

PRODIGIES VERSUS THE PRODUCTS OF THE FORMULA

At the age of three or four, the people we studied could read words. By kindergarten, they all had unusually good basic literacy and math skills. If they later struggled, it was at the honors level, trying to keep up with other exemplary students.

This brings up a common question asked about the products of the Formula. Are they off-the-charts smart or is their kind of specialness attainable for the rest of us? The people we interviewed are definitely intelligent, but maybe the best way to describe their kind of smart is to instead look at what they are not.

Howard Gardner, the psychologist and Harvard professor known for his theory of multiple intelligences, defines a *prodigy* as a child who displays "adult-level performance" not because they labored to earn their virtuosity, but because they essentially found themselves in possession of a natural-born talent. Gardner believes being a prodigy is like being given a gift that borders on miraculous. "Even if one refused to believe in miracles and looks only to probabilities," says Gardner, "the kinds of performances exhibited by the young Wolfgang Amadeus Mozart or Felix Mendelssohn, by the youthful Picasso or the English painter John Everett Millais, are astounding."

How does the high achiever raised by master parents compare? Using Gardner's research and our more than ten-year investigation into the Formula, we came up with the following contrasts:

- While the high achiever is **purposeful** in selecting projects and skills to learn, the prodigy is swept along in the tide of others' responses to their talent.
- While the high achiever **commits to mastery** and **seeks out new and challenging experiences**, the prodigy achieves early

mastery through mimicry or without struggle and later finds it difficult to raise their game.

- While the parents of the high achiever introduce experiences in order to feed curiosity and initiate a **thirst for knowledge**, the adults in the prodigy's life create opportunities centered around showcasing the child's prodigious talent, rather than introduce them to opportunities to learn and expand their interests.
- While the high achiever becomes **gutsy and courageous** in a gradual way by learning to take chances when reaching for high goals, the prodigy grows accustomed to success without risk because a parent or a teacher shields them from obstacles.
- While the high achiever **develops skills by collaborating with adults**, the prodigy displays skills by performing for adults.
- While the high achiever **grows confident** that they can learn and thereby achieve mastery, the prodigy is confident of their ability to perform, but not necessarily to learn.

Often, in their twenties, the prodigy experiences the ground shift under their feet, says Gardner. Adults are no longer fans but masterful rivals. Some of their contemporaries, who were never considered prodigies, had worked hard and purposefully and were now outstanding competitors. Finding it difficult to cope, Gardner writes, "many, perhaps most, do not fulfill their youthful potential."

Unlike for the prodigy, challenge for our high achievers led to growth. In college, where some of them discovered their peers were light-years ahead academically, they made the needed adjustments. For instance, when Rob Humble, a small-town boy known there for his intelligence, got into a top-rated college where every student seemed to be more brilliant than the next, he was nearly thrown off his game. But he knew if he was going to compete, he had to take action, know himself, and organize his time and life. He knew he wasn't made for last-minute cramming, so he devised a plan that fit his temperament: he started a study group, and completed homework weeks ahead. While other students were pulling all-nighters prior to finals, Rob was able to spend long hours, days before the exams, focusing strictly on the material that was going to be on the finals. He calculated how long he needed to study in order to be tired enough to get eleven hours of sleep the night before the exams. When test time came, he was refreshed and sharp, unlike his classmates. And as a result, he excelled.

In studying prodigies, Gardner concluded that their abilities are rooted in something other than agency or purposefulness. Rather, he says, it's "something in the structure or functioning of the nervous system of Mozart, of the chess player Bobby Fischer, or the mathematician Carl Gauss that made it preternaturally easy to gain the initial mastery of patterns involved in musical tones, the configuration of chess pieces or the possibilities of numerical combinations, respectively."

In contrast, there's no reason to believe most of the high achievers in this book were born supremely gifted, in the top 1 percent of hereditary potential like the prodigy. In fact, based on our conversations with them, as well as interviews with their early-childhood and high school teachers, parents, siblings, and mentors, plus copies of report cards, college references, and applications, there is much more reason to believe their natural abilities are well within the normal range of human variation, if perhaps in the top quarter. Instead, they are people whose parents understood that *smart* is like *strong*. It can be nurtured.

Genetics play a role, of course. Children come with innate capabilities that affect their ease of learning, just as some weight lifters inherit distinctive physiologies that make building muscle faster and easier. But a weight lifter's strength also depends often even more on diet, lifestyle, practice, and other environmental factors.

The high achievers in this book grew smarter in the same way that weight lifters get stronger: from the ways they spent their time and the things they paid attention to.

As it turns out, being smart is a lot more like bodybuilding than you'd expect. Just as weight lifting builds muscles, science tells us that learning builds denser brain pathways for storing knowledge and processing thoughts. Every time we learn, the brain physically transforms into a better tool.

Take the case of London taxi drivers. In a 2011 study, Eleanor Maguire and Katherine Woollett, both neurologists at University College London, followed a group of taxi trainees studying for an exam called the Knowledge, a grueling test of recall that can take from two to four years to prepare for. It's been called one of the toughest memory feats in the world because the test requires drivers to know all of the city's 25,000 streets and tens of thousands of landmarks, all within a six-mile radius.

Maguire and Woollett scanned the trainees' brains before they began studying and again after the test. The results were fascinating: the trainees that passed the test saw an increase in the volume of gray matter in their hippocampus, the part of the brain that stores spatial representations—meaning all the time spent studying, visualizing, and mentally navigating London's sprawling, ancient, and intricate roads and streets literally grew their brainpower.

Like those taxi drivers, the extraordinary people we met spent more time than most of their peers in activities that helped them improve cognitive skills. Physical changes happened in their brains as they got better at things, which then let them *keep* getting better at things, like a weight lifter who builds new muscles that allow them to easily lift what was once difficult. Our achievers developed new neural pathways through learning while maintaining older ones that might have withered away if left unused. In other words, unlike Gardner's prodigies, they became smarter over time.

WHO OUR ACHIEVERS ARE AND HOW WE CHOSE THEM

So where and how did we find individuals who met these definitions—smart, successful people with purpose and agency? The largest group of achievers in our research, and featured in this book, are Harvard graduates, who years earlier participated in the How I Was Parented Project. Those contacted for follow-up interviews five years later were chosen to include a cross section of geographic, socioeconomic, ethnic, and racial backgrounds.

Having survived the Harvard admissions process, they represented exactly the types of achievement that interested us. Being an academic star is not enough to gain admission to Harvard; many valedictorians are rejected. Aside from being academically superior to other students, successful applicants must have achieved excellence in extracurricular passion projects, written intriguing application essays, and received extraordinary recommendations from teachers and counselors, all attesting to their purposefulness and excellent potential to change the world (which those we interviewed again for this book are now doing).

Of course, Harvard is certainly not the only place to find that kind of person. At least sixty other people outside of the Harvard project caught our attention. Tatsha received referrals or met special people during her reporting and editing work, and both Tatsha and Ron noticed potential interviewees at meetings and conferences and through chance encounters. For instance, there was Maggie Young, the twentysomething world-class violinist, whom Tatsha spotted performing with spellbinding elegance and authority; and Chuck Badger, whom Ron noticed on a political affairs panel, where the young political consultant spoke with great depth and sophistication. Chuck told us about the ultra-successful Ryan Quarles, the Kentucky farmer and agriculture chief. Lisa Son, a professor of brain science with an innovative method of teaching her own very small children to read, was one of about fifty parents in an affluent New Jersey town who responded to Tatsha's Facebook post in search of parents of high achievers.

In nearly every case, we knew nothing about these high achievers' upbringing until we sat down to talk with them—we only knew that they were exactly the type of successful, fully realized adults we hoped to learn about. And in nearly every case, we saw the same commonalities in the parenting they'd experienced: the eight principles, or roles, that make up the Formula. Let's turn now to the Formula itself—those eight roles, and what they look like in action.

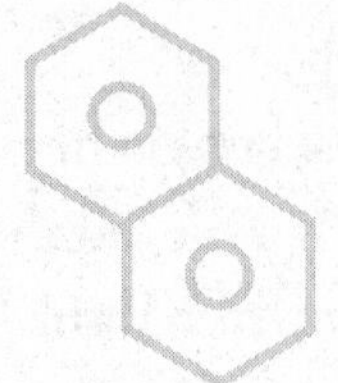

CHAPTER 3

The Formula

THE INCREDIBLE LIFE OF JARELL LEE

In Harvard graduate Jarell Lee's earliest memory, his mother is rushing out of the home where they were living with him cradled in her arms. Minutes earlier he'd been on the floor playing with his Ninja Turtle truck when, from nowhere, a knife slammed into the wooden floorboards next to him and stuck there, like a dart in a wall.

"I was three," Jarell recalled as we ate lunch at a Brooklyn soul food restaurant. The memory prompted Jarell, who couldn't remember anything more about the story, to call his mother in Ohio for answers. She told him that her boyfriend at the time (not Jarell's father) had thrown a knife at her that day. Mother and son fled, but there was no money and no place to go except for homeless shelters in their native Cleveland, Ohio. From kindergarten through third grade, Jarell attended nine different schools. He lived in nearly as many homeless shelters just during the first grade.

All that moving around left him with no childhood friends to speak of, but there were two constants in his life: his mother and learning.

When she became pregnant with Jarell at age twenty-two, Elizabeth Lee started reading everything she could about childrearing. "I read books on what to expect when you're pregnant; I read books on different things to do while you are pregnant, and about raising your child. After that, I read books about raising a one-year-old, a two-year-old, a three-year-old, and a four-year-old."

A former foster child and honor student who'd quit school in her senior year because she didn't like the cliques, Elizabeth believed if she did the things she read about in books, combined with what she could figure out on her own, the outcome would be a middle-class son and all that came with that distinction.

"I told him, 'I'm poor and broke and we're in the ghetto, but if you do good, get good grades, and go to college and be successful, you can get out of here,'" Elizabeth recalled.

Elizabeth started early with flash cards. She and Jarell would sit there, two partners in learning, on a bed at the homeless shelter going over the cards, which she used to teach him shapes, colors, numbers, and words. She'd show him a card and Jarell, who was about three or four, would read back the word.

"Not word for word but reading whatever he could remember," she said.

Elizabeth picked up early that her preschooler either had a good memory or caught on quickly; either way she knew he needed more than what she knew how to teach him. When Jarell was still too young for school, Elizabeth volunteered at his Head Start center, watching everything they taught during class and then replicating it when she returned to the shelter.

"That's how he learned. We went over everything. Later, we'd go to the library and we would get stacks of books. We'd sit on the couch and read books together."

She made it so much fun that Jarell never knew he was learning. She'd focus on six words a day. Mother and son would review those words for about an hour. This continued until she found work, which was about the same time Jarell entered kindergarten. By that time, Jarell had some basic reading skills and he knew a few numbers, which set him apart from other children. He recalls the kindergarten teacher exclaiming, "You can read!"

From there, Elizabeth set the agenda, ensuring that Jarell got into a habit of doing well in school, never falling short of his potential. To keep him challenged, she tried to get him into the best schools she could, or at least make sure he was always tested for placement in gifted and talented classes, where she knew he belonged. Sometimes the gifted program was in a school in a rough neighborhood, and sometimes it was in a school in a rich neighborhood, or in a Quaker school. Regardless of the setting, she did whatever she could to not only survive, but also prepare Jarell to thrive.

In the middle of all that surviving, Elizabeth had two daughters. Though she still lacked money for books, Elizabeth made sure reading continued to be a central activity in the family. The public library was a second home. The whole family would spend hours picking out books, then losing themselves in the stories and drawings. "I've always had enough books for my children. We read kid books like *Peter's Chair*. We got all the Dr. Seuss books, like *Are You My Mother?*" Elizabeth said. "That was one of our favorites by Dr. Seuss, and *One Fish, Two Fish, Red Fish, Blue Fish*. We read anything; it didn't matter what it was or who wrote it. They were all from the library and free."

Elizabeth was always trying to figure out ways to stimulate her children and expose them to activities that might provide them with a leg up later in life, even though she had little to no money to spare. "We went to parades, just any kind of event. There used to be something downtown called the Kids' Fest. Every year we'd go down there. We went to everything."

She was always teaching, even on city bus rides. "I'd point out stop signs, traffic signs. They could read signs on buildings and restaurants. We'd play those types of games."

Jarell describes Elizabeth's style of parenting as nurturing and kind, but she describes it as "lenient-strict." She believed in giving her children freedom, knowing she had already set a structure. Homework just needed to be done before bedtime. All three children could watch television on the weekend, but weekdays were for reading books. During the summer, they read a book a week and wrote a report. Sloppy work was never allowed. "I would not accept anything less than a good grade. I would look over Jarell's paper, and if it wasn't right I would tear it up, ball it up, whatever. It was over if it was not your best work. I expected better and I knew he could do better," she said.

Although her girls did fine in school, they sometimes resisted her advice. Jarell, however, was always receptive and responsible. "When he was in high school, he could stay up as long as he wanted because he knew how to get up in the morning. I didn't have any problems with him. His homework, he basically did it on his own. A lot of stuff he was doing I did not know how to do; a lot of stuff I couldn't do. If there was a paper he had to write, I could help him with that, proofread it, rearrange sentences, but as far as math, science, that was a wash."

A wash for her but not for him. In fact, math and science became his favorite subjects, because when Jarell was a toddler reading flash cards and pointing at objects from the bus, Elizabeth had taught him the love of figuring things out and how to teach himself things he didn't know.

After years of moving from one homeless shelter to the next, when Jarell was eight years old, the family was finally able to rent a small house. It stood less than a block from Harvard Avenue in a depressed section of Cleveland's East Side known as Union-Miles. Jarell called it "the wasteland," but not just because of the boarded-up homes or the former church across the street that had become a crack den. He also called it a wasteland because of the aimless boys that ruled the blocks, "wasting away" their potential. Jarell was not one of them.

Small for his age, with big ears and a boxy haircut called a "fade," he favored the protagonist of the 1990s show *Smart Guy*, a ten-year-old African American whiz kid, which often inspired teasing. Children would break out the theme song when Jarell walked by. Worse was when the teasing turned violent. He was assaulted by boys on the bus in second grade and hospitalized at thirteen when jumped by a gang just because he preferred to keep his nose in his books.

Jarell could have done what he really wanted to do: retreat into the house, and spend all his time reading books and playing video games. However, Elizabeth knew he couldn't hide from his fears; he needed to face those hurdles.

"My mother had to force me to get involved with things. I didn't become athletic until I was twenty-three, but when I was very young I played sports. I loved it. I just wasn't good at it."

Elizabeth gave him tools to succeed in the real world just as she gave him tools to succeed in the classroom. "She told me: 'You're a black man. Never get in the car with three other black guys because you will likely get pulled over,'" Jarell said.

Many of Jarell's neighborhood peers saw their own destiny in the poverty around them and had resigned themselves to it, but Elizabeth persistently shared the importance of striving to do better in life. She'd point to the "thugs" in the neighborhood and say, "Do you see the people out here? You see how they are living? You see how we're living? We're poor. You don't want to be like this for the rest of your life."

She taught him a different story line, and according to Jarell, her words guided him every day. "She'd say, 'The only way you can change your fate is by being in school and learning and doing something different with your life.' She made it really clear," Jarell said. "So I always looked at education as a way out. I thought, 'This is terrible. No one wants to live like this.'"

By the time Jarell was eight, Elizabeth's work was paying off. Jarell was a busy straight-A student involved with many of his own projects and coming up with his own goals, rather than just working toward the ones his mother had set for him. As he told us, "When

I was eight . . . I remember hearing about college. I wanted to go to the best college. What's the best college? Someone said a school called Harvard. I said, 'Okay, that's the college I'm going to.' I didn't know what that meant but ever since I was eight it was the only college I wanted to go to."

Elizabeth knew little about Harvard, and getting Jarell there was never her goal. All she knew was that if her son was going to get out of the ghetto and become middle class, he had to have high standards, be challenged, and associate with other smart children and good teachers.

To make that happen, Elizabeth continued to do her homework on which nearby schools were more advanced and had gifted-education programs. In fact, once, when Jarell was in early elementary school, she even chose a particular homeless shelter because it put Jarell in a better school district.

At the time, they were staying in a transitional home that provided Elizabeth's family with a particular kind of stability and the structure of a home. Jarell remembers it being "fantastic." After-school programs at the shelter provided him with rare friendships with other children. "It wasn't any ordinary shelter," Elizabeth recalled. "It was considered a shelter, but we had our own apartment, our own kitchen, bedroom, dining room, living room." The shelter required the parents to attend classes regularly if they wanted to keep living there. Homework time for the children was set from four to six. On Saturday, volunteers would come in to help.

Then Elizabeth learned about another, less homey transition house located in Shaker Heights, a suburb on the border of Cleveland that became famous in the 1960s for its creative and largely successful efforts to remain racially balanced. Its elementary school system was rated among the highest performing in Ohio.

Elizabeth had a choice. She could either remain at the more comfortable shelter and send Jarell to a Cleveland school, or move him to the better school system, but a shelter that wasn't as great.

It was a no-brainer for Elizabeth. It didn't matter that they would have to live in a not-so-nice shelter or that Jarell would only be able to attend the better school for just a few months before they were required to move to another shelter. Elizabeth gambled that the benefits would last a lifetime.

She was right.

Lomond Elementary in Shaker Heights sat on eight beautiful acres, and the main building showcased Georgian-style brick. Featured in *Newsweek*, the school was known for its academic excellence. The superb teaching cemented the basic skills Elizabeth had taught Jarell, giving him a leg up in later grades. And their short experience at Lomond provided a lasting impression, a taste for both of them of what it felt like to be in a first-rate school.

In fact, Elizabeth credits that short time at Lomond, along with Jarell having his sights set on Harvard, with Jarell's determination to attend a first-rate high school, in particular Hawken, an exclusive prep academy where he only gained entry after two determined attempts.

In retrospect, switching shelters to ensure that Jarell attended the right school was the first of two very important educational-opportunity decisions Elizabeth made that would lead Jarell indirectly to the doors of Harvard University.

Elizabeth's second decision, introducing Jarell to the right mentor, enabled his goal of attending college even more profoundly. By the time Jarell was eleven, Elizabeth started introducing him to role models to help him envision who he could someday become. One of those was the minister of the church the family started attending around that time.

Bishop Greg Dorsi still remembers how impressed he always was with Elizabeth and her three children. The little girls were polite and curious, and their brother was well behaved and smart. Elizabeth, he observed, was as strategic as any middle-class parent, despite her financial struggles.

"She's astute, and she is brilliant," Bishop Dorsi says of Elizabeth. He sees her as a model for all parents. "Regardless of where you live, regardless of your race, your culture, and even if you are a single parent, you need to notice the intelligence of your children from the age of one and up."

Dorsi was especially taken by Jarell's maturity and academic skills.

Believing it would enhance Jarell's social skills, Dorsi encouraged him to get involved in meaningful activities at the church. There, Jarell taught Sunday school to the youngest children. Dorsi also applauded Jarell when he joined the church dance and rap groups.

"Bishop Dorsi is the one who taught me how to tie a tie; he gave me a lot of his old clothes so I could have nice things to wear," Jarell said.

Dorsi also proved instrumental in Jarell receiving financial aid. By the time Jarell was applying to college, Harvard was still the place he most dreamed of going. He got an interview with a local graduate, who seemed to like him, but the admissions officers at the college were skeptical that Jarell's family was living on the small amount they reported. Admissions needed more justification to offer the financial aid package Jarell needed.

Elizabeth turned to Dorsi, a polished communicator who could help Jarell write a letter to convince the school that her son not only needed financial help, but deserved it.

Dorsi recalls sitting down with Jarell to make a plan. "I said, 'You tell them you were reared by a loving, caring mother and that your pastor mentored you since you were twelve. And you state that you have something to offer to the community.'"

Dorsi wasn't exaggerating. By the time Jarell was applying for college, his academic excellence and potential for success were clear to everyone who knew him. Here is what one of his teachers at Hawken wrote in his letter of recommendation to Harvard:

> Most students coming from outside of Hawken, especially in non-standard entrance years, have a significant challenge adjusting to the academic rigor at Hawken . . . However, from day one Jarell showed what kind of excellent student he was going to be . . .
>
> When he would leave class confused about a subject he would go home and re-read the information from the textbook. He then would come back to me the next day to ask if he now "got" the concept. Time after time I was amazed at his ability to self-teach himself when other students would give it up as "too confusing." With many students, it is difficult to get them to read on their own or to take responsibility for their own learning. Jarell <u>never</u> allowed that of himself.

Elizabeth's masterful parenting had paid off. The choices she made, and the roles she played in his childhood, prepared Jarell to not only compete but succeed at a prep school like Hawken, an Ivy League university, and beyond, despite having been raised in circumstances a world away from the people who traditionally attend those institutions.

Today, Jarell is married with a new baby, and employed as an educator. He's been able to climb the education ladder swiftly, becoming a principal in his twenties—an age when most teachers are just finding their footing in the classroom. Since 2014, he's worked in schools in New York City, New Jersey, and Chicago, where he recently moved. Still very young, he has developed a burning purpose in life to guarantee that children like the one he used to be have the opportunities he was fortunate enough to have.

Jarell believes he's changing the world through inclusion, "one young mind at a time," but his larger goal is to change the learning outcomes for entire communities of children.

In other words, Jarell has grown into exactly the kind of person Elizabeth envisioned back when she first got pregnant and began reading all those books about childrearing, hoping to secure a better life for her unborn son.

THE FORMULA: THE EIGHT ROLES OF MASTER PARENTING

Unknowingly, Elizabeth followed a particular parenting blueprint that helped Jarell reach his potential and become the smart, resolute, and purposeful young man he is today: the Formula.

The Formula is made up of eight different parenting roles, each played by one or both parents (or, in some cases, another family member or family friend) at particular points in a child's life.

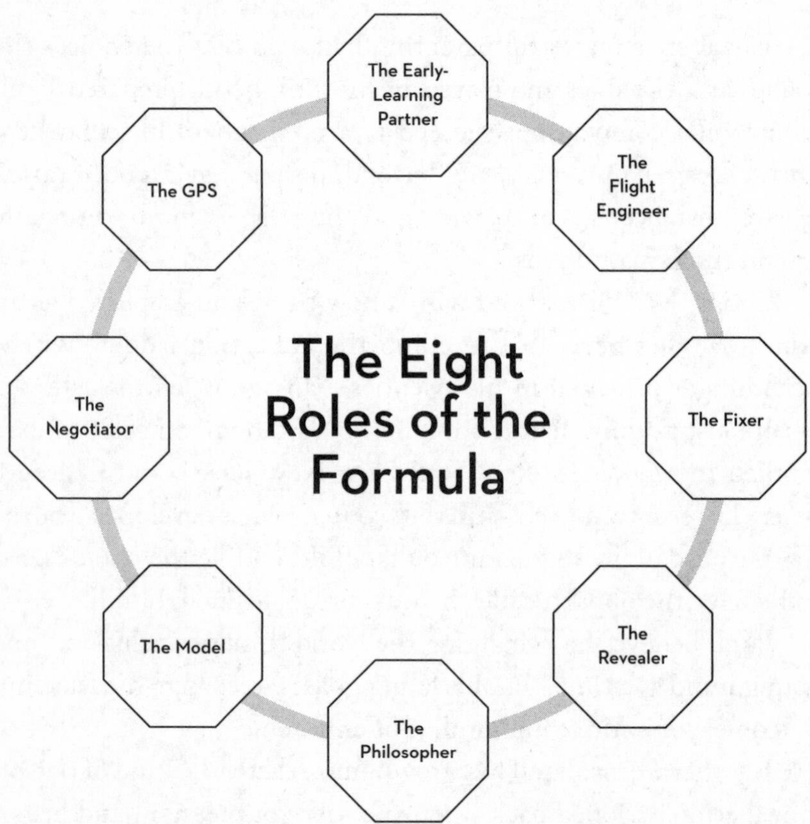

Each of these roles represents a strategic pattern of behaviors—overlapping actions and decisions implemented over the course of many years. And while the precise fashion in which a family enacts these roles differs based both on the family's circumstances and the parents' worldviews, the basic prescription for each is remarkably similar across all demographics.

The Early-Learning Partner

The Early-Learning Partner is front and center during the first five years of life, when the brain achieves 90 percent of its adult size. The parent as Early-Learning Partner spends a lot of time with the child in brain-building play and literacy activities, stimulating imagination while cultivating a voracious learning mindset.

The library books Elizabeth and Jarell read and discussed, the way Elizabeth pointed out things to be investigated, and their routine use of flash cards for developing early reading and math skills all set Jarell up to be more advanced than most of his peers from the time he started kindergarten. And Elizabeth's habit of intentionally asking questions that required Jarrell to work in order to learn the answers also helped him develop confidence as a learner.

The Flight Engineer

Once the child enters school, the Flight Engineer role takes prominence. Like the flight engineer for a spacecraft, who monitors all of the craft's systems and is able to step in to perform anyone's job if necessary, a parent in the Flight Engineer role ensures all of the people and systems working on behalf of the child are functioning properly and in the child's best interest. If something starts to go off course—discipline issues arise, the child receives perplexing feedback on a homework assignment, or the relationship between a self-assured child and a stubborn teacher becomes strained—the Flight Engineer intervenes to work with others in finding a solution.

Each time Jarell changed schools, Elizabeth met with administrators to make sure they tested her son for gifted and talented classes, because she knew the most rigorous classes would give him the highest-quality skills and knowledge, which he needed if he was going to stay competitive with other high achievers and qualify for the many opportunities those gifted programs come with.

The Fixer

The Fixer is also focused on problem solving, but where the Flight Engineer works within systems the child is already part of (usually their school) to find solutions, the Fixer is like an emergency responder, rushing in, often by themselves, to solve problems that otherwise could slam shut the door to opportunity.

Sometimes the Fixer's role involves finding an ally with more money or connections, or a better understanding of how to deal with complex institutions unfamiliar to the parent. Like the fixers used by foreign news correspondents to help them survive in hostile new territories, the parent as Fixer finds the right people and resources their charge needs to succeed, as when Elizabeth enlisted her minister to help Jarrell respond to Harvard regarding financial aid.

The Revealer

The parent as Revealer exposes the child to new ideas—things they can learn about, places they can go, and people they can be. They introduce the child to mind-expanding topics that grab their imagination, and also help the child learn what's possible for them by giving them glimpses of who and what they could become.

Elizabeth enrolled Jarell in activities at church, and took him to free concerts, museums, and parades that broadened his worldview. She introduced him to the Black Achievers program, which matched black professionals with poor children like Jarell to provide them with models of successful people who looked like them. In this process, she exposed him to a world that disadvantaged kids rarely get to see. These experiences also gave him insights for what today is the most meaningful part of his job as educator: serving as a bridge between people who've had great opportunities and those who have not.

The Philosopher

The Philosopher starts early in the child's life and remains active throughout it, helping the child find meaning and purpose. The master parent shares their worldview with the child, who uses that worldview as a guide.

For parents like Elizabeth who raise high-achieving children while living in poverty, a core tenet of the philosophy they pass along is that poverty is an unacceptable fate. When Elizabeth Lee took five-year-old Jarell on bus rides and pointed out the idle boys and men on street corners, he believed her when she told him he could escape such a fate if he excelled in school. Her philosophy of success through education drove him to believe he could and should compete with students of higher socioeconomic levels, even as the statistics screamed that someone like him would not and could not.

The Model

The Model instructs by showing and doing rather than simply telling—by conducting themselves in the same manner they hope their child someday will. The parent's behavior, which reflects their worldview, allows the child to observe firsthand the type of person their parent is preparing them to be.

Elizabeth took college courses while Jarell was growing up; he watched her study and read, even while she was caring for Jarell and his sisters. In doing so, she was modeling the high aspirations, determination, strategic behavior, and resilience that she wanted Jarell to develop as well. Without Elizabeth's example of another, more successful way, of living, Jarrell might have modeled himself on the people he observed on the streets, the "thugs and gangbangers," doubting that a different life was really possible.

The Negotiator

The Negotiator prepares the child to be an adept decision maker and an independent actor with the ability to effectively self-advocate. While the Fixer steps in to solve often-daunting problems that the child can't conquer alone, the parent as Negotiator prepares the child to fend for themselves.

This doesn't mean the child is allowed to make whatever choices they want. While the Negotiator nurtures and encourages independence, they also intervene when necessary to limit or punish behaviors, veto poor decisions, or impose beneficial requirements. The child has a voice and a chance to make their case, but master parents set consistent rules and boundaries.

Elizabeth always respected Jarell's intelligence, teaching him it was his right to challenge adults, as he later did with a teacher at Hawken on the man's interpretation of *The Scarlet Letter*. But when Jarell wanted to stay inside and read to avoid teasing, Elizabeth insisted he spend time outside of the home in order to meet and make friends. Jarell abided by her rules, but he had a say, too: he stepped out of the house just as she wanted, but he was the one who chose which (Elizabeth-approved) extracurricular activities to pursue.

The GPS

The final role, the GPS, is the parental advice and wisdom, residing in the child's memory, that helps guide them to their chosen destinations in life. Like the navigational systems in our cell phones or cars, the master parent as GPS provides direction consistent with the their philosophy even in the parent's absence or long after the child has left home.

Elizabeth frequently assured Jarell that he deserved to have an excellent education, a message that helped him feel that he belonged in the sometimes-intimidating academic and social spaces he wanted to enter—he just had to work to get there. Elizabeth's words echoing in his mind through the years drove Jarell to keep finding ways to persevere, even when it meant cleaning bathrooms for extra money at Harvard. Her guidance back then also compels him to share her uplifting message with the black and Latino children from low-income communities he teaches today, furthering Elizabeth's impact and driving his own: "You deserve to be in those same places and spaces."

The Formula's roles can be divided into two groups. The first group consists of those roles that foster qualities of success in the child and prepare them to compete out in the world. The Early-Learning Partner, for example, encourages curiosity and inspires a passion for learning new things. This group comprises most of the Formula's eight roles. The second, smaller, but no less crucial group of roles includes those that ensure the child's opportunities to succeed. The two roles in this group, the Flight Engineer and the Fixer, seek out and/or protect opportunities for the child.

Of the eight roles of the Formula, only two, the Early-Learning Partner and the Flight Engineer, are played in a particular order: as the child moves from being in the home to being out in the

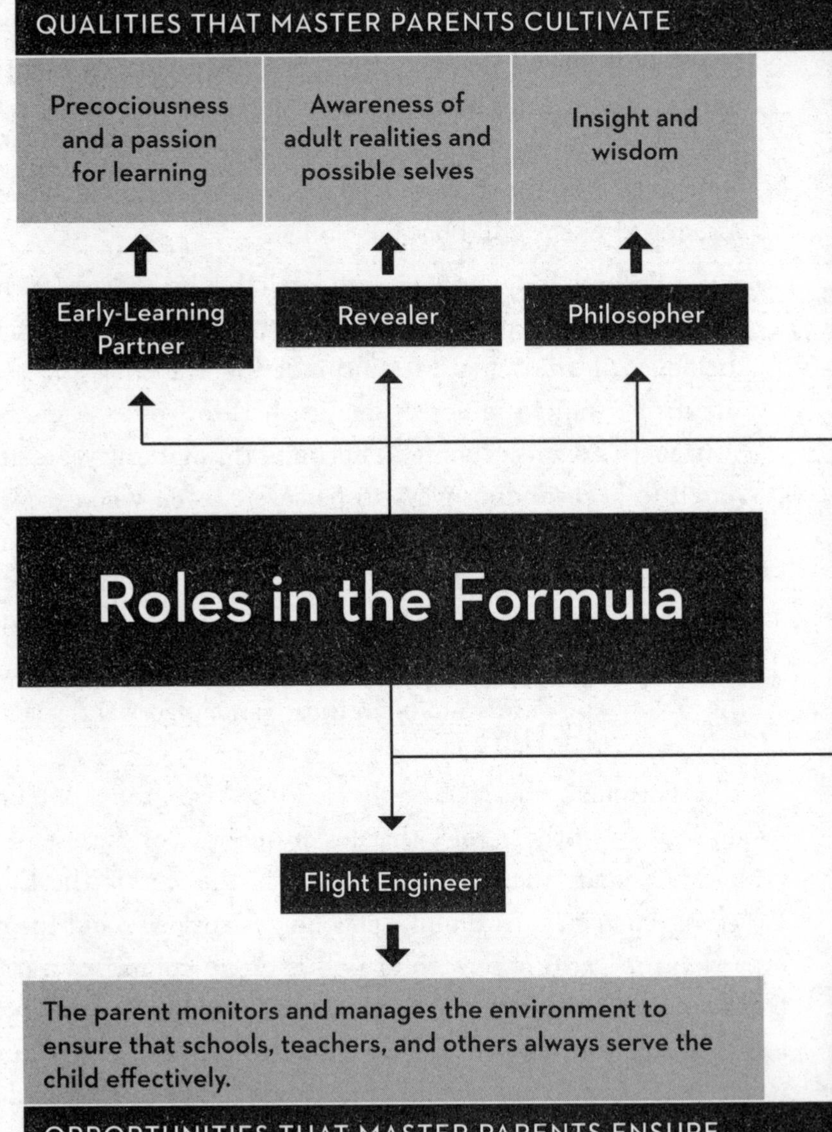
QUALITIES THAT MASTER PARENTS CULTIVATE
Precociousness and a passion for learning
Awareness of adult realities and possible selves
Insight and wisdom
Early-Learning Partner
Revealer
Philosopher
Roles in the Formula
Flight Engineer
The parent monitors and manages the environment to ensure that schools, teachers, and others always serve the child effectively.
OPPORTUNITIES THAT MASTER PARENTS ENSURE

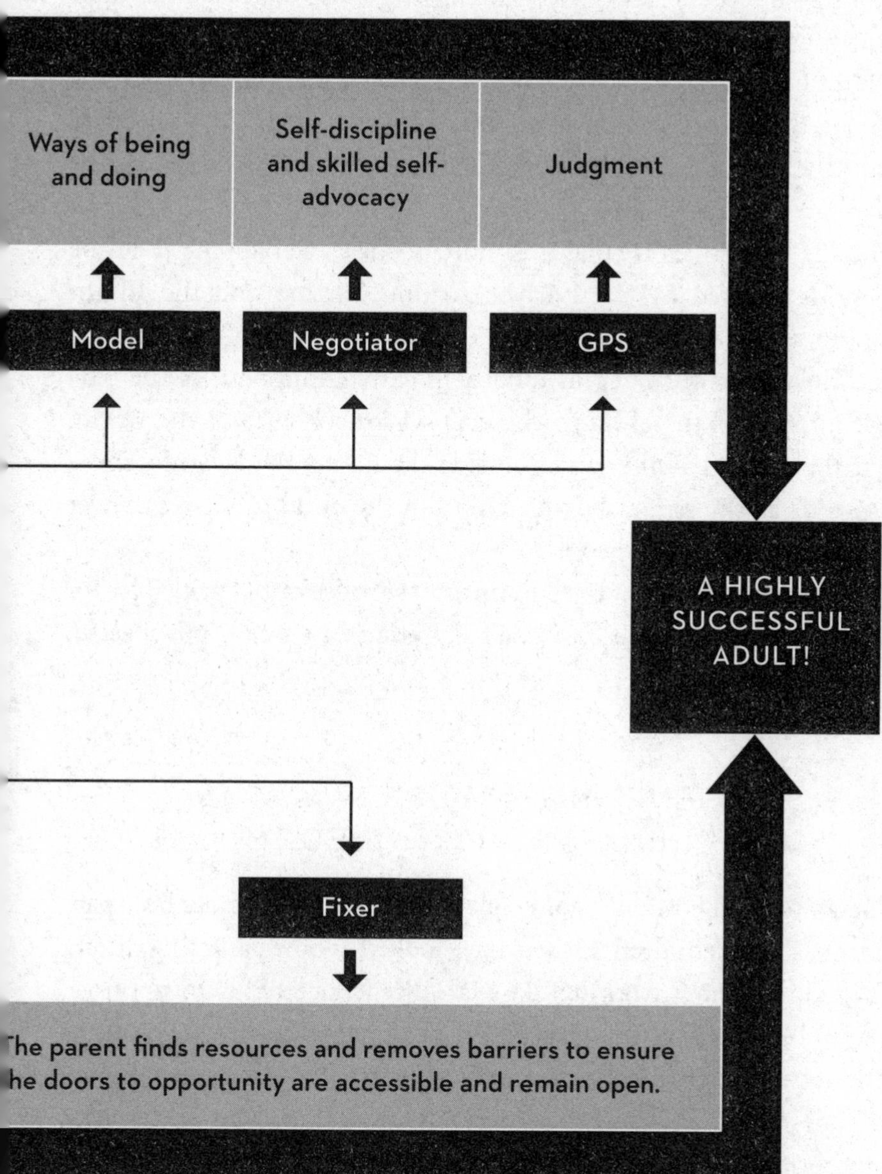
Ways of being and doing
Self-discipline and skilled self-advocacy
Judgment
Model
Negotiator
GPS
A HIGHLY SUCCESSFUL ADULT!
Fixer
he parent finds resources and removes barriers to ensure
he doors to opportunity are accessible and remain open.

world, the parent shifts from managing them up close (as their Early-Learning Partner) to managing them from a distance (as the Flight Engineer). These two roles are also foundational; the parents in these roles are responsible for launching the child successfully into the world, and the impact of these initial influences can be seen far into adulthood.

The other roles are played simultaneously, overlapping the time periods covered by the Early-Learning Partner and the Flight Engineer, though some rise in importance over time. For example, the Revealer's work begins quietly in early childhood, as the parent introduces the child to the everyday mechanics of the world, but then, as the child moves outside the home, the Revealer's role expands as the parent begins exposing the child to bigger, newer places, interests, and people.

Together, the eight roles comprise a set of essential principles for successful parenting: a Formula for producing a smart, purposeful, and confident adult.

PARENTING STYLES: WHAT IS DIFFERENT ABOUT THE FORMULA?

Of course, the Formula is only one of many theories about how parenting shapes children. Others have looked at how parenting differs in middle- versus working-class families (concerted cultivation vs. natural growth), at the pros and cons of being heavily involved in children's lives (helicopter parenting), and at how different parental approaches to managing discipline affect behavior and grades (authoritative parenting vs. authoritarian or permissive parenting). In recent years, a bestselling book even touted the supposed advantages of parenting grounded in Asian cultural traditions (tiger parenting).

The Formula is different in that we explicitly set out to discover what is distinct about the type of parenting that leads to superior achievement. We were not responding to existing notions about parenting and aiming to prove them right or wrong; we were not seeking to judge between competing ideas as to what makes parents most effective. And we were genuinely open-minded in asking whether young adults of diverse ethnicities, socioeconomic backgrounds, and national origins, all of whom by any reasonable measure are making the most of their lives, had been parented in a similar way.

However, the Formula does share commonalities with many well-studied parenting methods, and it's worth taking a moment here to compare them—both to see where the Formula overlaps with other parenting approaches, and to better understand what about master parents' approach is distinct.

Concerted Cultivation

In the 1990s, Annette Lareau, a sociologist from the University of Pennsylvania, along with her team of graduate students, intensely observed twelve families—six white, five black, and one interracial—every day for three weeks as part of a larger study of the families of eighty-eight poor, working-class, and middle-class third- and fourth-graders.

Lareau concluded that children from different socioeconomic backgrounds are parented in very different ways. She identified two contrasting parenting styles, the first of which she called *concerted cultivation*.

Most common among the middle class, this style of parenting teaches children to interact confidently with adults in general and authority figures in particular. Concerted cultivation supports high levels of extracurricular activity, including after school and on weekends. Lareau observed that parents practicing this parenting style often pressed their children into pursuits that the children themselves did not select. And they tended to overschedule children, which limited children's opportunities to develop their own interests or learn to use unstructured time.

Children reared by the principles of the Formula are also taught to feel comfortable speaking to adults, including how to negotiate with them to achieve their aims. Their parents also encourage them to engage in extracurricular activities.

But where parents practicing concerted cultivation largely dictate what those activities are, the children of master parents largely choose their own. The master parent provides the menu, but the child selects the meal. And while the successful people in this book were all involved in afterschool programs and enrichment activities when they were children, they also spent lots of unstructured time working on their own toward mastering "passion projects" that really captivated them.

Natural Growth

The second parenting style that Lareau identified is called *natural growth*, and is common among working-class and poor families, who tend to believe that, while they should care and watch out for their children's safety, children should grow up organically without so much adult interference.

In the natural-growth parenting style, children are given lots of unstructured time to play outside and develop their own friendships and interests. But because they are on their own or with other children so much of the time, it is harder for them to develop the comfort level with authority and the language skills to self-advocate that children parented with concerted cultivation do. Their parents give orders rather than allow debate and negotiation. And while middle-class children parented with concerted cultivation can be rude to their parents, the fact that they are not afraid of authority figures can, according to Lareau, be an advantage in the future. (Although products of the

Formula are raised to feel comfortable with adults and to even disagree with them when necessary, nearly all of our achievers said rudeness was usually not tolerated.)

Lareau also noted that working-class parents could be shy about making demands on instructors and administrators compared to middle-class parents, meaning their children sometimes ended up less well-served by their teachers and schools. Master parents, regardless of their socioeconomic status, were vigilant and assertive.

To be sure, natural-growth childrearing also comes with its own advantages. Children are typically able to choose from a larger swath of activities, and develop closer ties with their siblings and members of their extended family. Although lack of finances can prevent blue-collar parents from sending their children to enhancement programs, Lareau observed that working-class children are less bored compared to middle-class children. They're also less exhausted. And they learn to be more independent.

The Formula, too, allows for ample independence—once the master parent has instilled productive routines that become habits, which then guide the child on autopilot. Like working-class parents following the natural-growth approach, master parents allow for a more organic development of interests and trust their child to organize their own time. But where many working-class parents are forced to do so for financial reasons, master parents strategically choose to give their children this freedom—because they know the child will benefit from it.

Helicopter Parenting

The term *helicopter parenting* comes from Dr. Haim Ginott's 1969 book *Between Parent and Teenager*, in which a child complains that his mother hovers over him like a helicopter. This parenting style is ultra-involved and often intrusive, and the term is usually considered derogatory. But helicopter parenting is not without benefits. The abundance of attention helps the child feel cared for and provides ample opportunities for the parent to monitor the child and their teachers and to introduce the child to new things.

However, helicopter parents are often so omnipresent that it limits their children's opportunities to learn to handle obstacles solo and build confidence in their abilities. Children of helicopter parents find it hard to establish relationships that are truly their own, especially with adults. Helicopter parents also place a mental toll on themselves. They can immerse themselves so deeply in their identity as their child's caretaker that, when the child leaves home, they feel lost.

In the Formula, the parent monitors the child carefully, but is strategic about getting involved. In the roles of Flight Engineer and Fixer, the parent keeps their distance most of the time, intervening *only* when the child is not able to handle a situation themselves. This allows the child to build confidence in their ability to figure things out on their own, while still feeling safe and supported. And even though master parents make parenting a top priority, it's not their whole world. In other words, while parenting is a priority and a reason for sacrifice, master parents have their own interests and goals separate from childrearing.

Tiger Parenting

Yale professor and mother of two Amy Chua coined the popular term *tiger mother* in her 2011 memoir on tough love in Asian families, *Battle Hymn of the Tiger Mother.*

Like the Early-Learning Partner, the tiger parent spends a ton of time reading and playing games with their toddlers in order to help them adopt a habit of and passion for learning new things. Later, however, tiger parents place heavy demands on their children to achieve perfection in both academic and extracurricular activities. Master parents want their children to do their best and grades provide a useful indication of this, but they are not obsessed with whether their children achieve perfection or gain admission to an Ivy League college. It is less important to them for the child to work toward the parent's ideas of what they should be or do than it is for the child to find their own direction in life, and learn how to work effectively toward it.

Tiger parenting fails to encourage autonomy, and can stunt the development of purpose. Even more, it can do emotional harm, sparking feelings of inadequacy and resentment. A 2013 study of 444 Chinese American students found that tiger parenting was neither the most common nor the most effective way of childrearing among those families. Children parented by tiger parents had lower grades and felt less family-oriented compared to those children parented in a more "supportive" style. Master parenting, in contrast, brings the best out in high-achieving children by helping them identify their own goals in life and supporting them in their efforts to reach those goals.

Authoritative Parenting

The final parenting style instructive for understanding what the Formula is and is not is *authoritative parenting.*

In the 1960s, clinical psychologist Diana Baumrind was concerned that the existing debate on child discipline was misguided and damaging. In one camp were parents who believed they should avoid spanking their kids. Instead, they chose to hug and kiss them, even when the child was acting out. The other camp believed that parents should rule with an iron hand, being strict and quick to administer corporal punishment.

Baumrind believed both were wrong. She coined the phrase *authoritative parenting*, which represents a middle ground—or "lenient-strict," coincidentally the exact term Elizabeth Lee used to describe herself. Authoritative parenting as a style is defined as being emotionally responsive and loving, but also firm (though fair) when it comes to setting and enforcing rules. The child who has been parented using the authoritative style knows that their parents listen to and respect them, but also that their parents will enforce the rules they've set.

Authoritative parenting contrasts with parenting that exhibits too little responsiveness to the child's preferences (authoritarian parenting), too little boundary setting (permissive parenting), and too little of both responsiveness and boundary enforcement (neglectful parenting).

Of the parenting types we've discussed here, authoritative parenting has the most in common with the Formula. Authoritative parents, like master parents, effectively balance drawing boundaries and allowing the child to make their own decisions.

THE FORMULA'S STRATEGIC PARENTING

While the Formula shares some commonalities with all of the parenting styles above, it nonetheless stands apart as a road map for parenting children who grow up to be highly intelligent, purposeful, and successful adults. The reason for this? The master parent's strongly intentional, *strategic* approach to childrearing.

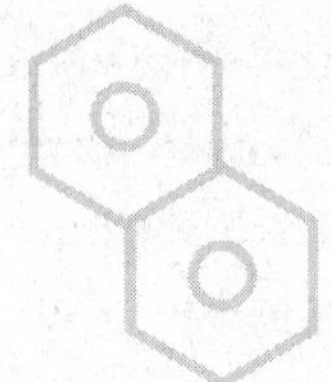

CHAPTER 4

The Strategists

THE STRANGE AND STRATEGIC PARENTING OF LISA SON

A psychology professor who specializes in the science of thinking and learning, Lisa Son pulls off a style of parenting that few of us would have the moxie—or expertise—to attempt: one based on lying, strategically, to her kids. Through this unorthodox style of parenting, she is raising smart, mentally nimble kids who enjoy posing questions, then figuring out the answers for themselves.

Born in northern New Jersey, the fortyish daughter of Korean immigrants lives in Short Hills, a wealthy New Jersey suburb west of New York City, with her husband, a computer programmer, and her children, a girl and a boy, eight and three at the time of our interviews.

Packed with captains of industry and executives of large Manhattan corporations, Short Hills was named the "richest town in America" in 2014 by *Time* magazine. The median home listing is $1.75 million, and seven out of ten households earn above $150,000. Learning three languages is held in such regard among families in their community that some children born to American parents learn Mandarin or Spanish before English to give the children a head start. Children's standardized test scores are among the best in the nation, according to *Time*.

All that money and success comes with pressure. Lisa has seen many children pushed to be the best at everything, and their harried parents rushing from one activity to another. But she's also seen those same parents too easily give their child answers to questions or shout the right answer in frustration when a child gets something wrong. Not Lisa.

"When my daughter was three and a half, she called her cousin in Korea for the first time. It was in the evening. I said, 'Oh, he's just going to be waking up for this morning.' And, she goes, 'What?' And that was very confusing for her. And I said, 'Yeah, it's morning there, even though it's night here.' And she was like, 'What?! Why?'"

One might have expected Lisa to explain the rotation of the Earth to her precocious little girl. But Lisa never gave her daughter the answer, keeping her in the dark for three long months. Every single morning when her daughter woke up, she'd ask Lisa about her cousin who was probably headed to bed. "She couldn't figure it out," Lisa recalled.

During that three-month period, Lisa provided her daughter with little hints—teaching her that the light from the sun was what made it daytime and what shape the Earth was—but never answers. Finally, she gave her a "mega hint"—the biggest one yet:

"I put my fist in a dark room and then out, and I took a flashlight because she, by that time, understood that light comes from the sun. So then if the sun's over here, here's the sun, and if I turn the flashlight on, okay, where are we? She understood by that time that the Earth rotates and spins, and so she figured it out on her own, but with all these hints. Now, I just think she'll never forget that."

An expert in cognitive psychology and memory, Lisa studies all types of strategies that enhance learning. One strange and unusual thing that works for her two curious children is fibbing to them about certain facts, which, like not giving them the answers outright, allows them to build confidence in their ability to figure things out for themselves.

"I've lied to my kids so often about just perceptual facts," she confessed. When her daughter was learning to spell, she asked Lisa how to spell *happy*. Lisa told her it was *h-a-p-y*, and then added, "I think."

Her daughter knew something was up. She wrote the word down, and then wrinkled her nose as she studied it. "I don't think that looks right."

"Well, I think it's *h-a-p-y*," Lisa replied.

Her daughter tried other ways to spell the word, finally writing *happy* on her own. "I never give her a straight answer if she asks me the spelling of a word, but I will give her a hint." One time her daughter asked how to spell the word *crazy*. "She couldn't get the last letter. She didn't know if it was *crazie* or *crazy*. So I said, 'Does *crazy* look better as *babies* or does it look like something else?'"

To figure it out, Lisa's daughter had to imagine what the word should look like, based on what she knew about other words.

Lisa isn't trying to confuse her children. "It's more about decreasing the use of feedback, which could backfire. The instinct for parents is to give all the answers to their kids, but that could slow down their learning process. It's much more important for kids to learn on their own, even if they are making errors."

Like the other master parents we spoke to, Lisa spent a lot of time strategizing about how to introduce the qualities she wanted her children to have: "I thought a lot about how to cultivate tolerance and opinion without disagreement. I wanted my children to be okay with it."

She achieved that outcome, too, through fibbing—in this case, by offering a wrong answer. "When he was about a year and a half, my son learned his colors. And then he would go around and go, 'Oh, that's blue.' And I would say, 'No, it's not. It's pink.' He would look at me very confused and he would think it's blue. And then he would go, 'Okay, but I think that's blue.' And I go, 'Well, I think it's pink.'"

The exchange was so memorable that she knew he'd never forget it. It taught him that different people have different points of view and opinions, and to trust his own judgment but also to respect others'.

"Ever since then, he realizes that I am not going to see things the same way he will but he's okay with it. I like the idea of being very flexible in terms of your thoughts and other people's thoughts. Both of them I've raised like that."

Lisa says that, first, "it shows them that there isn't always only one right answer. And second, it could help with their confidence. That is, even if others disagree with them, they can stand their ground."

Is Lisa Son's parenting style unique? You bet. But the strategic thinking behind it is typical of how master parents approach stimulating their children to become learners. Understanding that her children love to find their own answers and are unhappy when they're confused, Lisa cultivates just enough mystery to motivate them to search for a resolution. She makes it possible with hints that put them within striking distance of an answer. She pulls up to the end of the driveway and has them walk the rest of the way.

In the process, her children learn to not expect or depend on anyone else to give them an answer but to find it themselves—and to enjoy the hunt.

"Having kids learn on their own means you are putting the child in the driver's seat. This type of active learning makes up the core of metacognition, my research. Even with older kids, for instance, active discussion classes or lab classes are more beneficial than lecture classes where students often sit passively," Lisa said.

Though her children are still young, she can already see her efforts paying off. They are early readers, and are already becoming bilingual. Her son and daughter are flexible and independent thinkers, and comfortable with questioning adults—all qualities Lisa envisioned and took strategic steps to foster.

THE ART OF INTENTIONAL PARENTING

Master parenting is not happenstance. It is purposeful. Think of Elizabeth Lee, who, because she wanted young Jarell to do well in school and not have to live in inner-city Cleveland, strategically put her son on an accelerated learning track by teaching him to read and count as a toddler, and chose shelters based on whether they would give them access to schools that had gifted programs.

The parents of all the successful people we interviewed were, like Lisa and Elizabeth, strategists, pure and simple. A strategist envisions the future they want and works backward to figure out, then execute, the steps needed to achieve it. And that's exactly what these master parents did.

Being an effective strategist requires three things. Most obviously, it requires that the parent become *a student of their child*. The master parent learns their child inside and out, and calibrates their actions accordingly. If Lisa Son's children had become easily frustrated, leaving them to figure out the answers on their own the way she did might have backfired; they might have just given up. But because Lisa knew they would be persistent, she was able to turn their curiosity into practice in learning things for themselves. By observing their achiever as they grow and learn, the master parent is also able to adjust their approach to guide their child's development, keeping them on track for success.

But there are two other elements essential to an effective parenting strategy: the parent's vision, and the intense motivation behind that vision.

A MASTER PARENT'S MOTIVATION

A person's personal history is what shapes their worldview and values, which determine how they see and respond to the world. So it's unsurprising that it would affect the way they parent, as well.

In the case of master parents, their personal history often results in an intense, deep-rooted motivation that we call *the Burn*. The Burn is what drives a parent to go the extra mile and make the sacrifices necessary to apply the principles of master parenting. It's what drove Elizabeth—miserable and frustrated as she struggled to raise a son with no money and no home, but desperate to ensure that he grew up to have a better life than she did—to sit with Jarrell night after night in the homeless shelter, teaching her baby boy how to read and count.

The Burn, in other words, fuels the master parent's determination to raise their child to the very best of their ability. It also shapes how they go about doing just that.

Why Esther Wojcicki Raised the Smartest Girls in the World

Palo Alto journalism teacher Esther Wojcicki can't count the times people have asked her the same question: How is it that she and her husband Stan, a Stanford University physicist, raised three daughters who, as adults, have all become giants in male-dominated fields? It's a question she even asks herself.

Her daughters have been called the "Silicon Valley sisters." Susan, the oldest, is the chief executive of YouTube. Years before, she was Google's first marketing manager. *Forbes* has named her one of the most powerful women in the world. Esther's youngest daughter, Anne, is the CEO of 23andMe, the revolutionary personal genome company, whose methods *Time* magazine called the most important invention of 2008. The career of Esther's middle daughter, Janet, is perhaps less public, but just as laudable: she is an anthropologist and professor of epidemiology at the University of California San Francisco Medical School, a Fulbright scholar who speaks several African dialects, and a pioneer in understanding the relationship between nutritional factors and the progression of HIV infections, with a focus on sub-Saharan African populations.

In television interviews and magazine articles, Esther's daughters have tried their best to explain how their parents, especially their mother, helped them become who they are today. They've described how their mother taught them that almost any problem is solvable, and that it was okay, sometimes even necessary, to question authority. "I don't think we were ever intimidated by anyone," Anne said. Because of the way they were raised, they were not afraid to dive into difficult challenges. And they never accepted the idea that the status quo could not be improved.

Still, the real secret to Esther's parenting success is less how she did it, than what propelled her to do it the way she did—her Burn. Esther was driven by an intense desire to raise fearless girls who would challenge authority and have the opportunities her family tried to deny her.

Esther was raised in a poor Orthodox Jewish family and community where girls were second to boys. The oldest child and only girl in the family, she was told when the first of her three brothers was born that he was now number one: he'd be their priority, not her.

By the time Esther was ten years old, she was well aware of how poor they were. "We didn't have much of anything. We were below poverty level. That's when I decided studying was the only way out." But when she turned fourteen, Esther's parents announced that they would not help pay for her college despite the fact that she had become an excellent student, and would eventually graduate high school as valedictorian. "They said they were saving all their money for my three brothers."

Her purpose in life, they told her, was to marry a rich Jewish man. She soon defied them, taking a reporting job when she was still a high school student and attaining a college scholarship to the University of California at Berkeley, where she later received a BA in English and political science.

Esther grew up having something to prove to the world—that girls are just as good and just as smart as anybody else. It fueled her unrelenting determination to raise daughters who would be self-assured, in-your-face superstars. And she did.

You can also see, in Esther's background, the source of her daughters' willingness to question authority. Esther's youngest brother David died after playing with a bottle of aspirin and swallowing the pills. When her mother first discovered David had ingested the aspirin, she called a doctor who instructed her to put the child to bed, which she did. But he remained ill. When they tried to take him to the emergency room, the family was turned away by three hospitals because they had no proof of ability to pay. The fourth hospital took him in but it was too late.

His unnecessary death taught Esther that people in positions of authority can be incompetent and uncaring and, in those cases, did not deserve the deference her mother gave them. She began to question authority in ways that her mother had not—thinking for herself, challenging authorities to explain and justify their assertions—and, thanks to the strength of her Burn, passed this same view on to her daughters.

A MASTER PARENT'S VISION

Esther's Burn did not just motivate her commitment to parenting. It also inspired a clear vision for what she hoped her daughters would someday become (independent, and unafraid to challenge authority)—a vision that guided the way she parented.

For master parents, the image of who their child could be—the laudable characteristics they hope the child will someday acquire, shaped by the parent's personal history—is at the heart of their parenting strategy. We call this aspirational vision the *holographic ideal*: *holographic*, because the parent projects an image of their fully grown child in their mind's eye; and *ideal*, because the image includes all the best qualities the parent hopes the child will have.

For our master parents, the holographic ideal they envisioned before the child was born possessed a range of special qualities they admired in others and aspired to have themselves. Many parents envisioned a lifestyle free from poverty and hardship, with bountiful support for enrichment and growth. Though the parent may have fallen short of living this ideal themselves, they committed to do their best to make it real for their child.

This does *not* mean the parent used their child to make up for their own failures or tried to live out their own dream through their child. The master parent's goal is to help the child to be *their* very best self, not become a clone of the parent. The holographic ideal is a guide for the parent's strategy, not a straitjacket. The expectation is that the child will eventually take what their parent taught them and reinterpret the parent's vision to make it their own.

Elizabeth's holographic ideal was a son who no longer lived in the ghetto, who was highly educated, and who had a middle-class job. Lisa Son's holographic ideal was children who could think for themselves. But no one's holographic ideal was more vivid than Elaine Badger's.

Ms. Badger's Holographic Ideal

Elaine's Burn was a desire to not replicate with her young son, Chuck, a mistake she'd made in the past. Her oldest son spent time in prison, which Elaine attributed to her not being as involved as she should have been with his life and her failure to keep him off the streets. With Chuck, she swore, everything would be different.

Elaine Badger had limited personal knowledge of what success required. She lived in poverty, was socially isolated from successful people, and suffered from physical disabilities that limited her mobility. Still, she was dead set on Chuck excelling. Even before he was born, Elaine had in mind an image of what a successful man looked like. He dressed beautifully and used big words. People would stand back and respect not only his achievements, but his style and self-confidence.

It was a big vision. And she'd get Chuck there, despite her background.

Elaine insisted that Chuck should always be presentable as part of her own version of him "becoming middle class." She emphasized neatness in every aspect of his schoolwork, performance, and personal appearance.

For black Americans, looking and acting presentable has long been an act of social resistance to racist stereotypes—an assertion that "I'm somebody to respect." For example, perhaps no American in the nineteenth century was photographed more than Frederick Douglass. Through those photographs, Douglass offered a competing narrative to the perception in broader society that black people were inferior. He dressed formally, spoke with eloquence, and used photography to confront racists with his dignity. He often looked straight into the camera and he never smiled. Elaine instinctively took a page out of the same book in setting expectations for Chuck, who still has a fondness for wearing bow ties.

Chuck attributes a significant part of his success to his mother's high standards for him. He also traces his early comfort in leadership and speaking roles to performances his mother had him practice as a young child to present at church. As early as five, you could see in Chuck the man his mother had wanted him to become: confident, capable, well spoken, and well dressed. Today, the young man, still in his twenties, is a successful political consultant who has worked with congressmen and Republican presidential candidates and has done a stint in the White House. He's embraced the image of the successful man his mother strategically shaped him to be, and has taken it even further.

There's a video clip available on YouTube of Chuck on C-SPAN holding his own on a panel of nationally prominent thought leaders gathered to discuss the 2016 election. Well dressed (sans the bow tie), with a perfectly shaved head and a neat, thick beard, Chuck is elegant in the way he carries himself, but he's also a captivating speaker, who comes off as decades older than he is. He is the real-life embodiment of Elaine's holographic vision from before he was born: there are the big words she wanted, and the well-groomed man in a blazer and tie just as she envisioned, and the people admiring his confidence, just as she hoped, saying, as we did, "Wow, who is this impressive young man?" But as much as he turned out to be who his mother wanted him to be, the Chuck onstage, a young black Republican with his own moderate angle on the party's philosophy, is also 100 percent his own person.

STRATEGIC THINKING: THE FOUNDATION OF MASTER PARENTING

A strategic approach is not only a thread you'll see drawn throughout this book; it is hardwired in the DNA of the Formula's eight roles. But what really makes the Formula so effective is that parents start to be strategic very early—even before the child is born.

Our master parents were incredibly intentional about building their child a strong foundation for learning during their early years, which gave the future achiever a huge running start. That foundation was crucial, and directly linked to their later success. And there's no one for whom this was more true than Rob Humble, whose father performed the first role of the Formula, the Early-Learning Partner, in a masterful way.

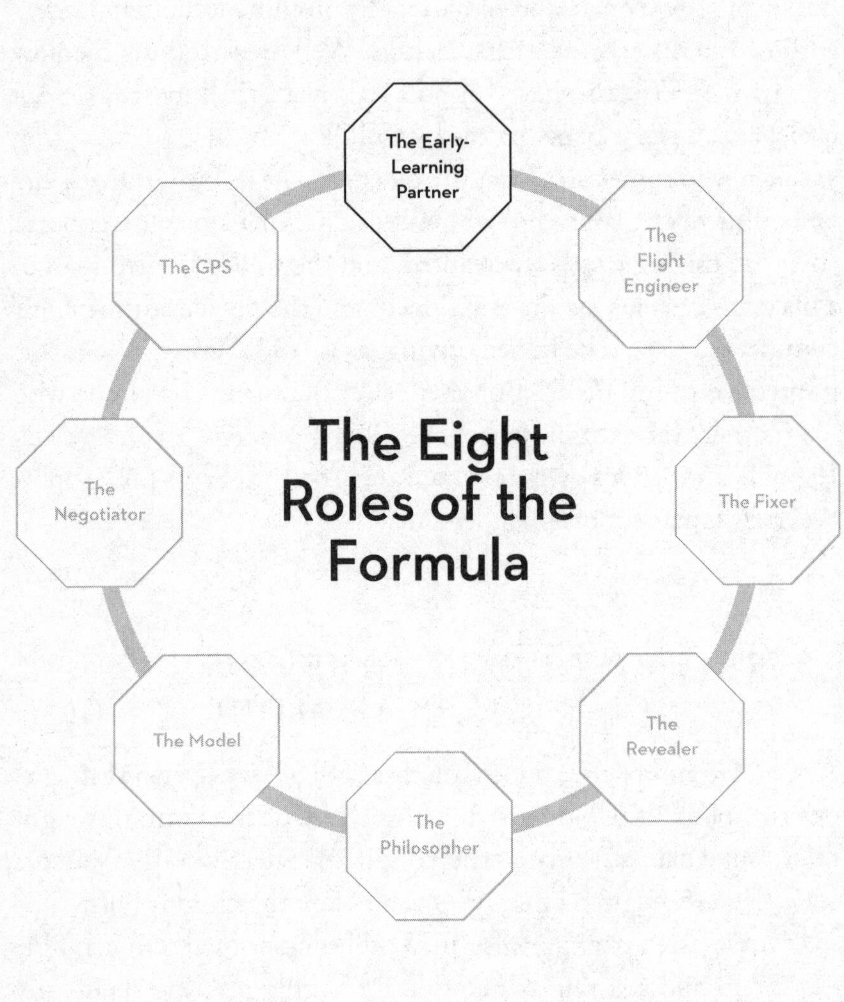
The Early-
Learning
Partner
The
Flight
Engineer
The Fixer
The
Revealer
The
Philosopher
The Model
The
Negotiator
The GPS
The Eight
Roles of the
Formula

CHAPTER 5

The Early-Learning Partner (Role #1)

ROB HUMBLE'S MOMENT OF TRUTH

Rob Humble was the smartest boy in his small town of Collinsville, Oklahoma. Few people there would deny this. Small for his age back then, with blondish-brown hair, he was nevertheless as sturdy and clever as his forebears: hardy people who came to seek their fortunes more than a century earlier in the bluegrass prairies above sprawling coal beds.

Always in the local newspaper for one award or another, Rob didn't just make straight As. He participated in all-state band, all-state orchestra, all-state choir, and was all-state in academics. He played football and soccer, ran track, weight lifted, sang in the choir, and could also knit. Nothing slowed him down. Only four days after a near-death car accident, he performed with his bassoon in an all-state high school band competition. But once he was accepted to the highly regarded Washington University in St. Louis, none of that mattered.

What mattered instead was that he found himself in a tight spot. He wanted to major in engineering, but his high school couldn't afford to offer calculus or physics—both requirements for freshman engineering majors. Rob's only recourse was to take a four-week crash course in both classes the summer before college and hope for the best.

That first week in St. Louis, Rob registered for the required Calculus II and calculus-based physics courses with a twinge of trepidation about his summer preparation.

"I'd learned everything I needed to know about differentiation that summer but was still clueless about integrals," he said. The apprehension was warranted. The calculation of integrals, a mathematical method for measuring the areas under continuous curves, was one of the first things the calculus professor asked students to do.

One thing was for certain. Rob's engineering schoolmates were academically light-years ahead of him. "I called my parents from college the first week literally breaking down in tears because I didn't know if I was going to be able to do it."

It's a wonder Rob didn't drop out right then. He considered going back home, but that would cause an additional burden on his parents and younger sister, with his mother recently diagnosed with bipolar disorder and out of work after losing her legal secretary job, and his father drawing only a schoolteacher's salary. Rob resolved to stick it out in St. Louis.

That year, his professors had outdone themselves, launching an elaborate engineering-design competition for freshmen. They set forth an intimidating obstacle course that Rob and his classmates would have to navigate with robots they created themselves.

This caused Rob additional anxiety, but there was something else, too: a fresh sense of excitement. His mind buzzed with ideas as he mapped out plans to build the best robot in the class. It was as if a voice whispered in his ear, *Now, here's something you can do.*

"My father always told me," Rob said, "if you take something apart, you can figure out anything."

One of Rob's earliest memories is sitting on the floor with his father when he was four, the two of them playing with Legos.

"I'd build a tower, and he would say, 'That's really interesting but can you do it with all blues?' Then I would do that, and he would say, 'Oh, that was really good, but can you do it with red and yellow stripes?'"

They spent countless hours playing together, Bob Senior challenging his son to construct the Lego tower better, more creatively—more efficiently. He'd wonder out loud if Rob could build the bridge to hold twenty pounds, or he'd help Rob construct a tower with steps that receded.

"I'd say, 'Take those yellow ones there and see if you could make the same house with those Legos,'" Bob Senior recalled in his Oklahoma twang. "He'd sit there and try to figure it out; the other ones were easy to figure out because they were uniform size but these weren't."

Rob's father was acting as an Early-Learning Partner, the first of the eight roles of the Formula, and the most important clue to answering the larger mystery in this book: How do parents raise high achievers?

The master parent as Early-Learning Partner engages the child from birth to age five in building foundations for life success. They welcome the child to a world where failures are not final verdicts, but rather puzzles to be analyzed and then solved. The parent's approach invites the child to share the driver's seat in their learning journey, and encourages the receptive child to think of learning as fun and a natural part of life.

Many of the successful people in the book recall "spending loads of time" with one parent when they were three, four, and five. If they weren't playing Legos like Rob, they were practicing reading words like Jarell, learning the violin like Maggie Young, or exploring nature or learning numbers like some of our other high achievers.

These weren't just isolated activities. Early play—whether tinkering with blocks, reading from flash cards, learning an instrument, or just gazing at the stars—stimulates the brain in a way that inspires discipline, imagination, and critical thinking, all of which cultivate the confidence and skills needed to engage fully in more difficult subjects later on like physics, calculus, or writing.

When Rob heard about the robot competition, he recognized his professors wanted the students to tinker and innovate. "This was one area where I knew I could kick butt."

With his knack for thinking through problems and figuring things out, Rob says, "I saw this as my opportunity to make my mark in a school that for every other reason seemed to really intimidate me."

He barely slept for weeks. "They actually ended up giving me a key to the lab where we built the robots because I wanted to spend more hours in there than it was open. And so I'd go in with the key at 7 AM on Saturday and I'd remain until midnight. Sometimes I forgot to eat."

The challenge was brutal, but Rob felt like the assignment was something he was born to do. On the day of the competition, he was as calm as a summer breeze. His robot glided through the obstacle course as if its wheels had been buttered. Each student was given two motors to create the robot, but Rob needed only one. "None of my friends came to see it, but my dad drove all the way from Oklahoma to St. Louis."

The moment he won the competition, a flag attached to the unused motor began spinning, a symbolic air punch from Rob to his rivals.

THE SCIENCE OF PLAY

It could be that the most important thing master parents do, beginning when their children are mere infants and toddlers, is engage them in activities that stimulate the brain, preparing it to problem-solve—to hold a jumble of puzzle pieces in their heads and reconfigure the pieces until they all fit together.

Whether Rob's dad knew it or not, playing Legos with his little boy was helping Rob develop sophisticated abilities—big things, such as spatial reasoning and intuition about the structural integrity of design (which are fundamentals of engineering, according to researchers at MIT, which has its own Lego lab). Lego play helps children develop a practical sense of geometry; it equips them to imagine a physical structure, plan how to combine different shapes and sizes of Lego pieces to build it, and then execute that plan to produce what they have imagined.

It gets deeper.

There's been a recent explosion of fascinating evidence obtained using MRI brain scan technology that shows how certain kinds of activity, playing with blocks in particular, literally reorganize the brain during play.

In 2016, researchers at the University of Indiana published results of a study that used neuroimaging to examine the effects of block building on brain activity. By scanning the brains of two groups of eight-year-olds before and after playing either Scrabble or building blocks for five half-hour sessions, researchers compared the impacts the two games had on spatial processing. Researchers also administered a mental rotation test (imagining what an object will look like after it's rotated) before and after the set of play sessions.

"The block playing changed brain activation patterns," the researchers observed. "It changed the way the children were solving the mental rotation problem; we saw increased activation in regions that have been linked to spatial processing only in the building blocks group."

That is, they did not see the same changes among the children that played Scrabble. The block-playing children also showed improvement in reaction time and accuracy of solutions.

If this is the case among eight-year-olds, imagine the impact on under-fives, whose brains are growing at an incredible rate, nearly reaching adult size by kindergarten.

Spatial awareness is bolstered when a child builds a house of cards, plays a game of chess, constructs her own dollhouse, or creates new worlds in *Minecraft*. It is particularly key in video games, which require a player to visualize and mentally rotate objects. But let's take a step back and really think about what superior spatial problem-solving skills equip a person to do.

An automotive designer must use spatial reasoning to conceive of a design, then transfer that design from their mind onto paper, by sketching what they've imagined. Once they begin building three-dimensional models of the car out of clay—first small, eventually full-sized—they must use that spatial reasoning to problem-solve, reimagining and refining their design to move it from conception to reality.

Even when solving a simple equation such as $x + 3 = 5$, a child, likewise, must use their mind's eye to figure out they need to remove 3 from both sides of the equation in order to isolate x. In geometry, that same student will need to picture in their head how an image involving multiple shapes will change when they combine them in different ways or change the angle between two sides of a polygon.

But STEM (science, technology, engineering, and mathematics) isn't all spatial reasoning is useful for. In sports, a wrestler imagines how to maneuver their opponent into a particular position, and a student of judo envisions dropping in a manner that cushions the impact before they hit the floor.

In essence, tinkering with Legos—especially in the ways his father guided him—not only helped Rob grasp basic concepts of math and science, but also taught him how to identify a problem, analyze it, and design a solution. Rob strongly believes this problem-solving orientation that he learned as a four-year-old was key to his ability to compete in—and win—that robot competition.

Scientific research supports the idea that what we learn as a very young child impacts our adult capabilities—far beyond just playing with blocks. Neurobiologists have established that many early life experiences, like counting, pointing, discussing, reading, and playing an instrument or a sport, can affect the physical structure of the preschool brain and help determine the ease with which a child learns particular skills for the rest of their life. What's more, every instance of constructive stimulation helps to strengthen the neural pathways along which new ideas travel, like widening streets to carry more traffic in a growing city. In short, the time Rob spent playing Legos with his father, basking in his attention while figuring out how the different-shaped blocks fit together, arranged the architecture of Rob's brain in such a way that similar forms of thought—tinkering and probing and, most important of all, imagining—became easier for Rob fourteen years later as he faced the engineering assignment that changed his life.

After his win, Rob felt as if he had crossed a threshold, entering a life he was confident he could navigate. Though he'd breezed through high school, his college years were tough. He got through, though, recalling inspiration from his father's favorite saying: "You know, if you work hard enough and long enough there's nothing you can't accomplish."

Using the same knack for thinking through problems and figuring things out that helped him win the robot contest, Rob was able to organize his college life. He eventually made a B in Calculus. It was the lowest grade in his whole life, but still a triumph, considering where he'd started. He found a way to not only succeed in his school work, but also to have a life, singing in chorus, joining school religious organizations, and even taking on a part-time job to help cover his schooling expenses.

After college graduation, Rob ran a department with a major defense contractor and held a director-level job at a Fortune 1000 company while still in his twenties. Then he entered the MBA program at Harvard University, where he met his wife, a graduate of the Harvard Divinity School. "After business school, I worked for a chemical company in Dallas and then went to work in corporate strategy," he said. In one year, he advanced in another major company from a manager of strategy, the lowest person on the totem pole, to top strategic planner. Now, in his early thirties, he's flying high as the lead strategist for a corporate enterprise in Austin, Texas, where he and his wife are Early-Learning Partners to their two small children, a boy and a girl.

THE CRITICAL PERIOD AND THE 400-FOOT LEAP

The Early-Learning Partner is the most important of the eight roles because of the early start the parent in this role provides their child. The play a parent engages in with their preschool child gives the child great advantages, in particular an academic edge that puts them ahead of other children.

Across species, early learning is vital to laying a strong foundation for life. Scientists have long observed that, in the animal kingdom, the trials of life and learning start at birth. All organisms are born with built-in behaviors—instincts—but those instincts must then be developed into skills for survival.

Consider the death-defying leap newborn barnacle goslings must take just hours or days after hatching. Barnacle geese build their nests on mountains or cliffs, high enough to be safe from predators, but far from food. Since geese do not bring food to the nest for their babies, the chicks will starve if they do not follow their parents to the ground by taking a heart-wrenching leap of faith—as much as a 400-foot drop. Real BBC footage of the ritual is almost unbearable to watch as the tiny birds, which cannot yet fly, spread their itty-bitty wings wide as possible—and jump.

This jump is necessary for the goslings' survival—there's no food up in that nest, after all—but it is not necessarily instinctual. Neither are the skills to forage for food, hide from Arctic foxes, or migrate across continents. What *is* instinctual is the gosling's impulse to follow their parent. Very young human children are similarly hardwired to imitate their parents during early life in order to learn what they need to survive. Just as geese build on their goslings' natural abilities to allow them to thrive in their environment, human parents, too, use their baby's instincts to mold them into successful (or not so successful) adults. Every child is born with genetic potential, but how much of it gets expressed depends on the parent, as the most important part of the child's environment. Human infants have instincts to talk, for example, but they don't learn language without a parent's help.

Biologists and developmental psychologists call the short but critical window of time when goslings are able to quickly grasp what is being taught to them "the critical period." This is a fascinating maturation period in which an organism's nervous system is extremely flexible and sensitive to stimuli that help them learn certain skills and acquire certain traits.

Austrian zoologist Konrad Lorenz was the first to popularize the concept of the critical period, but he is best known for discovering the principles of attachment within the critical period, better known as "imprinting." In the 1930s, he discovered that newborn graylag geese would "imprint" on the first befitting stimuli they laid eyes on after birth—even a human. Lorenz is often shown in old documentary films leading a gaggle of geese that had imprinted themselves on him and treated him like a parent figure. Lorenz later discovered the geese could also imprint on objects, like a pair of wading boots or a ball, and that imprinting had to occur within a few hours after hatching.

Lorenz's astonishing work, which won him a Nobel Prize years later in 1973, has also helped change the way we think about human parenting. For normal development to occur, his work suggested, organisms must be introduced to and learn certain tasks during a specific window of time—something scientists are just now beginning to understand is true for human children, too. This critical, or, better yet, "sensitive," period of learning peaks between birth and five years of age, stretches into the early elementary school years, and is also described as a period of "developmental plasticity." During this period, children are especially sensitive to stimuli and learn most easily; their brains soak up knowledge like sponges.

While the critical period provides an incredible opportunity for learning, it carries a dangerous caveat: if you miss that critical period, you can't make up for it later. Lorenz also discovered that when birds born in captivity don't learn the basic skills a parent in the wild would normally provide during that critical period, they may never learn to fly or communicate with other geese. Human brain development has that same use-it-or-lose-it quality. A baby's potential blossoms when nurtured. It also withers with extreme neglect.

Take Eugenia, who lived in a Russian orphanage until she was adopted by American parents at two and a half years old. At age eighteen, she was still dealing with the effects of having no support or cognitive stimulation when she was a baby.

Though the orphanage was so clean one could eat off the floors, sparkle is no substitute for nurturing. Eugenia was left alone, rarely touched, and never held. The caregivers saw themselves as staff members—that's it.

As an adult, "I don't like to be touched. Ever," she told neuropsychiatrist Dr. Bruce Perry and journalist Maia Szalavitz in an interview for their book *Born for Love*. Even clothing touching her skin could cause unbearable pain; she had to pick the softest fabrics to avoid discomfort.

She also struggles with emotional connection. "A lot of my friends hug and are very close, but I don't get that close to people," she said. "If I never saw them again, I wouldn't mind."

We've seen how early positive stimulation and activities—Lego play, reading, playing the violin—improved the natural abilities of our high achievers. In contrast, being denied stimulation as a toddler stunted Eugenia's memory. She's also been diagnosed with auditory processing disorder; as Perry and Szalavitz write, "she wasn't fully taking in what she was hearing." As a result, she can't always recall what people have said to her and has a hard time following direction.

Eugenia believes these auditory and memory problems are directly related to the time she spent in the orphanage, and Perry agrees: "Although people don't have conscious memories of infancy, babies' early experiences nonetheless deeply imprint themselves into the brain."

The master parents we interviewed put so much effort into teaching their child in the first three to five years because they sensed that time was critical for development. They believed that the skills they encouraged, and how they responded to their child's needs, during that early period of time would have long-term effects on the child's cognitive, social, and emotional development.

"My theory back then, and I didn't read it anywhere, was that whatever I did from the first five years was going to determine how they were for the rest of their life," said Esther Wojcicki. It's why Esther believed it was so important to teach her daughters to read and count before they reached school age.

Rob Humble's father theorized that it mattered what he exposed his children to even earlier. Bob Senior put his beautiful tenor voice to use by singing to his wife's growing belly, convinced his children could hear him in utero.

"Rob heard my voice through the walls of his mama's tummy. When he came out, he knew the sounds. He would warm up when I sang to him. I think it was comforting. His sister did the same thing."

In fact, we now know, as Rob's father suspected, that a child can hear months before they're born. Several years ago, Dr. Kathleen Wermke of the University of Wurzburg in Germany supervised a groundbreaking study that examined the wails of newborns.

Using digital recorders, Wermke and her colleagues spent hundreds of hours studying the cry patterns of sixty French and German babies between two and five days old. Then scientists used computer software to analyze the cries. What they found was astonishing. The cries of French babies tended to start off low and then rise, like the intonation of French speakers. The German babies' cries started off high and then dropped, the way German speakers did. The researchers concluded the babies had been listening to their mothers' voices during the last few months of pregnancy and were now mirroring their accents in anticipation of speech.

MASTERS OF A DISCIPLINE

For our high achievers, the impact of this early "imprinting" extended beyond the preverbal years. As their Early-Learning Partners actively shared their own interests and avocations during those early years, the achiever often took on their parent's interests with great enthusiasm, making them their own.

Still, teaching a very young child to do things like read and play the violin can make us uncomfortable, especially those who see it as an imposition on the child. "Let children find *their own* interests," they might say. But it's not that these master parents were trying to indoctrinate their children; they were just sharing what they knew and were passionate about. Teaching curiosity and a love of learning by sharing a beloved vocation or specialty with one's child is only natural. The parent is saying, "This is interesting to me and it might be to you, too."

In the process, these children didn't just learn about whatever their parent was interested in; they were also learning how to take in information and explore new frontiers. The children and their parent-partners planned and executed small projects that frequently foreshadowed later achievements. Encouraged and supported by their Early-Learning Partner, these children became little builders, storytellers, musicians, social-justice activists, engineers, reptile specialists, and decision makers, on course for developing the habit of purposeful mastery.

Rob's dad loved music, and Rob sings and learned to play a number of instruments. But what Bob Senior wanted most for his son—his Burn—was for Rob to embrace another passion of his, one that had been passed down to him from past generations: being a thinker and problem solver like two of his inventor forefathers. Bob Senior himself had taken to that passed-down love of tinkering and thinking as a child. In fact, Bob Senior was so good at math and science that if he hadn't broken out in his high school music scene, he probably would have studied engineering in college, as his son later would. (Instead, after he graduated from Oral Roberts University in 1976, he started to teach music at Collinsville High School, where he has now worked for more than three decades.)

Bob Senior passed down a predilection for quantitative, spatial thinking and for problem solving, in addition to music. And although Rob loved music, he grew up to be a corporate strategist—which, simply put, is a professional problem solver.

RAISING STORYTELLERS: CULTIVATING THE POWER OF EMPATHY

Parents we interviewed who lean toward literacy more than STEM or music tended to focus on storytelling and reading, like Myrna, the mother of Suzanne and Suzette Malveaux.

The Malveaux household was a veritable playwriting and storytelling workshop, an apprenticeship for the storytellers that the girls—now a CNN anchor who tells others' stories for a living; and a lawyer and provost professor of civil rights law at the University of Colorado, as well as director of the Byron R. White Center for the Study of Constitutional Law, for whom stories come in the form of legal synopses—would grow up to become. It was also a library for reading, and a stage for both freewheeling and structured play—drawing, singing, puppet shows, and dance. There wasn't anything they could throw away. Why discard an empty toilet paper roll or milk carton when it could be reused to create something fun and beautiful? And a giant refrigerator box was just waiting to be painted and turned into a little house.

The girls' favorite project, from age three to early elementary, was creating families out of paper dolls and pasting them on Popsicle sticks. Each family had its own story and look. The dolls represented Asian families, Latin American families, and families that were both black and white. "We would spend hours and hours drawing these little cartoons, and then cutting them out and then storytelling," Suzanne said.

The act of storytelling—of imagining the lives of real people—stretches the brain. Storytellers have to come up with the words their characters will use, the ways they'll move, and even their vocal inflections and emotions. They must imagine how characters will interact with one another and how what one does will affect what the others will do. Storytelling builds empathy: it teaches the storyteller how to put themselves in other people's shoes, which in turn increases their ability to "read" (and respond to) others' thoughts and feelings.

Storytellers have a highly developed "theory of mind"—what scientists call the ability to anticipate how other people think. For example, a very young child playing hide-and-go-seek might amusingly think if they can't see the seeker, the seeker can't see them. They aren't yet capable of understanding that different people have different fields of vision and different points of view. Researcher Raymond Mar, a psychologist at York University in Canada, found that the more stories a preschool child had read to them, the more sophisticated their theory of mind became.

The combination of being read to and then being encouraged to come up with their own puppet stories in early childhood created a cognitive foundation for Suzette and Suzanne Malveaux to discern, distill, and communicate the real-world stories they would become so expert at telling in the courtroom and on television news.

TEACHING A BABY TO READ: THE EARLY-LEAD EFFECT

One reason the Early-Learning Partner role is so important is the way that early advantage impacts future success. Learning to read before reaching kindergarten, for example, tips a child toward academic preeminence—but not for the reasons one might think.

Humans are especially talented at recognizing social patterns, and one of the biggest drivers of human behavior is the desire to hold or improve our social position. Our prehistoric ancestors used pattern recognition to distinguish social hierarchies—learning who in their tribe had more or less influence, and where they fit in—and so do we.

Social scientists are finding that, for most children, third grade is when they become conscious of whether they are ahead of, equal to, or behind their classmates. But by the time our high achievers entered kindergarten, they reported already having started to recognize patterns of social order among peers. In other words, they saw that everyone was not treated the same.

Children like the ones in this book, whose parents taught them early and intentionally to be observant, also become aware as early as kindergarten that they are more advanced than the rest of their peers, and that they received more attention because of that. This realization comes with a motivational boost: they want to keep having that exuberant feeling, and reaping the rewards, which requires them to work hard to stay at the front of the pack.

We call this phenomenon the "early-lead effect."

Elizabeth Lee's decision to teach Jarell to read early initiated a ripple effect that set him on course to become a high achiever from the day he entered kindergarten. Jarell clearly recalls the teacher sitting him on her lap that first day, having expressed excitement that he knew how to read, and paying attention as he did so. He quickly recognized that knowing more than most of his peers caused his teacher to react in a positive way. He recognized the pattern and wanted to repeat it.

A version of this tale was so common among our 200 respondents that it almost felt like *Groundhog Day*: almost to a person, they cheerfully recalled a kindergarten teacher who was nearly giddy as the child read some simple sentences.

One achiever recalls her preschool teacher being stunned as she watched the four-year-old write words on the blackboard. Another woman, a Canadian screenwriter, remembers her kindergarten teacher being so excited that she knew how to read in French that she dragged her to the principal's office so he could see for himself.

There's a practical reason for the ripple effect this kind of moment initiates. Kindergarten teachers typically focus on pre-reading skills, such as letter sounds and two- or three-letter words, especially at the beginning of the year. But the children of master parents are typically well past these thresholds. When the busy teacher's eyes sparkle with delight, it's not just simple amazement; it's because the child's existing knowledge makes their job easier and opens up exciting possibilities for the teaching and learning they can accomplish with that child.

We heard this story most often in regards to reading, but it also applies to other types of academic skills, including math proficiency. Regardless, these children all recognized they had made their teacher happy and wanted to elicit that reaction again. They began feeling special compared to their classmates. They did not yet fully understand the hierarchy they found themselves atop, but it felt good. For many of the achievers, this was the beginning of their distinctive social identity as an academic high performer.

WHAT IF THERE'S NO EARLY-LEARNING PARTNER?

The sad truth is, without a dedicated early-learning companion like Lisa Son, Bob Senior, or Maggie's parents, a child's opportunity to develop the skills and inspiration to achieve at a high level is sharply diminished, if not extinguished. That early period is, as we've seen, critical.

Think of Jarell in a parallel universe, without Elizabeth's determination that he escape poverty. His early days in the homeless shelter may instead have been spent just watching television or playing with little or no adult interaction. Those trips on the bus, instead of stimulating adventures exploring the city, could have been boring, even depressing, given the pervasive and grim signs of poverty. The hours in which they had conversations about books could have been filled instead with silence, except for directions on what he was, or was not, allowed to do. Fortunately, Jarell had a highly engaged mother who helped set his life on an upward trajectory.

HOW TO MASTER "THE BASICS"

If you chose to read this book, you're likely already aware, on some level, of how important early learning is for brain development. But most parents, especially those who don't look to the bookstore or library for parenting help, do not realize how crucial what they do can be for their children's future success. Experts write books and publish articles, but there are no schools or instructors providing widespread access to scientific, evidence-based guidance. Instead, each generation learns from the one before. We gradually incorporate new insights from our families and peers. But this leaves most parents behind the curve, missing opportunities to help their children develop.

Fortunately, a social movement has emerged that is working to reach parents from all types of backgrounds with a twenty-first-century understanding of what children from birth to age three need to experience for success. National campaigns are underway with titles like Too Small to Fail, Vroom, and the Thirty Million Word campaign. Each campaign is informed by research on how parenting and caregiving in early childhood affect brain development in areas associated with lifelong success: confidence, emotional self-regulation, interpersonal skills, curiosity, and imagination, as well as literacy, numeracy, and reasoning skills.

Another example, The Basics, began as a project of the Achievement Gap Initiative at Harvard University, led by one of this book's authors. It started as the Boston Basics before becoming a multi-city movement. In an attempt to erase the cognitive skill gaps between toddlers from different family backgrounds that arise before children even reach preschool, the Basics teach parents to adopt five simple but powerful routines important for brain development:

1. **Maximize Love, Manage Stress**. Too much stress can be toxic for brain development. Infants who feel secure grow up to be more socially intelligent and have more self-control.
2. **Talk, Sing, and Point**. Back-and-forth vocal exchanges teach infants to talk and toddlers to understand and express themselves, while pointing helps infants associate words with objects and further learn to communicate.
3. **Count, Group, and Compare**. Early activities involving grouping or comparing build on children's innate awareness of quantities and help them develop mathematical thinking.
4. **Explore Through Movement and Play**. Play that encourages exploration and discovery develops children's natural curiosity.
5. **Read and Discuss Stories**. Conversations during reading time build reasoning skills.

Learn more about the Basics at www.bostonbasics.org.

THE GIRL RAISED BY A VILLAGE OF TEENAGERS

The Early-Learning Partners we've seen thus far in this chapter have been mothers and fathers. But that doesn't mean the enrichment an Early-Learning Partner provides has to come from a parent—as the fascinating story of Pamela Rosario, who had not one Early-Learning Partner but many, demonstrates.

Pam's path to becoming valedictorian of her northern New Jersey high school and a Harvard graduate began in a small village in the Dominican Republic, where the lights flickered on and off because of the unreliable electricity. Born in Santo Domingo, the island's capital, Pam spent her formative years in the La Kennedy barrio, a neighborhood in the capital city made up of zinc-roof houses stacked on top of each other, and in Sonador, a village in the countryside with dirt-clay roads and latrines.

Her biological parents were very young when she was conceived, and unprepared for the responsibility of a child. "My dad was just, 'I'm seventeen, and I'm a dad?'" she says.

He and Pam's mother had a shaky relationship. "They got married when my mom was pregnant. I doubt they would have if I were not in the picture," Pam says. The teen couple was always fighting. Pam's father, who later played Major League Baseball, was chasing a dream, and her mother, who later became a journalist, was chasing him.

Because her parents were not mature enough to care for her alone, she spent her very early years, starting at age two, being raised by her father's teenage sisters, her aunts, each of whom she called "Mami." There was twelve-year-old "Mami Sergina," fourteen-year-old "Mami Ely," and seventeen-year-old "Mami Mary." "Mami Anna" was eighteen, and "Mami Anny" was nineteen and the main breadwinner.

When her biological parents weren't around, "I would just go find another parent. That's just how it was. There wasn't any moment where I could say, 'I really miss my biological parents.' Because for me, my parents were all of these other people who were around me. I never defined it by who was my blood relative."

It wasn't just those teenage aunts, or even the other members of their extended family, who helped rear her. There was also the "Cesa Family," a clan of neighborhood teens, each of whom taught her much of what they knew, including how to read, how to defend herself, and how to act and talk like an adult. "I was raised by a pack of teenagers," Pam says simply.

Those teenagers treated Pam like she was "a tiny adult" rather than a small child. "I experienced teen life when I was two years old," she says, and having so many people involved in her care "made me extremely adaptable."

For the rest of her childhood, from five on up, Pam's upbringing would be led by her paternal grandmother, "Abuelita." But during Pam's earlier, formative years, Abuelita was in Miami laying the groundwork to move the whole family to America. At first, Abuelita's husband Gregorino, Pam's paternal grandfather, worked out of town and would come home to where Pam and the others were for the weekends. But when Abuelita had a stroke, Gregorino moved to Miami to care for her.

That left the girls on the island by themselves, and left Pam blessed with a whole committee of mothers, an endless supply of Early-Learning Partners happy to share their passions with her. Mami Mary loved to read the Bible, so little Pam would read it with her. Mami Anna loved novels, and so the toddler would read them with her. Mami Anny loved eighties music, so Pam sang along to Air Supply with her. Whatever they did, Pamela also did.

Before Pam's grandmother left for Miami, she told her daughters to "make sure [Pam] stays smart." Their actions were purposeful, aimed at keeping the child feeling safe and engaged even when life was not perfect. When Pam was scared at night, her teenage mothers would get up and dance around, singing to make her feel happy, safe, and encouraged. They intentionally included her in their lives and interests, always talking to her as if she were another teenager.

While they had no way of knowing it, Pam's multiple Early-Learning Partners were following the Formula and providing her with early preparation for the challenging circumstances she would confront later as a Dominican immigrant in the United States. Even though she would spend most of her life speaking English, not the Spanish her aunts spoke, the understanding of language she developed would be a foundation for speaking, writing, and learning not only in English but also later in French.

The number of people Pam interacted with, each of them with their own interests, meant Pam had to process a great deal of information as a young child, which helped develop her memory. The ways her village of teen parents questioned her and pressed her to express opinions built comprehension and debate skills she'd rely on later in high school. She directly attributes her skill at reasoning and negotiation to her aunts' interest and respect; their willingness to treat her as a fully formed human being with ideas and opinions led Pam to always consider herself an equal to the "big people" in her childhood.

Pam's story tells us a few important things. First, that you don't need to be rich or highly educated to apply sound early parenting. But also, that an Early-Learning Partner doesn't need to be a parent at all to be effective, and that a child can especially benefit from having more than just one.

Despite lacking a traditional family structure, Pam's early-learning experiences resulted in her having many of the same opportunities more advantaged high achievers do. She was in the gifted school programs, learned to play the violin, and became proficient in English, French, and Spanish. In high school, she ran track, was the president of her school's chapter of the Future Business Leaders of America, and was involved in student government and French club. When she wasn't placed into AP French class, she had the gumption to ask the AP teacher to prep her for the exam anyway, which Pam later passed.

Long after she had moved to the United States, and when Pam was still in high school, the first lady of the Dominican Republic heard of her academic achievement through Pam's biological mother. She called on Pam to hold workshops with Dominican high school students on career planning, personal development, and community action. And later, after the 2010 earthquake in Haiti, the first lady called on then-nineteen-year-old Pam once again, this time to teach art therapy to Dominican and Haitian children affected by the tragedy. "I worked with children who had been raped, sold, and mistreated after the earthquake."

None of these opportunities and achievements would have been possible without the early preparation that started when she was only two, being raised by not just one Early-Learning Partner but by a whole village of them.

If we looked only for traditional parents in order to understand Pam's early development, we'd likely conclude she was functionally an orphan. We'd see her story in terms of the myth of the extraordinary child who does it on their own—and miss that Pam is, instead, the product of the Formula's masterful, strategic parenting.

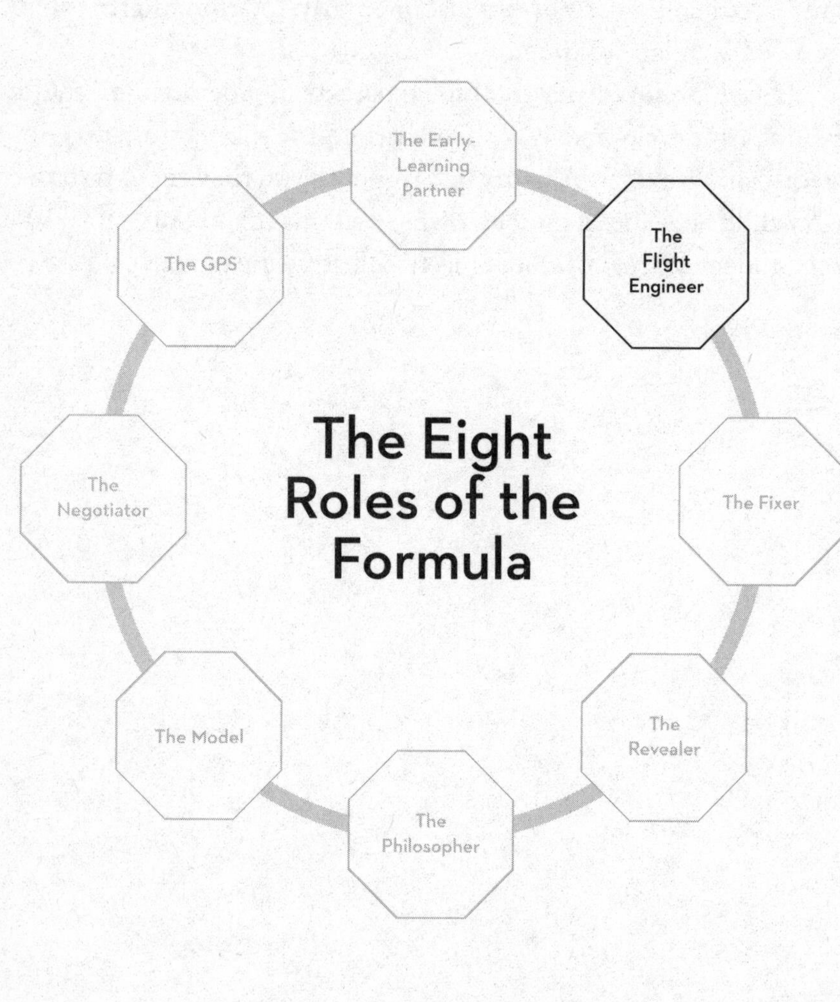
The Early-Learning Partner
The Flight Engineer
The Fixer
The Revealer
The Philosopher
The Model
The Negotiator
The GPS
The Eight Roles of the Formula

CHAPTER 6

The Flight Engineer (Role #2)

MASTERS MONITOR AND MANAGE (EVEN FROM THE WHITE HOUSE)

It was surprising to hear President Barack Obama speak so candidly about raising his two daughters. He had no way of knowing that one of the journalists interviewing him in the Oval Office that day was mentally checking off how the parenting practices he spoke of were similar to what she'd heard from other parents she'd been studying since 2003.

Sounding like so many other Early-Learning Partners in the book, President Obama said, "Michelle and I read to them from the time they were babies." But when the time neared to launch their daughters into the daily rigors of school, they prioritized developing independence and responsibility as well. "When they were four years old," he said, "they got an alarm clock so they started waking up on their own and making their own beds."

The time-management lessons they began teaching their preschoolers turned into habits, which stayed with them when they entered grade school.

"They're responsible for making sure they get to school on time. I mean, we monitor them, but they've gotten into a bunch of habits where they are expected to be prepared to learn when they go to school," President Obama said.

Although the Obamas set only a few rules for their daughters, they enforced them consistently. Homework was to be started soon after the children returned from school. Bedtime for the younger once she entered elementary school was 8:30 PM, and the older went to bed thirty minutes later. In their home, books entertained them—not television—and despite having assigned bedtimes, they were free to read until they fell asleep. Television was for the weekends.

"In terms of setting high expectations, we . . . always encouraged them to think about education not as a chore or a burden but as a great privilege," Obama said.

At the time of the Oval Office interview, First Lady Michelle and the president were in the thick of raising their girls, then ages twelve and nine. Despite their dizzying schedules, the Obamas helped manage their daughters' academic journeys, sometimes partnering with the school officials when necessary to ensure their children's interests were being tended to.

"I have not missed a parent-teacher conference since I've been president, and I didn't miss a parent-teacher conference when I was a candidate for president. And Michelle goes to all those activities."

The habits and routines established years earlier made it easy for the Obamas to monitor the girls, despite spending lengthier periods away from them as the girls matured and spent more time at school.

"We set very early on expectations for Malia and Sasha in terms of them taking responsibility for their own education," said the president. "And the last thing I'll say in terms of setting high expectations . . . Malia will tell you, my attitude was if she came home with a B that's not good enough because there's no reason why she can't get an A."

They required both girls to play team sports, checked homework when it seemed necessary, and stayed in touch with teachers.

"So those are all things that any parent can do. There's no doubt that Michelle and I have more resources and are privileged compared to a lot of parents," Obama said. "We understand that. But I don't care how poor you are—you can turn off the television set during the week. You can make sure that you're talking to teachers in the school."

WHEN THE CHILD ENTERS THE WILD, MASTER PARENTS STEP UP

The first time Barack Obama ran for elective office, Malia and Sasha were getting ready for grade school. As their daughters moved into the classroom, the Obamas transitioned from being Early-Learning Partners who talked, read, and played games at home ("We read to them from the time they were babies," the president said) to taking on the second role of the Formula, the Flight Engineer.

Like the Flight Engineer on an airplane or spacecraft, the parent in this role monitors and manages, staying alert to detect and resolve any problems that might emerge once the child has "launched" into their school years. The parent's responsibilities expand from engaging the child in the home to keeping track of what the child is doing as they become part of a multitude of new environments for the first time.

The work of Urie Bronfenbrenner, a Russian-born American developmental psychologist, focuses on how social environments or "ecologies" influence a child. His theory of human ecology asserts that—like animals, which science describes as living in complex "ecologies" that impact their overall growth and development—human children do not develop in a vacuum, but are affected by a combination of all the things they experience, at home, in school, and anywhere else they interact with other people.

A child's first small system of human interactions, or "microecology," is at home with parents and siblings. But once children start school, their world expands, and they become participants in additional microecologies. One of these is the classroom. Others might be a Bible study group on Wednesday afternoons or a tee-ball team on Saturday morning at the park. The child's encounters in these new places on any given day may go smoothly or not. For example, a child may clash with a teacher at school or get drawn into a self-destructive peer group. Their experiences in these new microecologies depend not only on the child's own decisions, but on what others say and do as well.

Aware of how strongly these other microecologies will influence their child's development, the master parent as Flight Engineer manages their child's experiences through collaboration with the adults in them or, if necessary, by making demands and asserting their authority as a parent.

The master parent in this role works to ensure these environments, the school in particular, are consistently doing three major things: (1) placing the child in the grade, course, or academic track that best fits their abilities and maturity level; (2) treating the child with respect; and (3) delivering high-quality instruction.

If, through monitoring, they learn that something has gone awry regarding these responsibilities, the Flight Engineer intervenes to manage and correct the situation.

CHECKING IN: "THERE'S A PROBLEM; LET ME FIND THE SOLUTION"

Bob Senior spent five years as an excellent Early-Learning Partner, playing Legos, reading, and teaching Rob songs and problem-solving skills. But then Rob turned five, and Bob Senior and his wife knew they would have to start partnering with other adults to make sure Rob's academic journey continued to go smoothly.

Now that others would be evaluating his children, Bob Senior wondered if his impressions of Rob and his sister as special and gifted might be inflated. He was a teacher and accustomed to the parents of his own students thinking their kids were so smart that their school should feel privileged to host them. He worried about becoming one of those people. The real test of his perceptions of their abilities, he knew, was how well the child performed outside of the home, when they started school. So after a few weeks, he checked in.

He didn't expect the first feedback he received from Wilson Elementary School. "We need some glue!" Rob's kindergarten teacher said. "To glue his little bottom down in the chair." Another teacher said, "He's loud and wild," going on to explain she could hear him in her own classroom all the way from the playground.

Bob could have gotten angry at Rob or the teacher, and either disciplined Rob or passively agreed to whatever his child's teacher thought he should do. Instead, Bob Senior investigated, observed, and asked more questions.

No parent, master parents included, has been trained for the complex oversight role they are suddenly thrust into when their child starts school. Still, master parents know their child well, and they are observant enough to figure out what the problem might be and assertive enough to press for solutions. The parent develops a strong sense for what *mission success* requires from other people in the child's life, especially teachers. They perform routine reconnaissance by checking in with their child and consulting informally with teachers to stay abreast of how their child is performing. When and if something seems awry, the master parent as Flight Engineer becomes an astute diagnostician, reading situations and applying a studied understanding of human nature to improve them, and seeking advice from others to do so when necessary.

What his son's teachers were really telling him, Bob Senior realized, was that Rob was socially immature compared to the other kindergarteners. In other words, there was an ecological mismatch.

Bob Senior himself noticed something else: Rob was smaller than the other boys. He just seemed out of place around the other children. "I knew he didn't belong there, but I didn't have a solution."

He began asking around, and that's when a teacher suggested Bob could do what she'd done for her own son, who also had seemed immature for his age. When the time came for first grade, she'd held him back a year and instead placed him into a K-1 class, an intermediate level between kindergarten and first grade designed to allow a student to catch up socially with their peers.

The practice of holding a child back to start school with a slightly younger age cohort is called "redshirting," after the practice of sitting college sports players on the bench their freshman year to extend their playing eligibility. Researchers estimate that between 3.5 and 5.5 percent of potential kindergarteners in the United States are redshirted, mostly white boys like Rob.

Economist Michael Hanse at the Brookings Institution wanted to know if redshirting helped, so in 2016 he reviewed the best research he could find on the topic. The results were mixed. According to Hanse, "In short, there's no reason to believe that redshirting your child will instill some long-term educational advantage. While a child's age at the time of testing does make a difference in early elementary grades, and redshirting will enable him to score closer to the top of the class rather than the bottom, being the oldest in the class does not appear to convey any advantage on its own."

Hanse also says that any benefit of being the oldest tends to grow smaller with time, and has little if any effect on their college admissions test scores.

Still, it seems almost certain that Bob Senior was correct in believing there was an advantage to holding Rob back, to allow him to mature in the company of children his own size. Of the twenty-two children in Rob's K-1 class, eighteen were boys, and Rob remained in classes with those same boys for the whole span of his school life in Collinsville. Together they excelled not only in academics but in athletics, too. They became great friends and academic rivals.

Looking back, Rob considers Bob Senior's decision "very astute" and, in Rob's particular case, it may have been. When Rob entered first grade, after his K-1 experience, Bob Senior again wondered where his son stood. He approached Mary Burr, who was now Rob's first-grade teacher. "Is he catching on to things well?" he asked.

She looked at Bob Senior, puzzled. "You don't know?" And then she clammed up and wouldn't tell him until much later in the year.

Eventually, he found out that there was no comparison academically between Rob and the other kids. Rob fit supremely well within his new microecologies, in the classroom and on the playground, far surpassing his classmates. Rob was so far ahead academically, he would have experienced the early-lead effect no matter what. However, having that extra year to mature socially gave him the best chance of being the all-around outstanding student he became.

The Flight Engineer as parent is savvy in the way they talk to their child and to the adults who teach and supervise them, and in how they interpret what they hear. They monitor situations to get a clear understanding, and then act judiciously to avoid unintended side effects. Rather than reacting in a knee-jerk, uninformed way, or letting fear of communicating with school officials dictate their actions, Flight Engineers do their homework and approach encounters with their child's schools with confidence. As a result, they tend to elicit respect from the educators they aim to influence, and they usually get what they want for the child.

Sometimes, though, polite attempts at collaboration are not enough, and a Flight Engineer must demand what they want for their child.

ASSERTING AUTHORITY: "YOU WILL RESPECT MY CHILD"

Lynne and Clarence Newsome, like Bob Senior, were Flight Engineers who knew they needed to be partners with the elementary school teachers they depended on to help raise their girls Gina, their eldest, now a psychiatrist; and Bree, an activist, writer, and film director who in the summer of 2015 received national attention for removing the Confederate flag at South Carolina's capitol building. But when they learned that a teacher was mistreating their first-grade daughter Gina, the Newsomes were compelled to step in and hold the school accountable.

Lynne and Clarence were both educators. Soft-spoken, rule abiding, and painfully polite, the couple had left North Carolina when they were very young for Columbia, Maryland, a planned community in Howard County that was consistently named by *Money* magazine as one of the 100 best places in America to live and famously known as a post-racial utopia.

But keeping with their desire of raising racially conscious children wasn't as easy as one might think, even in hospitable Columbia. Most of their friends and neighbors were white; the Newsome girls were usually among the few black kids in their school. None of the books they read had African American children in them, so

Lynne colored the characters brown, and to make it crystal clear they were African American, she drew Afro puffs in the little girls' hair.

When Gina was in first grade, she came home crying and announced sadly that she was dumb. Lynne and Clarence assumed it was because other students who looked like her were deemed troublemakers or in the lower reading group.

But Gina's explanation was even more poignant and upsetting. According to Gina, she was the one always raising her hand, but the teacher never called on her for answers. Even worse, the teacher insisted on placing frowny faces on Gina's papers whenever she missed a few answers, despite the fact that Gina was academically astute overall.

For Lynne and Clarence, this was unacceptable. The frowny faces were crushing to Gina, especially as she already felt she was being treated unfairly. When they confronted Gina's teacher, she resisted at first, but Lynne told her in no uncertain terms that there were to be "no more frowny faces." In fact, there should be "only smiley faces" on any paper the teacher returned, and, furthermore, this rule should apply regardless of Gina's grade on the assignment. Reluctantly, the teacher agreed. The family received satisfaction the next year when the same teacher presented Gina an honors award for high achievement.

Some people may disagree with Lynne Newsome regarding the appropriate level of assertiveness for parents to take with their child's teachers. But Lynne was smart and sensitive enough to discern the harm the teacher was causing Gina, and once a Flight Engineer knows something is harming their child, other people's opinions are mostly beside the point.

This commitment to vigilance and, when necessary, becoming the squeaky wheel, does not depend fundamentally on material resources. But it does depend on having trust in one's own judgment and not basing your approach solely and unquestioningly on others' opinions. Some parents treat school officials as authority figures not to be questioned, but not master parents. Like the Flight Engineer on a space flight, for whom knowing all of the mechanical systems and duties on board is what qualifies them to hold such a pivotal job, the master parent understands that their deep, nuanced knowledge of their child makes them the highest authority on what is best for their child, outside the home as well as inside.

DIAGNOSING MISBEHAVIOR: "HE DOESN'T HAVE ENOUGH TO DO"

The parents of US diplomat David Martinez knew their oldest son as a high-energy, academically advanced boy who loved to tell people what he knew. But to his kindergarten teacher, he was "disruptive"—so talkative, in fact, that she frequently isolated him behind a room divider.

Whenever his teacher asked the class a question, David says, "I would quickly raise my hand. I wanted to be first or I wanted to give the answer, because I knew it. And usually I'd get called on once, but would raise my hand again, and I'd get frustrated sometimes and just blurt out the answer, which would mean I'd get put on time-out or I'd be isolated," he said.

Lou, David's mother, being a student of her child and an astute Flight Engineer, interceded to rescue David from a bad situation. "I would just be in the corner doing math on my own. When my mother found out about this, she was livid because she realized this was almost a daily activity. Instead of doing what the other kindergarteners were doing, including playtime, I was literally behind a barrier."

Lou asked the teacher to explain, David recalls. "Then my mother said, 'You aren't stimulating David; you aren't giving him what he needs.' And she brought this up with the school administration," which prompted them to look into the situation. Based on the school's investigation, they figured out that David was having trouble because he was too advanced. The solution? Move him to second grade at the end of kindergarten.

David had no doubt that "I was disruptive in this class and it was probably a pain to my teacher." But while the teacher perceived the problem as a conduct issue, "my mother recognized that this was a stimulation issue. I wasn't getting the kind of stimulation I was used to at home, because I was capable of something beyond either the pace or the content of the class. She said, 'No, you're not giving him enough. The problem is the environment, it's not David.' Sure enough, when I went into second grade, my grades stayed high and my conduct improved, because I finally had something more of my pace."

Protecting David when he needed to be protected did not mean his parents, as Flight Engineers, defended him when he was wrong.

"When I was in third grade, we had this substitute teacher who told us to all stand up and then to sit down. And I said, 'Well, make up your mind!' I was sent to detention and a transcript of this was sent to my father and on the bottom of it my father signed it and added, 'David is required to make any amends necessary.' It wasn't 'My child was good,' or 'This was a misunderstanding.' It was, 'David screwed up, and you do with him what you see fit, and he's going to follow through with that.'

"If I otherwise didn't have support from my parents," David said, "that could have crippled me. It could have been, 'Oh my God, my parents don't love me.' But it wasn't. Why? They had established their support from the get-go, and every other way they showed us they loved us. But that didn't mean that we were immune from being punished, from being corrected or told this behavior was unacceptable."

ON AUTOPILOT BY THIRD GRADE

By the time they were eight to ten years old, nearly all of our high achievers had become self-regulated learners who rarely needed their Flight Engineer parents to review schoolwork, control their time and scheduling, or help them master projects that interested them. Simply put, by the third grade, they were on autopilot.

Like a pilot who points the aircraft in the right direction, sets the dials, and then takes their hands off the controls, master parents cultivate curiosity, build academic skills, and enforce clear rules and responsibilities early on, which then results in less need for parental oversight. This doesn't mean master parents stop monitoring their child; a pilot still monitors an aircraft on autopilot. But it does mean that as long as their child remains within the boundaries of what's permissible, they are allowed to make their own choices.

Other children take much longer to get to this point, where they don't need their parents to constantly check in and remind them of what needs to be done—sometimes as late as high school or even college. And some children never get there.

Kids on autopilot learn more and faster than their peers, according to a 2017 study of 1,700 German children. Researchers interviewed hundreds of parents about how independent their third- and fourth-grade children were, asking them to rate their children on four criteria: being self-starters, persistence, proactiveness, and being inclined to make their own decisions, regardless of what other children decided to do. The study discovered that children who rated high on this kind of "personal initiative"—a perfect description for our achievers—outpaced their peers in skills like reading comprehension by fifth and sixth grades.

There were rarely times when the achievers we studied were not doing their best, even without encouragement from their parents or other adults. Thanks to the passion for learning their parents had instilled in them, they enjoyed challenging schoolwork as much as they did sports and other extracurricular activities. At the same time, they took their schoolwork very seriously, treating it as their responsibility, like going to work was for their parents. Repeatedly during interviews, our achievers, especially the Harvard students, referred to school simply as "work," as in, "I always did my work."

The parent's role as Flight Engineer, then, was often simply support, especially as the child got older. When the achievers reached middle or high school, that work became much tougher, which sometimes meant staying up into the wee hours in the morning to finish a project or advanced homework. Several achievers mentioned a mother staying up with them just to be helpful or supporting the achiever by bringing them a cup of tea.

The achievers we interviewed also sought out learning opportunities beyond what school and their parents offered. At about this same age, eight or nine, they began choosing their own topics to explore or skills to master. These ever-important "passion projects," as we call them, not only energized the child to learn more deeply about their chosen interest, but also produced a variety of skills. Some of these projects led directly to the child's adult vocation, while others simply built skills the child later drew on for their academic studies or other pursuits.

Many parents have to push their child to find outside interests. Master parents, though they might introduce an interest, for the most part facilitate their now-on-autopilot child's self-chosen hobbies. They encourage the pursuit of those interests but also, as Flight Engineer, slow the child down when necessary, pointing them to bed if their work continues too far into the night.

KNOWING WHEN (NOT) TO STEP IN: "*YOU* CAN DEAL WITH YOUR TEACHER THIS TIME"

According to Luca Parmitano, an astronaut who filled this role aboard the International Space Station, the flight engineer must monitor all of the systems and be prepared to step in as "the plumber, the engineer, the cook, the scientist, the commander, or the pilot." The master parent in the Flight Engineer role is similarly a jack-of-all-trades, ready to mobilize any of an assortment of corrective responses when problems arise. As needed, the Flight Engineer parent might coach the child or the teacher on how to respond to a situation, as Lynne did when she corrected the hurtful grading practices of Gina's teacher. They might collaborate to find a solution, like Bob Senior did when Rob was struggling because of social immaturity.

But in other instances, the Flight Engineer might decide that the best path is to take a hands-off, wait-and-see approach. And if that fails, they might step up proactively to fill an unmet need.

When each of her three girls reached school age, Esther Wojcicki, in the role of Flight Engineer, was a great monitor, keeping track of what her children were learning, how rigorous their studies were, and generally how things were going. Having worked as a teacher herself, she wanted "to avoid seeming bossy" when it came to school, choosing instead to believe in the teachers and her children, whom she had trained to be independent. So she tried to manage from a distance, by coaching the children when there was a problem with a teacher, instead of going to the teacher herself.

"When they didn't get along with a teacher, they would use me as a sounding board. If they thought the subject was being taught poorly, they would use me as a sounding board then, too, and I would give them advice [on] how to cope with that teacher, or the subject matter that was taught. I became the sounding board for all their friends, as well. They would say the teacher didn't teach a certain way, so they didn't understand. They wanted help with the teacher. It was in all subject areas. I would say that some percentage of teachers fall into that category of being poor teachers. I told them you can't change classes; you have to cope. That's life. It's not fair, but you have to cope with it. You have to get around it."

But sometimes Esther did step in if she knew it would make a big difference, as when she noticed the girls' high school writing program was of poor quality; the school was not teaching what the students needed to be college ready. A professionally trained journalist, she volunteered to step in and teach an afterschool writing class. "My kids came, and so did twenty-five other kids. I thought it was fun. I taught them all how to write."

THE MISSING FLIGHT ENGINEER: ALFONSO'S UNMANAGED JOURNEY

If any role in the Formula is missing for a particular child, the risk increases that the child will fall short of their full potential. Every achiever in this book had a Flight Engineer parent who made sure schools and teachers did their jobs and that the child's behavior allowed them to make the most of their schooling—that is, every achiever except for Alfonso Hernandez.[1]

Alfonso's father Reynaldo was an expert learning partner, though he never pressed his children to do well in school. For him, learning was as natural as breathing, and something you sought opportunities to experience yourself, not something you depended on a school to provide for you, or even to judge.

Reynaldo was a dedicated father who had primary custody of his three boys after his divorce from their mother. A lover of

---

[1] Alfonso and Reynaldo Hernandez's names have been changed.

surfing and political debates, he was also an expert at introducing his children to thought-provoking books, philosophy, classical music, and more. He got enthusiastically involved in whatever passion projects his children chose, and never stopped learning new things himself.

As Alfonso said, "Dad showed a lot of support, buying me sketchbooks and materials for drawing, painting, and everything else that you do in an arts program or an arts magnet school. He would also write little poems. He would talk to us about some artist who was famous in history, like Picasso or Van Gogh, or people along those lines."

There was a special comics convention Alfonso liked to attend. Instead of just dropping Alfonso off, Reynaldo would attend, too.

"I don't remember ever resenting my dad or not wanting him around," Alfonso said. "I remember really enjoying my time with him."

Reynaldo believed lessons should be focused on whatever a person finds interesting, not what some committee of educators decided a person ought to know, and his middle son Alfonso developed the same orientation toward school and learning. He liked reading, drawing, and playing guitar, but, as he explained, "school was kind of in the way. I had to go because it's mandatory, so I went, but I wasn't into like algebra or history or English. I was like, okay, 'This is what life is, you do English, and you do history . . .'"

While Reynaldo was a masterful parent in many ways, the fact that he was not at all a Flight Engineer had consequences. Alfonso doesn't remember any communication between his parents and schools. He also doesn't remember his father looking at report cards or his father or stepmother helping with school projects or making sure he did homework. "I must have done it like right before class or something . . . I didn't make an effort to be the best student in class or anything. I was in the advanced classes, but not because I worked hard, just because I could do it."

In middle school, Alfonso hung out with friends who were just like him: nerds whose passion projects were video games, music, and comics.

"We got into rock bands like Nirvana and Pearl Jam. I think that's an age when kids get into anything. It could be sports and you really get into it. You begin reading on it. We started reading *Rolling Stone* and *Spin*. It becomes intellectually stimulating without having an academic application," Alfonso said. "Talking about what Nirvana means for music was something that we might have done without knowing that we were exercising that part of the brain that maybe could have been just as useful in doing homework or writing a paper."

In the evenings after school, Alfonso and his brothers made their own decisions about what to do. Even in comparison with others in this book, whose parents allowed them plenty of unstructured time to pursue their interests, he had lots of freedom. "We would just stay out at our friends' houses and play, or in the neighborhood and play. And so in my early childhood and even in my early adolescence, homework wasn't that important."

In the ninth grade, Alfonso got expelled from school for selling marijuana. There were warning signs leading up to his expulsion—warning signs that Reynaldo didn't see. Before high school, the family was evicted from their housing because Alfonso and his brothers were throwing rocks and eggs at cars and houses. By high school, he was feeling rebellious, acting out in school, "not turning in homework or taking tests and giving these nonsense answers deliberately. I thought it was kind of punk rock and I might have started rebelling."

The day Alfonso was expelled was the last time he would ever enter a high school. We'll see how his father helped him turn things around (Alfonso would eventually graduate from Princeton, and credits much of his success to Reynaldo) in an upcoming chapter.

But meanwhile, the lack of a Flight Engineer in Alfonso's life led to additional hardships and stress for the entire family.

What happens on a spacecraft with no flight engineer? If all systems operate as planned, the answer is "nothing out of the ordinary." However, if a mechanical system malfunctions or a crew member becomes incapacitated, the voyage might be headed for disaster.

Most educators do their best to inspire the children in their care and guide their progress, but that's not always enough to prevent trouble or put things back on track if the child derails. Without the Flight Engineer, none of the children in this chapter would have been as well served by the schools they attended. Rob would have started first grade before he was mature enough; Gina might have gone on thinking she wasn't smart; Esther's daughters and their classmates would not have developed the crucial-for-college writing skills that Esther taught them. There is no way of knowing what mishaps were prevented for the Obama daughters by parents who held both the girls and their teachers accountable. Just imagine if these other parents had been as disconnected from their children's school lives as Reynaldo.

But what if the parent plays the Flight Engineer role, and all the roles of the Formula, successfully? Does that mean all their children will be superstars? The young people we've read about so far ended up in this book because they became impressive young adults. However, a number of them have brothers and sisters who achieved less. How could it be that master parents produce children who do not become high achievers? Does that mean they aren't really master parents at all—that their high-achieving child was destined to succeed even without them? Or are some of them masters of one? Let's take a quick detour to find out.

CHAPTER 7

Siblings

CAUTIONARY TALES

Most nights, in the quiet moments just before sleep, Ronnie's mind would wander home to Cleveland. Secure in his freshman dormitory bed at Cornell University, he'd think about his brother Darrell, only eighteen months younger, who had been kicked out of the house for selling drugs and was on the streets, living a very different life.

"Here I was at an Ivy League school, just getting started," Ronnie said. "The sense was that 'the future is bright and the world is yours for the taking.' I'm meeting all these new friends, people I could really identify with; high achievers who were smart and cool at the same time. The parties were good and the world was right. That is, if I didn't think too much about Darrell."

The central question of this book is how parents raise highly successful human beings. But with that question comes another: What accounts for differences between siblings? If parenting makes so much of a difference, why, when both are raised in the same household, would one sibling do much better in school and life than another? For anyone with a sibling, this is of more than academic interest. It is an existential question that goes to the very core of their personal identity. Of the 200 people interviewed for this book, many spoke of a sibling who was "just as smart," but didn't find the same success.

It's something Ronnie has been thinking about all his life: the distinct way each of his siblings was parented and the theories he had, even as a child, about how it mattered. After receiving a PhD from MIT and becoming an educator at several prestigious universities, Ronnie still ponders these questions. How did parenting and family dynamics contribute to his parents having one boy grow up to attend and teach at world-class universities, another become a physician, and another compete around the world for years as a frequent champion on the US national karate team, but two others struggle with alcoholism, drugs, and frequent financial hardship? What accounts for such disparity between children raised in the same household?

THE RECEPTIVE CHILD

Ronnie's second-youngest brother in the birth order, Homer, who, like Darrell, struggled with drugs, has one answer. "Ronnie took heed to the lessons we were taught," he said. "I didn't. I took it halfway. He followed by the book and made the best of the advice he got." His explanation echoes that of some of our high achievers, who say that their less successful siblings just didn't apply themselves.

But where do these differences in receptivity and effort come from? Is it just about personality?

Ronnie, Darrell, Homer, Kenny, and Stevie grew up within an extended family where their mother, father, grandfather John, and grandmother Nana all had an influence. As Stevie, the future medical doctor in the family, put it, "I was blessed to have four parents."

Their young mother was a loving homemaker who was more on the permissive side. Their father, who worked long hours as a housepainter and contractor, gave his boys hugs and kisses, but was the disciplinarian of the two parents, dishing out "beatings" when the kids misbehaved. Violations were never responded to with measured conversations and reasoning, said Ronnie. "Go get my belt and take your pants off," was all he would say. When it came to school, it seemed that behavior mattered more than grades to both parents, and there was very little conversation or pressure attached to academics when Grandpa John was involved, either.

But there was an outlier among the brothers' four "parents." When their mother, who had been sickly as a child, became pregnant with Darrell, it was Nana, always protective of and close to her daughter, who took responsibility for one-year-old Ronnie, the first son. Nana, a special education teacher, was such a master at teaching that many of her former students attended her ninetieth birthday party to show their appreciation. She used her same teaching skills with her first grandchild, constantly focusing on learning.

"She just gave me a ton of attention, beginning before I can even remember. She talked about how she took me on the train to New York City when I was eighteen months old. I was talking to everyone on the train," Ronnie said. "I can remember as a four-year-old sitting with a green chalkboard and her teaching me to write my name and other things on the board. I think all the attention and early instruction she gave me cultivated an impulse to learn."

Nana's Burn to help Ronnie become a high achiever was influenced by the rejection she experienced when her childhood mentor, Jane Edna Hunter, a prominent African American social worker and attorney, banished Nana from a group of young women she was grooming for leadership when Nana married at twenty. Ms. Hunter told her, "You have thrown your life away," especially by marrying a man who smoked cigars, drank whiskey, and, as far as Ms. Hunter could tell, lacked lofty ambitions. Seven decades later, Nana wrote in her journal, "What a mistake I had made!" The disappointment fueled her Burn to see her grandson Ronnie rise in the world, inspiring her to become a very intentional Early-Learning Partner.

The time she spent with him paid off. Like other children in this book, Ronnie remembers experiencing the early-lead effect in kindergarten and first grade, when he knew more and could do more than his classmates, and began thinking of himself as the best student in the class.

"Nana was teaching every minute. She was that way with all of us," he said.

But why did Ronnie sink his teeth into learning more than the others did?

The reason, he thinks, is those first three or four years, "I had more one-on-one time with her and that put me in a mode where I was always looking for stuff to think about."

For a child who's been intellectually stimulated at an early age, the world is like a room where someone has flipped the light switch on or turned the dimmer up to bright. The world is illuminated, and the enlightened child searches to absorb it all.

"During early elementary school, I spent a lot of time by myself building things with blocks and an Erector set that had little nuts and bolts. And then after second grade I got into a summer book club. I remember sitting in the corner in the shade reading these eight books during that summer," Ronnie said. "I think they were advertised in the Scholastic *Weekly Reader* and I asked my mother to order the books, and she did. I also went to the library a lot. It wasn't that the adults were guiding what or how much I was reading in any way. But that really early stimulation had set up a certain kind of hunger."

Master parenting by an Early-Learning Partner exposes the child to stimulating experiences, like young Ronnie's trip to New York City at eighteen months old. But how the child responds during those experiences matters as much as the parent's efforts to initiate the experience itself. If the child is highly receptive during those early experiences—for example, talking to everyone on the train during that trip—the master parent and child become hooked. They establish a fun partnership and stay involved—learning together, building on what they've begun in a positive feedback loop. Nana helped create Ronnie's thirst for learning, for sure, but the fact that he was receptive from the beginning may have been just as important as her master parenting skills.

After second grade, Ronnie took art and modern dance lessons at the Cleveland Karamu House, a cultural center in Cleveland's black community. By fourth grade, he was also taking private lessons on the clarinet and playing in the band and orchestra at school. His mother and Nana could be counted on to attend every performance and exhibit. Seeing them in the audience motivated him to stay engaged and keep getting better.

We know the children who receive intensive early stimulation are likely to develop a greater thirst for learning than those who do not get that attention. Even so, receptivity is a tricky thing. When a parent is trying to engage a child with blocks or simply by reading a book to them, one child, in the moment, will be fascinated, which rewards the parent and encourages the parent to do it more. But another child under the exact same circumstances might not be interested.

The master parent in such moments follows the child's lead, taking the long view by understanding that every child develops at his or her own pace, and tries again later, or tries to engage the child a different way—maybe with Play-Doh instead of blocks, or taking them on a walk instead of looking at a book. What's important is that the parent is providing some kind of learning experience. The more learning the parent and child do together, the more receptive the child is likely to be to learning in the future.

However, even the most committed parent will find it hard to keep trying if their child doesn't seem engaged. Elizabeth Lee said Jarell loved learning, "but my girls, even though I pushed them as far as I could push, gave me a lot of resistance. So I told them you are going to live by the choices that you make. I'm not going to fight with you. I didn't have to fight with him. I'm not going to fight with you to try to teach you something that's going to make your life better. You'll see in the long run that I was only trying to help you. You'll live by the choices you make, you made your choice."

Her daughters were also smart—one finished community college and the other finished a four-year school—but they were not as receptive as Jarell.

A MASTER OF ONE

There are other reasons why every sibling may not benefit fully from being in the home of a master parent.

Practicality is one of those reasons. Being available to play the roles in the Formula can be difficult for families with financial burdens or time restraints. The mother of one of the Harvard study participants, Gabriela "Gabby" Vargas,[1] was always available during Gabby's early years, but by the time her younger sisters came along, Gabby told us, their parents' marriage had dissolved and their mother had to work. Gabby stepped in as the Flight Engineer for her younger sisters, going to the school to deal with issues that arose, but as a child still herself, she could not replicate the amazing parenting her mother had provided to her.

Conversely, when Chuck Badger's older brother was young, his mother was not yet mature enough to do the things that she later did as a master parent for Chuck. Sometimes, whether due to available time, energy, or interest, parents are able to be at their best with some of their children and not with others.

Often, they are only master parents of one.

---

[1] Gabby's last name, and her mother's name later in the book, have been changed.

Families are like dynamic puzzles, in which a child's development depends not only on their parents, but also on their siblings and extended family. This, too, impacts a child's upbringing. For example, it's not unusual to hear a parent say, "Oh, this is my smart child," or "This is my future athlete." But a child whose average grade in school is a B can be the "smart child" or not, depending on what the other siblings achieve.

In another family, Ronnie's middle brother, Kenny, who grew up to be a national karate champion and successful businessman, might have been the family success story. But by the time he was a preschooler, life was bustling at home and quiet Kenny was easily overshadowed. For an early elementary school child, there's no substitute for being in the company of adults who interact one-on-one with them, listening to their thoughts, learning about their interests, and responding to their ideas. But at home with the family, Kenny mostly flew under the radar.

Given this, we might expect Kenny to have floundered. However, he was lucky enough to have godparents who lived two blocks away and had no children of their own. He visited them almost every weekend, and they gave him the attention he wasn't getting at home. "That's where it was my turn to feel special," Kenny says. The attention his godparents paid Kenny gave him confidence and a stronger sense that "I deserve this" when he later found himself in positions to stand up and be counted instead of blending into the crowd. The time they spent with him one-on-one helped support the emotional security and executive function skills that experts say are so important as foundations for success.

He didn't get the academic foundation that Ronnie got from Nana, but "I tried to follow in Ronnie's footsteps, the best I could." For four years, starting at age eleven, he successfully managed the early-morning *Cleveland Plain Dealer* newspaper route he took over from Ronnie while also working with his grandfather cleaning carpets. At age sixteen, he worked parking cars at the Stouffers Restaurant in Shaker Square, as all the brothers did.

Always disciplined, Kenny attended Kent State University, mainly because Ronnie went to college. That's where he was persuaded to try karate. By his senior year, he made the US national karate team, of which he remained a member for many years, traveling all over the world, more than once as the US national champion. Now a well-known businessman in Cleveland, he once ran a karate studio with hundreds of students.

Family context likewise mattered for Stevie, the fifth son. When Stevie came along, four years after Homer's birth, there were four older boys in the house—quite a load for their mother to manage. Nana once again stepped in to help relieve the childcare load, by keeping Stevie some evenings, on weekends, and during the summers. (Ronnie, then nine years old and on autopilot, no longer spent as much time with her.)

Speaking of how inspirational Nana was, Stevie recalled a frequent saying of hers: "Shoot for the moon and even if you miss, you'll land among the stars." And that's what he did, deciding at age five that he was going to be a doctor. Although the early-learning attention he got from Nana wasn't as intense as what Ronnie received, and although he struggled with slow reading because of undiagnosed dyslexia, he received a good enough foundation to follow his dream. When he wasn't at Nana's house, Stevie shared a bedroom with Ronnie. He remembers always seeing his brother at a desk in the bedroom studying. Stevie's brothers call him stubborn, but he prefers to think of himself as possessing a strong sense of agency. He signed himself up to attend a Catholic high school and talked his father into paying for it, because Stevie believed he'd get a better education there than at the neighborhood school. Years later he talked a medical school into admitting him, despite low test scores. He's now a doctor serving low-income rural communities in North Carolina.

Of all the boys, only Homer didn't receive additional special, one-one-one learning attention beyond what their parents could provide, largely due to his position in the birth order. (Darrell got it from an uncle and grandfather, but took it in the wrong direction, as we'll see in a moment.) Nana was still spending a lot of time with Ronnie then, and was a busy special education teacher while also mentoring a dozen or more young female protégées. Other potential external supports for Homer like grandparents or godparents were already taken by his brothers. And when Stevie, with his cherubic face and scene-stealing personality, was born, he grabbed the baby-of-the-family spotlight, taking attention from Homer.

The end result was that Homer received less of the early developmental attention that some experts say is the foundation for developing executive function skills—skills concerning the ability to regulate one's behavior to achieve goals. As as small child, Homer didn't get much practice following through on intentions under the watchful eye of an adult, and may have developed less self-discipline as a result. And by his own admission, he wasn't receptive to adult guidance during his teen years.

High achievers who respond to very early guidance from a master parent develop a sense of agency and stick-with-it-ness. Think of Maggie Young and her long hours of self-directed violin practice, and Sangu Delle, who at the age of fourteen got himself a scholarship to study for four years in an American high school by applying on his own to a school he found on the internet.

Without an adult focused on helping Darrell or Homer build a clear, productive vision for their future, they formed their own shorter-term goals. Both were at least average students, handsome, gregarious, very well liked, and popular with the opposite sex. But neither saw academics as a way to distinguish themselves or to achieve success.

Instead, their preoccupations were making money, having fun, being cool, and becoming star athletes. Especially for Darrell, success was being dressed up with lots of cash in his pocket. That's what Grandfather John, with whom Darrell spent a lot of time, seemed to value most. He was also influenced by Uncle Bill, a former Harlem Globetrotter and well-known high school basketball coach. Both Darrell and Homer envisioned professional sports, basketball for Darrell and football for Homer, as their ticket to fame and money.

But it was quite clear by sophomore year of high school that neither had the ability to play professionally. And so, lacking any other sense of direction or purpose, as high school students they both sought fun and popularity in ways that led to trouble.

TOO BIG TO FOLLOW

Kenny and Stevie both looked up to their oldest brother Ronnie, which affected their choices and aspirations while growing up. But Darrell's and Homer's relationship to Ronnie's success was not as straightforwardly positive.

Older siblings are most effective as role models for younger ones when their achievements are not only valued by the family, but also within reach for the other children. A younger child typically chooses to follow in the footsteps of an older one, but if the sibling believes that no matter how hard they try, they cannot live up to their sibling's example, then they may look elsewhere for attention and goals. The people we've followed—Sangu, Rob, and Gabby, for example—often modeled academic behavior that younger siblings sought to emulate, but sometimes they overshadowed their younger siblings' achievements.

By the time Darrell got to school, he was a B student but never an A student. "Even when we were little kids," Ronnie said, "I got all the praise for doing really well at school, and Darrell became really good at cleaning the house. Nana in particular would just lavish praise on him about how well he cleaned the house. Darrell had to find a different light under which he could shine, a different way than school to distinguish himself in the family. So kids fall into roles in the family and maybe in some families only one can be the star."

Homer saw both Ronnie and Darrell as role models. Ronnie was his model for conventional types of success, but Ronnie's achievements were always out of reach for Homer. "Who could follow behind that?" Homer said.

Darrell was charismatic and handsome. "He was cool," said Homer, who watched his two older brothers with wonder and awe. "I can remember Darrell driving to school with the Chevy Impala convertible, and how he dressed so sharp. He was cool on the street side, very hip," Homer said. "Ronnie was smart! I can remember he had so many books walking to school that he had to use his hip to help him carry them. I said, 'I want to be smart like Ronnie and cool like Darrell' . . . The mix was a confusing thing to me. Darrell did drugs and that was hip and cool."

It was easier to follow behind Darrell.

"I think a lot about whether if I'd paid more attention and spent more time with Homer and Darrell when we were teenagers, if they might have made different choices," said Ronnie. "But I was gone, already in college, when they really went way off track."

Ronnie is Ron Ferguson, one of the authors of this book, who grew up to be a Harvard economist and an expert on achievement. And one day, years after those late nights he spent in his dorm room at Cornell University worried about Darrell, he was sitting in his office at Harvard, speaking with a colleague, when the phone rang with the news.

Darrell was dead of alcoholism at thirty-eight.

"I can remember being angry. 'What a waste of life.'" The anger dissolved to sadness, and then to feelings of guilt for being so much in the spotlight as a child, perhaps crowding Darrell out from a more constructive pathway.

WHY "I RAISED THEM THE SAME WAY" IS A MYTH—AND WHY IT'S BETTER THAT WAY

What we see in the cautionary tale of the Ferguson brothers is how the differences in the experiences each child had with parents, grandparents, and one another led to five quite different life trajectories. But it's not just changes in environment and family dynamics from one child to the next that impact how a child develops. As we saw with receptivity, the child's personality also makes a difference.

If there is one common thread in the family stories in this chapter, it's that while a parent may love each child the same and interact with them based on the same parental philosophy, that does not mean they actually raise each child the same way. Any parent who believes they do should ask themselves two questions. First, "How are my children different from one another?" Second, "What things work when I say them to one of my children, but don't when I say them to another?"

The answers are a reminder that all children are different. They each have their own likes and dislikes, strengths and weaknesses, that lead their parents, even if they don't realize it, to treat them differently from their siblings—to treat them as individuals.

Joe Bruzzese, a former educator and academic coach, believes that every child requires their own tailored approach to succeed, and that this is as true within families as it is between them. For example, Bruzzese worked with three brothers over a course of several years to fine-tune their organizational and study skills. Their parents pressed all three boys to be top performers academically, but because each had his own set of strengths and weaknesses, they each had their own unique challenges in getting there.

The First Son

"The first son ended up going to Princeton," Bruzzese said. "He was a soccer player. He played at the top level, and he also was a very efficient student, but his work ethic is what enabled him to achieve at such a high level."

To get the grades he did, he had to work very hard. "He was a great student in that he learned to understand a lot of advanced content, but this is a kid who had to spend hours every night getting his homework done, preparing for tests, studying."

This first son knew he was expected to excel. "His parents drove him hard from a very early age. He graduated college after studying Mandarin Chinese and economics. He now works for a top-level corporation and is on track for a high-level executive job."

Although hard work was the secret to this first son's success, Bruzzese always wondered if the expectation, at the time, was too much for that particular son. "There was no alternative other than getting As in classes," he said.

If economic success is the only yardstick, it's hard to debate the end result. Especially when that result is getting into an Ivy League school and securing an excellent job with strong financial prospects. "He succeeded in that goal," Bruzzese said.

But if the aim is to produce a fulfilled child, as it is for the master parent, the first son's outcome is uncertain. "How happy or how fulfilled he feels now, I don't know. Whether that's even a question for him now, I'm not sure."

The Second Son

The next brother was a couple of years younger. He had recently graduated from Stanford when we spoke to Bruzzese, and was considering studying neuroscience in graduate school.

"He was a great athlete, and brother number two was perfect for the family's academic environment, all the way up to high school. Essentially, he could read, write, and remember everything almost to the point of having a photographic memory. I asked, 'How do you study for tests?' and he said, 'I just read through my notes a couple of times,'" Bruzzese recalled.

To achieve at the same level as his older brother, the second son required far less studying. But he was so laid back that he would only have succeeded in a home where high performance was expected. "This is a kid that if the expectation for him to achieve at a high level hadn't been there, he wouldn't have," Bruzzese said.

The Third Son

Bruzzese believes the youngest son was the most intelligent of the three. "This kid could, in middle school, sit down with you and over the course of a few minutes tell you the entire history of medieval times, but if you asked him to write it down on a piece of paper you could be there for weeks while this kid was trying to get out what he was trying to explain."

The third son had a different way of learning, one that wasn't respected in the classroom. "The real challenge is that today's academic environment does not cater to kids who have a more auditory learning style, kids who will listen, remember, and then are able talk about what they have learned," he said. "You can't grade that on a Scantron form."

Eventually, when the child reached high school, the parents realized the third son was not on track to attend a world-class university like his brothers. Bruzzese said that was a huge revelation for that particular family. The parents finally looked at their third son as an individual, and not as just another son who'd attend an Ivy League school.

"They finally figured out, 'You know what, he's different, and unless we start recognizing that he's different and that he's not achieving at the same level, we are going to lose him.'"

They decided the best option was to homeschool him for the remainder of his high school years. He earned a high school diploma and went on to nursing school.

Were the boys' parents master parents? For the second son, perhaps. These parents had high expectations and obviously knew how to raise smart children. And those high expectations were key to keeping their less motivated middle child on a path to success. But their single-minded focus on academic achievement, rather than the whole child, may have led the eldest child to lean too much on external markers of success, crowding out other worthwhile activities that produce the emotional development needed to achieve fulfillment. And their failure to understand their youngest child as an individual earlier, and adjust their parenting strategy accordingly, resulted in lost learning time.

The master parent, as we've seen, is a savvy student of their child. Master parents who are more than just masters of one get to know each child as an individual, and constantly adapt their parenting to do what works best for each child. This failure to adjust, even by very involved parents, is another reason that success can differ between siblings.

"MY SIBLING WAS JUST AS SMART, BUT . . ."

Let's look at another, similar case—one where, because the family had a broader view of what it meant for a child to flourish that emphasized developing the whole child rather than just grades, three different siblings each found their own unique path to success.

The Croal siblings are all very intelligent in their own ways, just like the three brothers Bruzzese coached. Growing up, all three read the same books and played the same games in the same intellectually rich home environment. But one of them failed to achieve on the same academic level as her outstanding siblings.

In school, Nneka (pronounced en-ay-kah) made Bs, Cs, and the occasional D. Born and raised in Vancouver, where she still lives, Nneka says she didn't put much stock in grades.

Her siblings, however, did. Her twin sister Aida, now an Emmy-winning screenwriter in Los Angeles and co-executive producer for the Netflix series *Luke Cage*, was a straight-A student who skipped the eighth grade. Their older brother N'Gai, a former *Newsweek* video game critic once compared to Roger Ebert who now runs a successful video game consulting company, was his year's top-scoring International Baccalaureate student in all of Canada.

N'Gai and Aida each made big waves with their intellectual nimbleness at an early age. N'Gai's first-grade teacher recognized that him being "a disturbance" in the class was actually a symptom of boredom, as it was with David Martinez. She had him tested and discovered he was doing math on a third- and fourth-grade level and reading on a seventh-grade level. "She went to the principal, and they went to the school board to persuade them to allow me to be placed in French immersion, two years before my peers would have been studying French, rather than skip me ahead to third grade," he said.

The parents worried that the girls, who were about to enter kindergarten, might have an experience similar to N'Gai's, so they immediately went looking for ways to challenge them. They ended up enrolling the twins in kindergarten French immersion classes, too, even though the parents could not speak French themselves.

Halfway through kindergarten, the French immersion teacher couldn't believe Aida was already reading French. As she tells it,

"The teacher said, 'What are you doing with that book?' I said, 'I'm reading.' She said, 'No, you are not.' She asked me to read, and I read it, and then she was like, 'Oh my gosh.' She took me to the principal's office and had me read French . . . I was painfully shy. I was petrified. That's when I realized something different was happening." As happened with many of our high achievers, the teacher and principal were singling her out in a way that made her feel special.

As they got older, Aida and N'Gai both continued to perform well. While Aida was usually the top performer of the three, N'Gai's grades shot up in eighth grade once he decided that he wanted to be on the honor roll. He started working harder, and before long he was the top student in high school.

Aida had until this point considered herself the superior student in the family and at school, but now her older brother was exceeding her accomplishments. She was proud of him, and resolved to follow in his footsteps. "My sibling was the best in the school, and meanwhile all those years, I never had to chase another person; I was always pushing myself without anyone ahead of me until then," she said.

Nneka, in contrast, chose not to compete at all, feeling, as Homer did about Ronnie, that she could never match Aida's accomplishments. "I created a persona where that just wasn't going to be me. I valued a social prowess," she said. She believed that making high marks like her siblings wasn't her way to navigate the world.

Was aptitude the problem? Aida believes "Nneka had the same or very similar aptitude as I had." She explained, "There was one teacher that we had in the sixth grade who told Nneka she knew she was capable of more and she held her to that expectation, so she became an A student for that teacher. After that, she didn't have that expectation on her, so she became a C student again. It took very little change in effort that year for her to do well for that teacher, so I know she could do it."

Nneka recalls the teacher who inspired those As. "I don't know if it was people pleasing, but she really believed in me, so I applied myself for that class, and subsequently other things that interested me."

If most of the time Nneka wasn't making the grades, how was she able to suddenly do so well in that one teacher's class?

The answer lies in the Croals' home, where learning was a constant. Their mother Yvonne, a former early-childhood education teacher, and their father James, a retired mathematician, grew up with humble means in Guyana, but the two master parents created an excellent home learning environment filled with computers, books, and Lego blocks. They were outstanding Early-Learning Partners.

When the children were young, James would take them to spend time at the computer lab at Simon Fraser University, where he worked. "He would do his work and we would play games on the Apple II computers," N'Gai said. And a few years later, in 1989 (years prior to the point home computers became commonplace), they got a home computer before any of their friends. That gave the Croal children a clear leg up—especially N'Gai, whose later writing and consulting career was steeped in technology.

"When we were really young, there was a lot of exposure," N'Gai said. "I think what my father was—either by design or just out of interest or his own curiosity about the world—trying to instill in us was that learning is everywhere; it's all around you."

Said Aida, "What we were doing at home was never presented as learning time; it was just the household atmosphere. You'd walk outside and my father is talking about the nature of the spectrum of light and what we can and can't see . . . What my mother and father were doing threw us ahead so far beyond what we were learning in the classroom."

As James described their home life, "There were always books, there was always conversation, the children were always busy doing things with us and each other."

When James was a child, his own father would gather James and his brothers and sisters together every Sunday night for a discussion about whatever they wanted to talk about. At some point, when his own children were in elementary school, James decided to do the same.

During these Sunday night discussions, James noticed Nneka was the most talkative. "She would often take the lead and express the most opinions, and she was more tuned-in to subtleties than the other two were. She would pick up on an issue or an idea that the others didn't glimpse."

Nneka wasn't lacking in intelligence, or in interest in learning. Academics just weren't her priority.

What Do Grades Have to Do with It?

James and Yvonne realized early on that Nneka's talents expressed themselves in a different, more social way than her older brother's and twin sister's. Unlike the parents of the three brothers, the Croals looked at each of their children as individuals. They had high expectations for all of them, but they didn't push Nneka to make the same grades as the other two, knowing that strategy would have backfired with this vivacious, socially precocious child.

Rather than applying a one-size-fits-all approach to raising their children, the Croals respected that Nneka's intelligence was not well measured by standard academic-reporting tools, like report cards, and judged her growth accordingly. If there'd been a social skills grade, where the ability to communicate and empathize were measured, Nneka would have outscored her siblings hands down.

"I never needed a grade from school to tell me how Nneka was doing. I could make that judgment myself," says James.

He saw no difference in terms of how well his three kids were learning. "Of course, each one had their own ways about them, but that's only natural," James said. "We never were trying to force them into any mold. N'Gai and Aida got better grades in school, and Nneka was a more social person from the time she was a baby."

That's not to say they didn't have high expectations for Nneka. "The expectation was that I should apply myself to learning," Nneka said. "It really wasn't that different [from my siblings]. But I wasn't expected to be as academically successful as Aida and N'Gai. I wasn't reprimanded for Bs or Cs. It was more like, we have an environment here of learning, and whatever grades come out of that, come out of that."

However, when N'Gai came home with less than an A, his mother told him she'd be proud if it was his best, but she knew it wasn't his best. That was never a conversation she had with Nneka. Aida believes their parents let Nneka know that they wanted her to do her best, but because early on "she wasn't getting the grades that I was getting or the grades that the teachers said N'Gai was capable of, they didn't push her as hard. When she came home with C+ or B, they didn't say, 'You're in trouble.' If I came home with those grades, they would say, 'What happened here?'"

Aida believes her parents did the right thing with her sister. "To put any more pressure on her probably wouldn't have worked. They did try it, but it didn't work."

Said Nneka, "I surrendered the high-achiever role to Aida, believing I couldn't compete with that."

But she wasn't envious of her twin—only proud. Their father says Nneka "would go around telling everyone that Aida did this and Aida did that."

Aida was just as proud of Nneka, and of how popular her sister was—so much so that Aida had her own moments that she thought she couldn't live up to her sister's example.

"When Aida was in fifth or sixth grade, she told us she was tired of being in Nneka's shadow socially and wanted to be assigned to a different class so she could make her own friends," James said. "So we allowed her to change classes."

Nneka told herself during those childhood years that her lesser academic performance compared to her siblings' successes didn't bother her, but now she's not so sure. "It must have. I think it did."

Would things have been different if Nneka had understood what everybody in the family knew: that she was just as smart as her siblings? Would she have claimed her high-academic position at the school for which it seems she was surely qualified? Or would she still have chosen to focus her energies in a more social direction?

We can't really know. What we do know is that her not making academics a priority had its costs. She missed out on experiencing the joy and satisfaction of earning high marks for a job well done, and the adulation from adults that affirms the importance of doing one's best, which affected the way she thought of herself, and as a result, what she believed she could accomplish. Even today, as a successful actor, Nneka says, "I have never considered myself a high achiever," which she very clearly is.

This self-doubt slowed Nneka's journey, delaying the full impact of the Formula's power to create purposeful children who grow up to be impactful adults. Nneka acknowledges her brother and sister were purposeful by high school. They knew what they wanted, and they figured out how to get it. That didn't happen for her until later.

If she'd had less strategic and thoughtful parents, Nneka's life could have turned out very differently. Though the Croal children described their parents as emotionally distant at times, Nneka's parents were fundamentally loving and attentive, and played all the roles of the Formula effectively with each of their children. That, and especially the freedom they gave Nneka to hone her social skills through the years, helped her become the actor she is today. "As an actor you need emotional intelligence. Empathy is a large part of where my strengths lie," she said.

It took her a little longer than it did her siblings, but she did eventually find her purpose.

Nneka was already a professional actor when she applied to a graduate program at New York University that allows artists to step away from their practice for a year to learn more about the role of artists in society. She didn't have the undergraduate grades that were typically needed to qualify, but she moved the admission's gatekeepers with her story. "It was basically a story about an outlier who had a certain amount of struggle inside and outside the home but overcame it."

In graduate school, she became the straight-A student she'd always been capable of becoming.

"I really stretched my legs in an academic way. It was like, 'Oh! I can do this!'"

Before attending the program, Nneka had been struggling with the question of whether a long-term career in acting was meaningful and purposeful enough for her. But during the program, she says, what really spoke to her was the idea of using her art to affect larger issues in the world. And that became her purpose.

IS YOUR OLDEST CHILD REALLY SMARTER, OR WERE YOU JUST TIRED WITH THE REST OF THEM?

A high number of the achievers you'll meet in this book were first-born children. Of those we've met so far, Nneka's brother N'Gai, plus Rob, Jarell, Gabby, David, Pam, and the Malveaux twins were all oldest children. This aligns with common knowledge about birth order and success: first-borns are more likely to excel and be leaders than their younger siblings.

The most common explanation given for this is that the first-born gets more attention, which creates a stronger foundation of knowledge and skills to build upon, and then retains their advantage as they get older by virtue of that head start. This explanation is supported by a massive 2018 scientific study from Sweden, which found that later-born children do in fact tend to be less successful because parents devote less time and attention to them than they did to their first-borns. And while this idea might make you wince, it's not really surprising. Maintaining the level of energy and commitment that many parents, who have often spent years anticipating raising a child, devote to their first-born can be difficult once subsequent children are born.

Another theory suggested by the research is that first-borns are more likely to excel academically because they are often asked to take on responsibilities in the home, such as caring for younger siblings, that require them to develop greater organizational and self-management skills, as well as a stronger sense of duty.

But as we've seen, a child's natural receptivity is also important, and so are other inborn tendencies. So when the second or third child doesn't perform academically as well as the first, it's hard to really know if it's because the zeal of parental engagement has dimmed, because the child lacked the academic capacity, or something else.

All Rob Humble knows about his own sister is that "life wasn't fair to her." By the time she came along, Rob was already considered an extraordinary child, and coming second in the birth order, behind a star sibling, "that's really hard to follow," Rob said. "And it's compounded by the fact that my sister was smart but not by society's standard measures of smart. She's very artistic, but she's just not academic. So I was always the smart boy with the brilliant future, and she was always the cute girl that could dance. I think to a certain extent we lived up to those expectations in our respective ways."

Was it because of something their parents did, or didn't do? Rob says, "I think our parents definitely parented her differently, but they were the same parents."

Bob Senior believes his daughter just decided not to compete. "They both seemed to be going along the same path until seventh grade, when my daughter had to take higher-level math and she couldn't do it. She had trouble with algebra and fractions and things. We did not discover until her junior year in high school that she had attention deficit disorder," he said. "By then, she had given up on competing with her brother. She'd almost turned herself in a different direction."

Much like an overachiever can distort the grading scale in a classroom where the teacher grades on a curve, a high-achieving sibling can distort a child's perception regarding what's good enough to consider success. If a parent or other adult does not intervene explicitly to assert a more reasonable standard, the child may, out of frustration or a sense of hopelessness, unwisely abandon his or her academic pursuit.

"She tried to compete with Rob and she couldn't. So she just chose a different path," Bob Senior said. "We had to monitor her. We never had to worry about what [Rob] was doing, but we had to with her."

Rob's sister became pregnant before graduating from high school and later struggled to find her footing. But Rob said she has always been a devoted mother to her children, a boy and a girl, who are doing well in school. "What she always had was tenacity," Rob said. "For instance, she had a job interview at a bank. Her car broke down on the way. She walked two miles in 102-degree weather. She got the job on the spot."

Bob Senior believes it's easier for everyone if the high-achieving child is not the first-born. Then, he explained, the lesser-achieving child isn't having to grow up trying (and failing) to meet the standards the achiever set.

And there are, of course, families where middle or youngest children are the superstars.

One of the youngest of four boys and one girl, Sangu was his family's academic standout. Most (though not all) of his older siblings excelled in school, but Sangu's precociousness was in a whole other league. Part of the reason may have been just natural abilities. Even as a child, Sangu had a photographic memory. But we also know that Sangu was a very receptive child who got a lot of one-on-one attention from his father, as well as his mother, who taught him to read at a very early age after a nursery school teacher noticed Sangu had an outstanding memory and caught on quickly. And while Sangu's mother paid attention to all her children, checking homework and supplementing their schooling at home, she held Sangu's work to a higher standard. Sangu did more than respond well to that; he thrived.

One of Sangu's older brothers, however, was known as a slow learner, and even with the age difference, Sangu quickly began to overshadow him.

"I know he was very frustrated growing up," Sangu recalls. "There were no special schools, there were no programs for learning disabilities, none of that stuff. And the teachers were a bit cruel because they would always compare me to him and they would use me to embarrass him. It was bad. We'd be in class and they might call him to the front of the class to answer the question. And so let's say he's two grades ahead of me, so if he's in fifth grade and I'm in third grade, he's struggling to answer the question, they would call me from third grade and I'd answer the question.

"We're lucky, because that could easily have led to resentment, but he loved me. He named his son, his only son, after me."

But while Sangu's brother loved him, he hated school, so much so that he gave up trying, despite his mother hiring tutors. "It didn't help a lot because he rejected it," Sangu said. The brother became incredibly street smart but never good at academics like everyone else in the family, and especially not like Sangu.

Eventually one of his tutors discovered Sangu's brother was good at math and built up his confidence by encouraging him to work harder. He later became an entrepreneur and started his own business, but it was not until he was older that he realized the extent of his own smarts.

Other high-achieving younger siblings in this book suspected their parents were able to be master parents for them in part because of what their parents learned from raising older children. In such cases—beyond any inborn differences in personality or aptitude—life circumstances and opportunities were simply more favorable for the younger sibling.

After Chuck Badger's older brother ended up in prison, his mother realized that she needed to spend lots of time with Chuck, especially during the Early-Learning Partner years, to get him headed in the right direction. And because she believed the older brother had gotten in trouble partly because he used his free time unwisely, she was sure to keep Chuck busy with enrichment programs. When her efforts were successful and his academic abilities eventually surpassed her own, she relied on others to fill in the gap, making sure he'd be on the same footing as other smart children and stay away from dangerous environments.

WHY A CHILD'S INTELLECTUAL CAPACITY MATTERS

From a broad perspective, of course, there is no ironclad rule for how birth orders affects either parenting or child development outcomes. There's also no one-size-fits-all solution to raising children, even though there are universal principles, such as those captured in the roles of the Formula, that always apply.

Each of the siblings in this chapter, from the Ferguson brothers to the Croals to Rob and his sister and Sangu and his brother, has a unique story with its own inherent logic, and its own dynamics. But similar stories play out in families around the world, and the patterns those stories represent can be instructive.

There are always differences in how children are raised, even in the same family, and these differences can lead to very disparate outcomes. But for most master parents, differences in parenting, as much as possible, are strategic; they adapt their parenting to fit the needs of each child.

As David Martinez said about how his parents raised him, an extrovert, and his brother Daniel, who was more introverted, "If I could sum up their approach, it would probably be setting very high equal standards for both of us, according to our capacities and our abilities. They assessed our personalities, our intellectual capabilities, and our emotional readiness to adapt to a learning environment, and then built everything around that."

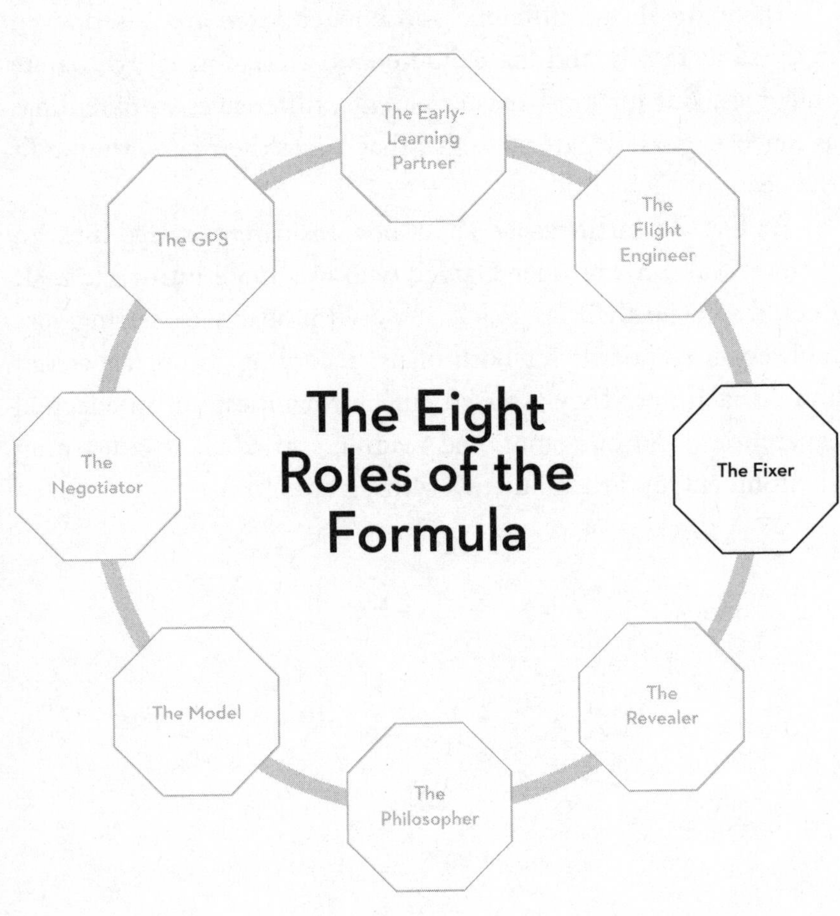
The Early-Learning Partner
The Flight Engineer
The Fixer
The Revealer
The Philosopher
The Model
The Negotiator
The GPS
The Eight Roles of the Formula

CHAPTER 8

The Fixer (Role #3)

THE FIXER TO THE RESCUE!

There's a scene in 1978's *Superman: The Movie*, where a passenger train is speeding across the desert when an earthquake causes a break in the rails ahead. The train is certain to careen off into the valley until, out of the blue, Superman appears. He bends one rail back into shape and braces his body to fill the remaining gap on the other side. The train passes safely over as though nothing had gone wrong.

The master parent as Fixer is the superhero who comes to the rescue when circumstances threaten to derail their child's progress. Especially when time is of the essence, this clever and resourceful guardian acts with laser-focused resolve to keep their child's journey on track.

Like the Flight Engineer, the Fixer is *vigilant*, monitoring what is happening in their child's life. But while the Flight Engineer always works within the ecologies or systems the child belongs to—collaborating with teachers and school officials when malfunctions arise in a system—the Fixer goes it alone, like Superman flying in at a moment's notice. They take often-heroic steps as an independent actor to remove blocks or repair cracks that threaten their child's place in that system.

Master parents in the Fixer role have a lot in common with the "fixers" journalists hire when they report from foreign countries to anticipate and remove roadblocks to the reporter's mission. Behind the scenes, these fixers create and protect opportunities for the reporter by providing access to informants, translating information, and helping them navigate safely through sometimes dangerous territory. They risk their lives to make a way when there seems to be no way, while rarely getting credit for their contributions. The parent as Fixer also makes *sacrifices* to keep their charge's journey on course, sometimes relinquishing prized possessions, making significant life changes, or devoting large amounts of personal time to continue their child's momentum.

Not unlike the mother who lifts a car off a trapped child, the Fixer must find strength to take extraordinary actions. The Fixer is *resourceful*, summoning up stamina and gutsiness beyond what most of us are willing and able to, and finding whatever resources they need to do what needs to be done. This ability doesn't depend on a parent's socioeconomic class status. Middle- and upper-class parents may have an easier time finding financial resources and well-connected allies, but master parents of all income levels are strategically ingenious in discovering ways to keep their child's journey on course.

Perhaps most important, Fixer parents are *relentless* in prioritizing their child's journey. Whether they are striving to excel in a high-stress career or struggling to make ends meet on a poverty-level income, the master parents as Fixers don't allow the other pressures they face to distract them from their commitment to their child's success. They find the bandwidth to fight for and protect opportunities for their child whenever the need arises.

VIGILANCE: HOW ONE MOTHER DECONSTRUCTED THE SAT

Esther Wojcicki's three ultra-successful daughters arrived at the pinnacles of their fields in science and technology through opportunities that their Fixer mother made sure they didn't squander. In high school, they took the PSAT, a practice test for the SAT college entrance exam. A less vigilant parent might have paid no attention to the scores, or noticed but not realized their importance—after all, the PSAT is a just a warm-up for the SAT, not recorded on any transcript. But Esther, a well-respected teacher, knew PSAT scores were supposed to be good indicators of SAT scores, and SATs mattered a lot to admissions officers at top-tier universities.

"They did terrible on the PSAT, and I said to them, 'This is crazy!' With scores like these, there was no way they would ever be admitted" to the universities that Esther and her husband Stan knew they had the ability to attend.

"I said, 'You are going to have to get into college, so you'd better pay attention and you're going to have to study a little bit for the exams.'"

She did not agree necessarily that the SAT should be a requirement for college admissions, but it was, and so her daughters needed to do well on it—an uncertain prospect, based on their PSAT scores. She knew she had to do something—and soon.

"I told them, 'Before you take the stupid test, you have to go to bed at night—no hanging out at midnight with your friends; you have to get a good night's sleep.'"

And then she started doing her own SAT studying.

Esther believed she could figure out how to solve almost any problem by breaking it down, a strategy nearly all of the master parents in the book described employing at some point. They stood back and observed, and then decoded what was in front of them, be it a financial problem or a recalcitrant child.

First, Esther obtained a sample of the SAT test and analyzed it, taking it apart "like someone would take apart a car engine. I looked into the SAT itself and I just categorized the types of learning they were looking for and then I focused on the vocabulary words. You can't learn the words overnight, but you can study over time with flash cards."

She bought a box of a thousand vocabulary cards and displayed the cards around the house. "I stuck them all over the place." The girls also each carried ten cards in their hip pocket every week. And "there were other cards taped to the dashboard of the car," Esther recalled. "The idea was to familiarize them with those words. I realized that if they had multiple short encounters with the words, they would learn them—and it worked!"

While she had been a journalist and writing teacher for most of her career, she also deciphered the math section: "I'd been a math teacher for some tutoring clients, so I also figured out the types of math problems that are on the test," and had her daughters practice them until they knew them cold.

Because Esther was so vigilant—and then, once her vigilance had alerted her to the problem, so resourceful and relentless in sacrificing the time and energy to deconstruct and master the SAT and to cajole her daughters to study it—Susan achieved a 1590 out of 1600, missing just one question on the math and English sections combined, and Janet and Anne did nearly as well.

THE KNOWING-DOING GAP

Life is full of things we know we should do, but seldom follow through on. We don't decide not to do them; we just don't quite get around to them.

Stanford University professors Jeffrey Pfeffer and Robert Sutton call this phenomenon the "knowing-doing gap." And though Pfeffer and Sutton's focus is on business (their work explores why so many companies facing big challenges fail to apply the insights and ideas they've worked to develop), their commonsense idea of the knowing-doing gap can be applied to any context in which people don't fully use what they know—like parenting.

Every parent has hopes and dreams for their kids. And we all know there are things we could do, like spending more quality time to understand their interests and ideas, to improve our children's life prospects. But we're busy. We'll do them later. There are also things, like how to help our kids connect their particular interests to potential careers or how to answer their deep questions about life, that, though we don't know, we could learn—but, again, we're busy. Who has the time?

Pfeffer and Sutton found that, for businesses, knowing-doing gaps diminish when a company stops wasting time listing what they could do to solve the pressing problems they face, and instead takes the first steps to fix them—even if they don't know every step they'll need to take to go all the way. When companies focused on what they *didn't* yet know, it resulted in inertia, whereas for businesses that got started trying to solve the problem based on what they *did* know, the answers they needed emerged during the act of doing.

The same applies to parenting. Master parents find ways to address both *knowing* gaps, by learning things they didn't already know, and *knowing-doing* gaps, by just jumping in and getting started with the things they knew they should do.

When master parents encounter an important but familiar idea about parenting, instead of thinking, "That's not new. I've heard it before," their reaction is, rather, a question: "Do I do that as much as I should?" Perhaps the greatest difference between parents who follow the Formula and other parents is not what they know. Instead, it's how relentlessly and strategically they use the things they know in helping to enable and support their child.

This is especially important when it comes to the Fixer role, where *doing* is key. The Fixer is not all-knowing; they don't always have the right answer up front. But they get to work on the problem anyhow, and usually find that answer along the way.

SACRIFICE: DAD SAYS, "WE NEED TO LEAVE—NOW!"

After being expelled for selling marijuana, fifteen-year-old Alfonso Hernandez was supposed to be headed to court-ordered reform school when his father Reynaldo decided to rescue him from serving the sentence. "We took off. My dad was like, 'Screw this. We're getting the hell out of here.' He refused to let the state take me away because he's a really great dad and was really protective."

If he had been a better Flight Engineer, Reynaldo might have learned earlier that Alfonso was selling pot and intervened to stop him. But he hadn't, and now he needed to make a major sacrifice as a Fixer to protect his son. The option of remaining passive and acquiescing to the order to send Alfonso away was off the table. He found it simply unacceptable to have his smart, promising son be placed in the justice system. So, instead, they immediately left the suburb of Chicago where they had been living.

The circumstances were daunting. It would not have been easy for any parent to make such a move, but it was especially difficult for Reynaldo, an undocumented immigrant from Costa Rica. He'd flown his entire family to the United States a decade or so earlier to take a job offered by a friend at a Midwestern university with whom Reynaldo had previously done some anthropological work in the Amazon jungles. But after they arrived, Reynaldo discovered the job offer had been retracted. Reynaldo had only been to a few places in America, had almost no funds, and lacked personal contacts, so although he had some years of college under his belt, he was stuck doing menial jobs.

After fleeing the Chicago area, Reynaldo took Alfonso's two brothers to live with their mother in Tampa and agreed with his current wife, the boys' stepmother, that they would, at least for a while, not be together. Reynaldo and Alfonso then moved far away to a college town in California. (The other two boys later left

Tampa to move back in with Reynaldo and Alfonso once the two were settled.)

With his father by his side, Alfonso started an unorthodox but ultimately successful academic journey. Come the next fall, when it was time to make a decision on school, "we explored the possibility of getting back to school formally, but I think it might have started getting too complicated," Alfonso said.

It was supposed to be Alfonso's tenth-grade year, but the father and son found another way. "We discovered an opportunity to take this test that, if I passed, would allow me to enter a community college. I took it, and I thought it was really easy. I got this certificate, which allowed me to go to community college at the age of sixteen."

It's virtually certain that if Alfonso had instead gone to reform school, his life would have taken a different course. Researchers believe that even less intensive forms of discipline, like long-term suspensions from school, often lead to dropping out, frequent arrests, and sometimes lives spent in prison. Rather than becoming a statistic, because of his father Alfonso ended up graduating from two elite universities, becoming fluent in Chinese, and traveling the world as an accomplished international business professional.

By making the sacrifice he did, and taking a big real-life risk, Reynaldo gave Alfonso a better set of options and a different path to travel.

RESOURCEFULNESS: THE GIRL WHO NEEDED A FLUTE

Today, Sara Vargas's daughter Gabby is a Harvard-educated immigration attorney helping people with the problems her mother once faced as an undocumented immigrant having fled the civil war in El Salvador.

But back when Gabby was in the sixth grade, she was just a girl who needed a flute.

Having the instrument was more important to Gabby's status and success in school than one might think. Gabby was thriving socially and academically among roughly thirty other high-achieving classmates, most of them—unlike the Vargases—affluent. The other top students were joining the middle school band, so Gabby needed to, as well. She couldn't remain on the same playing field as her classmates if she didn't have an instrument. And Gabby wanted that instrument to be a flute.

"I wanted a brand-new flute, not a cheap or used one," which would make her stand out, and not in a good way. "I wanted something as nice as what everyone else had. And I knew that however she could, my mother would figure out a way to help me get it."

Sara understood the importance of fitting in. She knew that Gabby needed to be with other high-achieving children in order to reap the benefits of being in that peer group—perks like having high-income parents as accessible role models—and she couldn't do that if she didn't have an instrument. But obtaining a brand-new flute was a huge problem in a family where there were no funds to spare.

The single mom and her three daughters were surviving on a cashier's salary—not even $6 an hour. A decent flute would cost $1,000. Sara did not have the money. And unfortunately, there was no one else she could ask for help. Being an undocumented worker, she had no savings account or credit card. If she was going to get Gabby that flute, she had only one option: pawning her wedding ring.

The ring was typical of the late 1980s, with a gold band made of two interlocking rings and three diamonds. But most importantly, it was a lifeline in a household where money was tight and deportation was always a looming threat to both Gabby and Sara.

Still, Sara didn't hesitate. "I said, 'I can do this if I go to downtown.' I started looking on the streets for pawnshops. I found one on Broadway. I went to the pawnshop."

She gave the man at the counter her wedding ring and she got the money for a down payment on the flute.

"Your child needs an instrument and there's no option. There was no other choice. Music was one of the areas that Gabby did well in . . . so she really wanted to do it. The only way I could buy the flute was to pawn my ring," she said.

She purchased the flute on a rent-to-own basis. "It was a sad and happy day," Sara recalled. "The ring had sentimental value but at the same time it was the only option for something that my kid really needed. I was going to help my kid, and that's it."

Having the flute in their home, at least in Sara's view, "was like winning the lottery." It was an invaluable symbol that Gabby belonged on the same playing field as her more affluent schoolmates.

When Sara was able to take time off work, she'd go see her daughter's concerts. Sometimes she even brought her friends to come along with her. "I was so proud."

Gabby's musical interests yielded her all the benefits that Sara believed it would. Being part of the school band broadened Gabby's outlook. It positioned her to travel, to discover the importance of teamwork, and to build close friendships with classmates who were likewise raised to do well in school.

Today, Gabby is still blown away by her mother's resourcefulness. "No one just pawns their wedding ring to get you a flute! That just sticks with me. It did then, and it does now."

Sara made her regular payments and eventually got the ring back. Then, whenever her girls needed something else and Sara didn't have the money, she would pawn it again. "I never stopped making payments. Every time I got my check, I paid for the ring. . . . My goal was to keep making the payments, not to lose the ring. I kept paying, and then I'd pawn it again, and get more money."

Without access to credit cards or bank loans, the pawnshop was like the bank, the ring collateral for high-interest loans. Every instance of pawning the ring carried the risk of never getting it back. But Sara always found a way to make ends meet, and she never gave up.

RELENTLESSNESS: ELAINE BADGER'S MIDDLE-CLASS DREAM

Terri Chapman will never forget the day she received her first phone call from Elaine Badger. Terri ran an entrepreneurship summer camp called the CEO Academy that exposed children from poor families to middle-class possibilities. Terri recalls, "I typically recruited children from the schools. I would tell the teachers about this wonderful summer camp. Teachers would make recommendations and parents would call. Ms. Badger found out about the program from another parent at the church."

Elaine wanted her fourth-grade son Chuck to participate in the program, but Terri explained there was a waiting list. Elaine was determined. She wasn't giving up. "But I just found out about it," she said. Then she began to tell their story.

Elaine explained to Terri how she and her ex-husband had moved from New York City to Nashville when Chuck was a baby, how Chuck had a much older brother who was later incarcerated, and how that had motivated Elaine to ensure Chuck kept busy with his education rather than having free time to get into trouble. "Elaine told me, 'What I am trying to do is build up his eight-week summer.'"

Elaine was ultimately persuasive. Terri recalls, "I said there is something about this kid. If there is a mother living in Section 8 housing and adamant about me meeting her son, I have to meet him."

Terri did not say yes immediately. She always went on a home visit first to see people in their "natural habitats." Like the other families in Terri's program, Elaine's home was not in the best part of town, and it wasn't fancy, but where they lived was not what mattered most to Terri, who is African American like the Badgers. What struck Terri most was Elaine, an older mom who seemed even older because of her many health issues. In fact, she had a stroke when Chuck was in second grade, which resulted in her sometimes needing a cane to get around.

Terri remembers being impressed: "Here Elaine was, a parent on disability, on public assistance, but was raising this young man. She could have been his grandmother. He comes out of the room wearing nicely ironed black pants and a nicely ironed button-down white shirt, unlike the other kids in the neighborhood. His mother was very adamant about him making a good impression."

That meeting was the beginning of a partnership in which Terri became Elaine's agent in connecting Chuck to the larger world. Without Elaine's persistence in her pursuit of protecting Chuck from his brother's fate, Chuck never would have received the early networking with political leaders he'd later work with as an adult. He'd have missed the mentoring by business and political giants who groomed him to be a leader in school and the astute campaign manager, consultant, and political commentator he'd become.

WHAT A DIFFERENCE A FIXER MAKES

How might their children's lives have turned out differently had Esther not been so vigilant, Reynaldo less willing to sacrifice, Sara not so resourceful, and Elaine less relentless?

It's not too dramatic to say that if Esther's daughters had not aced the SAT, the world would be a different place. Harvard is where her oldest daughter Susan first took the computer classes that later, in 1998, contributed to her becoming Google's eighteenth employee, first marketing manager, and later senior vice president of advertising and commerce, before encouraging the company to buy YouTube, of which she became the CEO. Janet might not have been in a position to make the contributions she has to addressing the HIV epidemic in Africa, had she had a different educational journey. And regular citizens would not have the same access to their genetic ancestry or their risk of developing certain diseases had Anne not built the company 23andMe, where she is the CEO.

If Reynaldo had not sacrificed by fleeing with his son, things might have turned out quite differently for Alfonso. Even if he had managed to complete a high school degree in reform school, he might never have been exposed to the opportunities that led him to excel in education, business, and life.

Without her flute, Gabby might have drifted away from the high-flying peer group that reinforced her educational aspirations and motivated her to become the lawyer she is today. If she hadn't, imagine the impact on the life courses of the immigrant families she supports and defends.

Finally, Chuck would never have met Terri and, through her, the others who helped him achieve his political dreams. The outcomes in the campaigns that he managed and won might have been different, and none of the many ripple effects from those campaign victories would have occurred.

By acting as Fixers, these parents found resources to access opportunities or prevent disruptions that might have knocked their children off high-achievement trajectories. As a result, they not only helped their children become successful, but touched untold numbers of other lives as well.

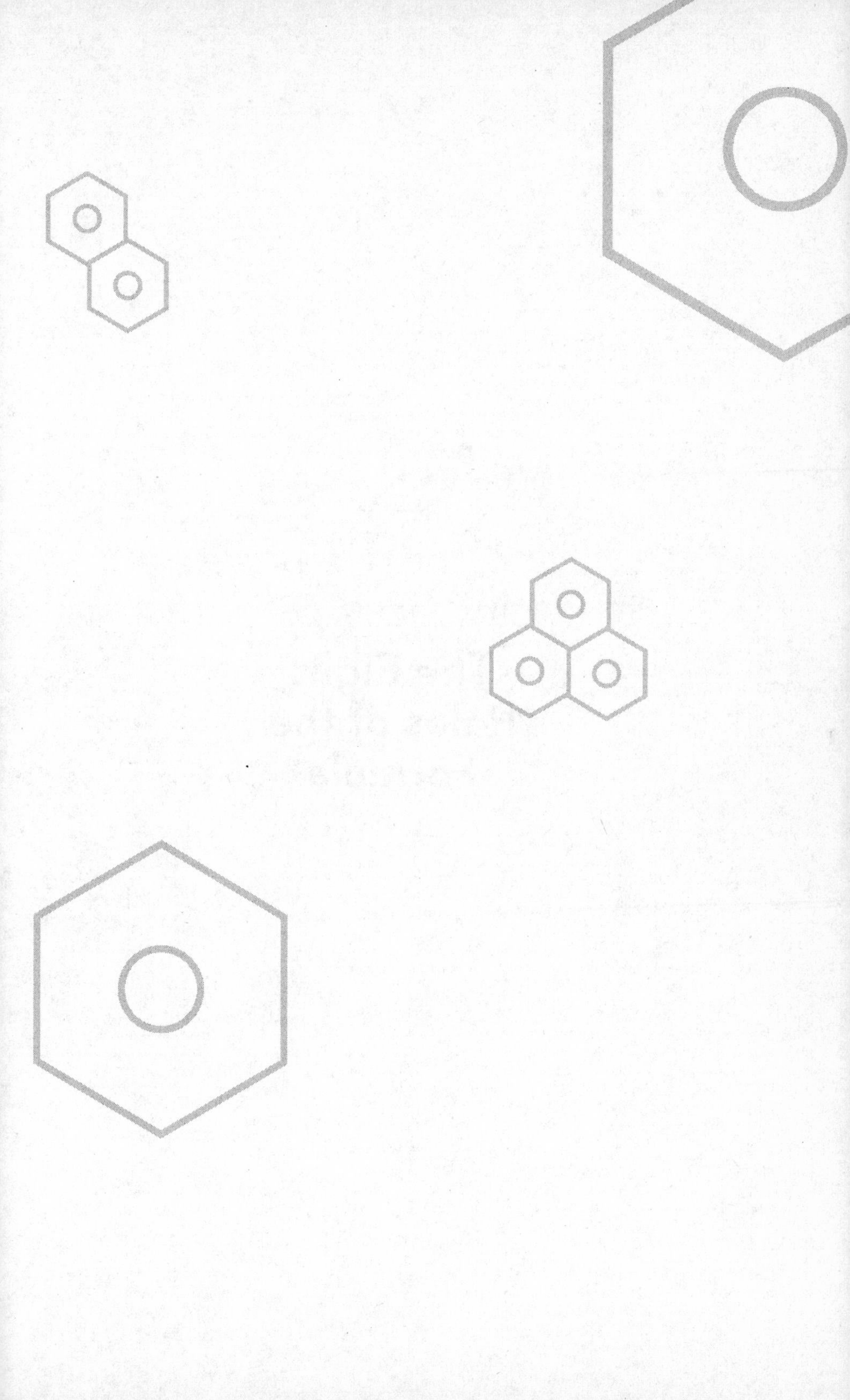

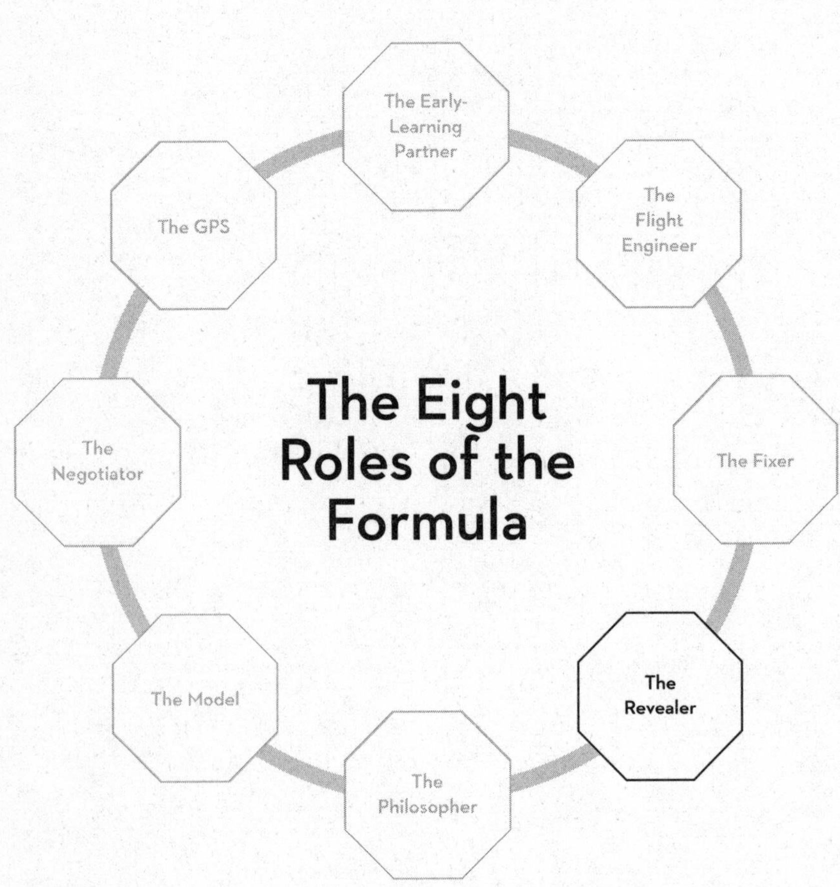
The Early-
Learning
Partner
The GPS
The
Flight
Engineer
The Eight
Roles of the
Formula
The
Negotiator
The Fixer
The Model
The
Revealer
The
Philosopher

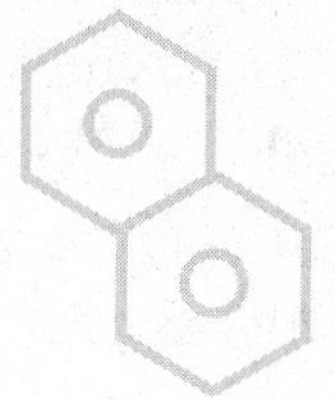

CHAPTER 9

The Revealer (Role #4)

ALBERT EINSTEIN'S MASTER PARENTS

Before Albert Einstein became the wild-haired physicist superstar who'd change our understanding of the universe with his theory of relativity, he was a boy in the late 1800s who disliked school—a lot. But that didn't mean he wasn't learning. It just meant he wasn't learning at school.

The fact that Einstein wasn't good in school is fairly well known. What isn't is how much, and how intentionally, Pauline, Albert's mother, supplemented his school education. She gave him toys and books, insisted he try the violin to improve his attention, and arranged access to mentors in areas that interested him. While Albert was perceived to be ill-mannered, bored, dimwitted, and "a freak" by his classmates and teachers, at home he was happy and so focused that relatives compared him to a little Buddha, as he cocooned himself in the garden, entertaining himself with mathematical equations and devouring everything from popular science to philosopher Immanuel Kant.

Pauline strategically created this warm, stimulating home learning environment, where he could build a fourteen-story house of cards, play with blocks, listen to music, or read all he wanted, to encourage Albert, along with his younger sister Maja, to be curious, disciplined—and self-reliant. When Albert was only four, for example, Pauline began introducing him to the world around him by encouraging the boy to cross the street and investigate their suburban Munich neighborhood all by himself, according to his sister's unpublished diaries.

As Albert grew older, his curiosity was further fueled by Thursday lunches at the Einstein home, where he was allowed to sit at the table with Pauline, his father Hermann, family members, and scientist friends they invited to share the meal. It was during these "lunchtime seminars" that Albert was exposed to worldly adults who challenged the adolescent boy's thinking while introducing him to the newest technology and modeling what it meant to be a scientist.

Special in this regard was his Uncle Jakob, who showed up at the regular lunches "armed with tricky math problems," according to author Denis Brian in his book *Einstein: A Life*. "When he solved them, Albert yelled triumphantly like a soccer player scoring an unlikely goal."

A poor Jewish medical student named Max Talmey also attended these Thursday lunches. He famously mentored ten-year-old Albert, often sharing books on math, physics, and philosophy and updating him on the latest science breakthroughs. Einstein loved to show Talmey equations he'd solved earlier in the week. (Eventually, Talmey recalled, he could no longer keep up with the boy.)

The Einsteins were strategic in finding the right people to enhance the child's education, but it was an even simpler act of out-of-school enrichment that Einstein pinpointed as originally setting him on a lifelong journey to becoming a scientist.

Five-year-old Albert was sick in bed when his father, a struggling businessman and a pioneer in a then-new field called electrical engineering, brought him a magnetic compass to keep him in good spirits. The compass not only puzzled the boy, but jump-started his fascination with spatial reasoning. The curious child twisted and turned it with amazement and took pleasure in trying to understand what was making the needle wiggle and point north.

Later, at sixteen, Einstein imagined what it might look like to chase and catch up to a beam of light, and his search for an answer would eventually change our understanding of space and time and result in the theory of relativity. His ability to theorize scientific ideas by working out imaginative thought experiments—like pursuing a beam of light, riding in an elevator in free fall, or sending one's twin up in a rocket ship—was a trademark of his revolutionary work. And Einstein believed this childlike, wonder-driven way of thinking began at home, with that five-year-old boy trying to figure out the toy compass his father had brought him. Even six decades after receiving the compass, Einstein still relished its memory: "That experience made a deep and lasting impression on me. Something deeply hidden had to be behind things."

Pauline and Hermann Einstein were Revealers. Master parents in this role unveil the world to the child while introducing them to possibilities for their potential future selves.

Since Revealers are well aware that learning doesn't just happen in a classroom, they supplement what the child has learned in school—or for children not yet in school, what they will learn in the future. They deepen the child's knowledge of the things they already know, and expose them to things they don't.

Like taking the child to the top of the Empire State Building and pointing out all the places they could someday go, master parents in the role of Revealer expand the child's horizons in three main ways:

1. by exposing the child to targeted learning experiences and environments, in particular those that further the child's interests

and allow them to interact with like-minded achievers (their "tribe");

2. by familiarizing the child with truths about the adult world to which they will someday belong, including harsh realities of life; and
3. by introducing the child to adult mentors who help them gain deeper knowledge on whatever they are passionate about and exemplify who the child might become.

The result is a well-informed child with an expanded vision of their future possibilities, which gives them a tremendous head start on becoming a successful adult.

THE ART OF SUPPLEMENTING EDUCATION

As we saw in chapter four with the Early-Learning Partner, the home is not only the first learning environment a child experiences, but also the most important. It is during the period from birth to age five that the essential foundations for brain development occur. Everything that a child is expected to know when they get to kindergarten, from their numbers and letters to how to interact with other human beings (at least on a basic level), is learned in those early-developmental years, usually at home. This period before grade school sees the development of achievement gaps (educational disparities between children from families of widely disparate advantages), but it's also when home activities provide opportunities for nipping such gaps in the bud before the child enters school—as Pauline Einstein did when she made her pre–grade school son take violin lessons with a tutor to improve his focus.

Pauline was the daughter of a Jewish baker who amassed a small fortune in the grain business, enabling him to provide his daughter a good education, including in the arts. Her passion for music led her to become a quite proficient piano player. So when she noticed her five-year-old son wasn't focusing and had a bad temper, she theorized that introducing him to the discipline of learning music would help. And she was right. Playing violin and piano helped keep Albert Einstein focused years later as he imagined and worked up breathtaking theories.

Elizabeth Lee was more formal in the way she supplemented Jarell's education. The home-based read-a-thons she initiated were structured like a class: after reading each book, her three children were all required to write a report, to strengthen their critical thinking. Jarell loved reading the books, but hated writing the report. Elizabeth pushed him because she knew Jarell needed to spend extra time on what he struggled with the most—his writing skills.

Setting up mini-classrooms in the home was a common theme among the people we interviewed, especially the participants in the Harvard project. These little home classes often started when the child was preschool age and continued until they formally entered school, but in some forms could continue much longer. The now-adult achievers spoke lovingly about getting so much time and attention from their parent (usually one in particular), but also about how fun that parent made learning.

One participant in the Harvard project talked happily about "Mommy school." When she was only a toddler, her mother set up a little classroom in an extra bedroom where it was just mom and the toddler playing, singing, drawing, and reading. When she was old enough to attend "real school," she remembers lamenting that there would be no more "Mommy school."

Other parents set up "classes" at home during the summer, or on the weekends. A few of them created actual classes or workshops to help not only their children but also others, as Esther Wojcicki did at her daughters' school when, in response to the school's lack of a writing instructor, she started an informal writing class for her girls and their friends.

One couple we talked to created a large alternative math program for students of color when their youngest daughter didn't get into an AP math class. Both of their daughters eventually ended up attending MIT. Many of the other students they taught attended respectable colleges across the nation.

These out-of-school educational experiences frequently extended beyond the home. In fact, some of the most formative experiences that parents created or made happen for our high achievers were in community centers, churches, institutes, or conservatories—where the child benefited not only from more specialized instruction, but from exposure to influential peers.

EXPOSURE TO THEIR TRIBE AND NEW LEARNING EXPERIENCES

From the age of ten, and until they graduated from high school, Maggie and her siblings were enrolled by their parents in the prestigious Juilliard Pre-College division, where they studied their instruments and improved their musical knowledge every Saturday in the company of talented peers. Before they got scholarships the second year, the family scraped by, saving pennies to afford the cost of the program. Maggie recalls her mother putting a jelly jar back on the grocery store shelf because the item was ten cents more than another jar. "I remember being very aware that it was a big burden."

This weekly reunion with other young musicians was the most important event in the week, and everything that the family did, from Maggie and her siblings' daily practice (to which their mother listened in), to going to bed early on Friday, was linked to Juilliard. On Saturday morning, Maggie, her siblings, and their parents piled in the car for the two-hour-long trek to New York City.

The Saturday Juilliard program was a magical place for Maggie, but it also felt like home. She found lifelong friendships among children from all walks of life, ethnic groups, and cultures—all of whom were just as dedicated to music as she was.

Those Saturdays were filled with music and possibilities. There was an orchestra class, and a class that focused on training the ear; there was also one on conducting. There were theory classes on the basic components of music. There were recitals and concerts. Students also performed and were critiqued in chamber.

"Real life" for Maggie Young wasn't her middle or high school on Long Island. Her "real" world was in New York City at Juilliard.

"We'd leave Juilliard at six o'clock at night and then drive two hours home. But I have to say, oh, I loved it," Maggie recalled.

At her school on Long Island, she felt different from others—probably why she didn't keep in touch with any of her high school classmates after graduation—but at Juilliard she was with her kind of people, her tribe.

Master parents as Revealers expose children to opportunities like Juilliard to show them what is possible and heighten their aspirations. Those Saturdays were when Maggie first heard about world-class venues such as Lincoln Center, where she'd later perform. Eventually, she'd even attend the prestigious graduate school at Juilliard. And exposing a high achiever to other successful peers, like the musicians with whom Maggie spent those Saturdays, can show them new levels of artistry toward which to aspire.

Programs like Juilliard's also have another important effect on achievers' life trajectories. Nearly all of the participants in this book who were placed in gifted programs during the elementary and middle school years, whether for academics or extracurriculars like music, described how utterly exhilarating it felt to be picked as equals to other high achievers and to be in the company of people they felt understood and appreciated them. That feeling of belonging to their tribe of achievers became so important to them that, once they were in that group, our achievers were careful not to do anything that might exclude them from it.

Smart and talented children like Maggie (who would eventually be accepted to Harvard but decided instead to attend a small music school in Philadelphia) also understood that being considered "one of the gifted kids" came with rewards, including the respect of adults and being picked for unanticipated special experiences and thrilling opportunities that others might never have, like studying in faraway places.

EXPOSURE TO THE WORLD—AND HARSH REALITIES

Nearly all of the achievers interviewed for the book had their own study space in the home. Sometimes it was just a corner of their bedroom, but there were always books, a table or a little desk, and a chair. A young Korean man in the Harvard project recalled that his father created a "map room" specifically for the child to study in. The small room with a map of the world sprawled across the wall, created just for him, made the boy feel special. But just as important, the map exposed him to the places he'd one day travel to. Interestingly, several other achievers also said a parent had created a map room to remind the child that there is a big world out there that they were a part of.

Revealers acquaint their kids with the world, including its shortcomings, in other ways, too. Several master parents taught their children it was fine to question those who assert expertise. Esther encouraged her daughters to ask doctors, scientists, teachers, or professors to verify their proclamations, while Alfonso's father warned him not to take what authorities said as gospel. Jarell's mother called attention to the fallibility of authority when she warned him not to enter a car with several other black boys because they'd attract negative attention from the police, who might falsely assume they were doing something wrong.

Similarly, throughout Sangu Delle's childhood, his father warned him never to assume others' good intentions. "I told him that society is fraudulent," Dr. Delle said, "and so he should be very critical of what people say and do. I also warned him about sycophants and told him not to be swayed by praise."

These lessons started very early. At five years old, growing up in Ghana, Sangu was already learning the bitter realities of liberation politics. Civil war was raging in the nearby West African countries of Sierra Leone and Liberia. His father, Dr. Delle, who was not only a physician but also the founder of the African Commission of Health and Human Rights, hosted late-night meetings outside the home, near the pool, where political refugees, often victims of torture, would come to the home for safe harbor, and to tell their horrific stories and talk strategy. Little Sangu had a front-row seat. He recalls hearing a grandmother tell of being raped by a child soldier, and a famous refugee tell of being tortured for writing against Charles Taylor, the former president of Liberia.

Understanding these were important meetings, Sangu would dress himself in a shirt, jacket, and tie and sit with the grown-ups, listening and watching their planning and activism. "I'm talking like 11 PM. People would show up at the house and they would have at it until dawn," Sangu recalled. "They're discussing freedom, liberty. Their political party at the time was banned by the government. And my dad would allow me to be there and see all of this."

Although Dr. Delle grew up in a Catholic school system where children were seen but not heard around adults, he never treated Sangu that way. He would even pause the meetings to allow his little boy to ask, "But why?"

At an age when most children have no clue about struggles for political power and their effects on human lives, Sangu was being exposed to tough realities while watching history unfold. Nothing was hypothetical; everything was tangible and real. He observed and interacted with grown-ups who had accepted responsibility for saving others' lives and protecting human dignity. The five-year-old boy was wounded by these horrific stories, but he listened as the grown-ups planned what to do, pondering options alongside them as though already in their shoes.

With so much exposure to problems that needed solving, Sangu was motivated to become an advocate of human rights. Now a brilliant social entrepreneur and citizen of the world, his thoughts and actions assume few limitations.

"I think it goes back to those meetings with my dad. I really truly felt like I could just have conversations with anyone older and with authority," he said.

This engagement with adult problem solving, fed by exposure to adult conversations, wasn't unique among our achievers. Ryan Quarles, the farm boy who grew up to win Kentucky's agriculture commissioner race, like Sangu—and like Albert Einstein in those Thursday lunches with his parents' scientist friends—was also allowed to sit in on grown-ups' conversations.

Almost every day when Ryan was a boy, "a group of farmers gathered around lunchtime at Cedar Post, a diner where farmers hung out to talk about what was going on in their world."

Like a popular professor, Ryan's father—who every night sat down with newspapers and magazines to keep up with the latest agricultural news—was always looked to for answers during those informal lunches. And Ryan sat either at the table with the adults, or, if there wasn't room, nearby, listening.

Ryan now says those lunches might as well have been legislative hearings. By listening to those conversations, he gained a deep understanding of issues like crop insurance and the economics of tobacco farming.

"It didn't matter that it was dirt, grease, and sweat as opposed to fine suits at the table," he says. "I was watching the farmers discuss, share information, and build nonpartisan consensus on what was best for agriculture." Those round-table lunches "exposed me to the deliberative process that I exercised later in life as a legislator."

When master parents in the Revealer role discuss and debate serious grown-up issues with their children in the room, achievers like Ryan or Sangu picture themselves in the adults' positions struggling with those same issues. It's like a graduate course at an elite college that uses the case method, where class discussions revolve around authentic, real-world situations in which decision makers faced choices that had real consequences for people's lives. Just as the graduate students listening to classmates debate pros and cons, the achiever listening to the adult conversations—and sometimes even participating, as Sangu did—gets to practice the type of thinking they'll one day have to do in their own lives, and as a result be better prepared.

INTRODUCTIONS TO POSSIBLE SELVES

When the achievers in the book were between the ages of eight and ten, sometimes even earlier, they began developing interests in specialized topics such as politics, music, or zoology, and their Revealer parents took it upon themselves to find high-quality opportunities for the achievers to indulge and further those interests.

The Kentucky Capitol Building with its great dome had fascinated Ryan for as long as he could remember. When he was a little boy, driving across the county with his father on routine trips to the additional plots of land they farmed, he'd stare out the window as the truck passed by the Capitol. When they stopped at the old water company to fill up the 500-gallon tank hitched to the bed of the truck, Ryan would dutifully drop coins in the slot to release the water, but his eyes were always fixed on the Capitol's dome in the distance. The view on the return trip seemed even better: the building seemed to look right back at him through the dirty truck window. Ryan could only gaze and wonder. How high were the ceilings? Who worked there? Look, there were so many stairs. Such large doors. What was behind them?

When he finally found out, the experience was overwhelming. “There was smoke everywhere and people were spitting tobacco!”

That first visit was arranged by his mother and teacher as a reward for an excellent report card when he was nine. But after seeing the impact that visit made on him, his mother helped ensure he had the opportunity to serve each year until his senior year of high school as a legislative page to the state representative, giving him an intimate look into the big arena where he’d one day realize his dream of serving as an elected political leader.

“Paging at the Capitol gave me an occasional rare glimpse into what I might be as a very young man,” Ryan says. “It motivated me to work hard so I could earn the privilege to return again and again, and it caused me to pick up the newspaper every day to keep up with state politics. Those formative years shaped my outlook that, if I worked hard enough, I too could achieve to a level that I once considered unattainable or beyond the reach of a farm kid.”

Years later, in a twist of fate, Ryan, in his first run for office, defeated that same state representative he had worked for as a page.

Ryan was not the only achiever whose early interests, facilitated by a master parent, put him on track early for a career in politics. Chuck Badger was five years old when his mother Elaine saw him pretending to be a minister. She soon figured out that he loved public speaking and, like Ryan’s mother, found ways not only to perfect his social and communication skills, but also to put him in situations where he could imagine his future self based on what he observed in other people. When other children were playing sports or video games, Chuck, at the age of eleven, was speaking at youth conferences about his personal biography and schmoozing at political cocktail parties with the business elite.

Dressed in a suit and tie, young Chuck worked the cocktail parties like a little man, passing out his personal business cards with a confidence usually only seen in a child groomed by prominent parents, like politicians or CEOs. That confidence intrigued the grown-ups he met because they knew he came from the projects. During one of those cocktail parties, he recalls meeting a woman who, obviously recognizing something in him, turned him to face a large window overlooking the city skyline: "This could be yours. Look over the town here."

That and other the-world-is-your-oyster statements worked on Chuck's psyche, "expanding my sense of possibilities, the scope of what was possible for me in life," and who he could someday become.

HOW PASSION PROJECTS FACILITATE MASTERY ORIENTATION AND A SENSE OF AGENCY

The kind of interest in specialized topics that Ryan developed in politics and Chuck pursued in public speaking, or that Maggie had in the violin, we refer to as a "passion project." Unlike in the concerted cultivation approach of the stereotypical middle-class parent, who loads the child's calendar with as many extracurricular activities as possible, the Revealer rounds out their child's education thoughtfully and strategically, keeping the child's future always in mind. Encouraging the child's chosen passion projects was a key part of this.

Our high achievers were often drawn to these passion projects and spent much of their free time pursuing them while the master parent ensured they had whatever tools or opportunities they required. For example, US diplomat David Martinez's passion project was reptiles, and his parents would spend hours in the desert collecting lizard eggs with their son.

"We would be driving on the highway and I would tell my dad that I saw a lizard on the rock back there and we would turn around and sure enough, it was there," recalled David.

His friends' parents were not as accommodating of their own children's interests. "They were like, 'Reptiles? That's not acceptable. I hate snakes. We're gonna get you a dog and we're going to push you towards that; we're going to push you towards fish.' My parents did not do that," David said.

"They saw it was something I was passionate about very early and they encouraged it . . . It was, 'David, let's see how many dinosaurs you can name,' and 'I have this puzzle here; it's a 150-piece puzzle and it's all the frogs of the rain forest.' And of course I was willing to do that, because I'm focused on the reptile. I'm focused on this thing that is really cool in my young world. They're focused on me doing something that is going to encourage my brain and encourage my mind."

When the Revealer introduces a child to something that sparks their interests and encourages excellence, and then supports the child in pursuing that interest, they help their child develop two major qualities: first, *mastery orientation*, an internal drive to learn about a particular topic and produce high-quality work, while feeling encouraged, not discouraged, when a task turns out to be difficult; and second, a *sense of agency*, an awareness of one's ability, right, and responsibility to take purposeful action in the world. Each hobby the achievers embraced produced new learning experiences on a journey toward full realization that fed their curiosity, piqued their imagination, and developed these special habits of mind and behavior.

David's mother Lou, a judge, remembers the intensity of David's love affair with reptiles and the sophistication and expertise he achieved through his single-minded quest to master his understanding of them. "He was in second or third grade when we started subscribing to scientific journals for him. By the time I think he was ten, he would ask us to take him to the university."

One day, Lou says, "they had a meeting of herpetologists. The professor conducting the meeting described a particular lizard and David raised his hand to say, 'I saw that lizard at my friend's house here in Las Cruces.' The professor gawked at him and said, 'Well, that's ridiculous. It hasn't gone past some place in West Texas.' David was really offended by how he had been put down. Two or three months later, the professor called him and says, 'Where did you see that lizard?' David told him the address. The professor wrote a paper on it. It was true. That lizard had migrated into New Mexico."

David's expertise became widely known in their town. "By the time he was like ten or eleven, the pet stores would call him because they couldn't figure out what kind of reptile they had or if it was male or a female. David would go over and tell them. He had that much knowledge."

Even when a childhood passion project does not continue into adulthood, as with David's interest in reptiles, the mastery orientation a child develops through it becomes an asset in whatever field they eventually enter. Because of the time David spent as a child learning how to master his knowledge of reptiles by "dedicating myself countless hours to a task, being subjected to reviews and critiques, and continually focusing on improving my skills," he saw other skills—like the Spanish he later needed to learn to become a diplomat—as undertakings he was capable of conquering through similar devotion.

In some cases, however, the more subject-specific skills gained through the pursuit of passion projects directly prepared our high achievers for their future careers.

David's younger brother Daniel, at the age of ten, became just as enthused about roller coasters as David was about reptiles. During every family vacation he insisted his mother and father drive to the local amusement park, where he'd check out the "coasters."

He eventually visited fifty coasters in all. His favorite? The Viper at Six Flags Magic Mountain. "I loved that one. It was one of the last of the seven-loopers."

Daniel wasn't always a roller coaster devotee. "At first I was scared of coasters, until David encouraged me," he told us. "I never liked roller coasters because I thought the drop would be too scary, but it turned out that I loved the sensation of going through drops and loops and everything about the coasters. There was an amusement park I never got to visit, even to this day. It's in Ohio. When I was a kid, it had over a dozen coasters, and it has even more today. I knew about every single one of them."

He remembered statistics and spouted them off to everyone. He'd say, "This one is 220 feet high and has a drop of fifty feet and reaches a speed of eighty miles an hour."

His passion for detail led him to study everything about coasters—including their mechanics, which taught him science and math skills, and gave him a predilection for both. "It's the reason why I wanted to major in mechanical science. I wanted to be a roller coaster designer, so even in middle school, I knew that mechanical engineering was the appropriate fit."

Eventually, his intense childhood interest gave way to more mature intentions. Midway through college, he moved away from the idea of designing coasters, "but I thought, there are other fascinating and rewarding things I can do as an engineer, which is why I stuck with it."

By supporting passion projects, the Revealer not only cultivates a mastery orientation in their child, but also helps them develop a *sense of agency*. Treating the child as capable in the area they're passionate about, as they develop their expertise—just like sharing the realities of the world with the child (in age-appropriate ways) and giving them opportunities to practice working out problems in their head by discussing complex issues with adults—promotes the initiative and confidence that foster success.

Because of how his father patiently took the time to discuss the world with him in conversation, it never occurred to Sangu not to converse also with the grown-up refugees who came to his home or, for example, to write a letter at the age of five to the president of Harvard to ask how he could get into college there. (He received a response from Harvard's president that said he was "too young" for Harvard and encouraged Sangu to apply later.)

Sangu's passion as a small child was seeking answers to big questions. The seriousness with which his father took that passion led Sangu to believe that he could find the answers—and that he could have a hand in solving big problems. "For years, I remember, during the war and genocide in Rwanda, they'd talk about it on the news. I'd ask my dad, 'Well, why doesn't the UN intervene?' And, he'd say, 'Well, why don't you write Secretary General Kofi Annan a letter and ask him?' And I did."

He was only six.

Years later he'd take the initiative again to do something big, but this time without nudging from his father. At the age of fourteen, Sangu announced to his parents that he was leaving Ghana. His destination was a boarding school in the United States. "I told them at different times. To my mom, I said, 'Look, this is the situation.'" Sangu had applied to the school in New Jersey all by himself. He'd been accepted, secured a full scholarship, arranged his own visa, and paid for the $800 one-way plane ticket with money he'd made creating study guides for his schoolmates.

"I told my father a week before I was leaving, 'I'm moving to the US.' He had this smirk on his face, but he said nothing." Years later, Sangu's father would admit that he was pleasantly shocked.

Sangu's exposure to real-life situations related to his interests, and his father's encouragement to get involved in them—like Ryan at the statehouse listening to the politicians and assisting as a page, and Chuck networking with business people—were key to developing the sense of agency that would later bolster him in his efforts to raise money to aid underdeveloped communities in his homeland.

THE FUTURE SELF: SEEING IT, PURSUING IT, BECOMING IT

The Revealer encourages their child to visualize the adult they could one day become, and the important problems they might help solve. Can this visualization inspire a child to take the steps necessary to become that person—in other words, to express *agency* in developing the *mastery* needed to achieve that goal of self-realization?

Daphna Oyserman, a social psychologist at the University of Southern California known for her studies on identity-based motivation—how a person's self-concept helps determine their goals and behaviors—set out to answer that question. She and her team were interested in young people's understanding of the connections between their present and future selves. She wondered if young people who develop clear and compelling images of what they can become are more motivated to work hard and persist, expressing agency and striving to achieve mastery in order to achieve those images.

In a series of experiments, she assigned middle-school students to treatment and control groups, then led the two groups through different guided visualizations. In one experiment, for example, the young people in the treatment group were asked to identify pictures in magazines of people they wanted to emulate, and then use the pictures to discuss what they needed to do now in order to achieve their imagined futures. Those in the control group were assigned a different task, unrelated to their future selves.

Following each experiment, the group that imagined their future selves worked harder and more consistently than their peers who did not. After one experiment, for example, the group "taught to integrate thoughts of the future with the now had improved grades, spent more time on their homework, had better attendance, and achieved higher standardized test scores. They came to view difficulties as important rather than impossible, and to see schoolwork in terms of advancing their lives."

What should we take from this experiment? Oyserman's findings reinforce the idea that the more clearly a young person is able to envision the future, the more it bolsters their sense of agency and inspires their quest for mastery, which leads to future success.

A REVEALER IN ISOLATION HELPS A SON FIND HIS POSSIBLE SELF

As a child, Chuck Badger dreamed of being a great orator. By age thirteen, he was traveling and giving motivational speeches based on his life. "I was basically imitating Les Brown and Zig Ziglar," he said, two orators that Terri, his mentor, encouraged him to study.

Later, as an older teen, he dreamed of being a political operative—which is exactly what Chuck, today the young head of a political consulting company, became. But growing up black and in the projects in Nashville, Chuck started out with a much narrower sense of what he could do with his future, and no entrée to the types of people he'd need to help him become the person he is today.

How precisely did Elaine, a marginalized single parent on a restricted budget, battling health issues, produce a political expert who, from a very young age, had such a strong sense of agency? How did she know what to expose him to? By contrast, Maggie's parents were professional violin instructors. Esther, the mother of three powerful women in the technology industry, grew up, despite her upbringing, to become a talented academic and married a brilliant professor. Gabby, Jarell, and Alfonso all had parents who struggled financially, but were worldly in their own ways: Jarell's mother Elizabeth and Alfonso's father Reynaldo were avid readers, and at least in the case of Reynaldo and Gabby's mother Sara, their previous lives were more middle class than their hardships as adults might suggest.

But Elaine Badger had none of those benefits.

Elaine wasn't particularly academic, likely because her parents had no aspirations for her beyond working for the government. But she knew it was her responsibility to shape her talented son and bring out all of his potential.

Other parents in this book built their children's literacy skills mostly through reading stories. Elaine used word games.

"Six thirty in our house was a sacred time," said Chuck. "My mother never, ever missed an episode of *Wheel of Fortune*." Chuck would sit by her, figuring out the words in his head. But Chuck's most vivid early memories are of him and his mother playing Scrabble, his favorite word game. Even before grade school, the two would sit and play for hours.

Dead set on winning, he kept a little word book. "I probably spent more time with the Scrabble dictionary than the real dictionary," he said. "I remember being very fascinated by it."

The word games improved his basic skills, and were the start of Chuck becoming an avid reader and a writer.

"I just wanted to make sure that he had the best, because I saw something in him at a young age, and I did not want it to die, and I knew that I had to help bring that out, whatever it was," his mother recalled.

Elaine caught a glimpse of who and what he might become when he was only five. An observant child who attended church regularly, with a big vocabulary for his age resulting from those word games and Elaine's custom of conducting adult-like discussions with him, he would imagine himself as the minister. "He put on a robe and made him a makeshift altar at home and had the Bible and thought he was up there preaching. That was the furthest thing from my mind, him being a preacher, but it just impressed me so that whatever I was doing and what I was exposing him to, that's what it led to," she said.

That's when she began to transform into Chuck's Revealer, actively exposing him to people and opportunities that would supplement his education and bring him closer to the person he'd one day become. Although her work as a Revealer was as impressive as anyone else's in this chapter, Elaine did not come by the role naturally. It was a bumpy journey that took years and required extensive planning and outside help.

For Elaine, raising Chuck to become the man she wanted him to be was like solving a puzzle. She had some of the pieces already—she'd raised him to be smart and polite, and eager to learn. She also had some inkling about what the missing parts might be. But what she knew for sure was that she lacked some of what was needed, like social connections, to expose her son to important people who could help him reach his potential and find his purpose.

She resolved to find surrogates who possessed what she didn't have, who could help her locate the missing pieces. But first, she spent almost a decade working with him by herself, exposing him to what she thought he needed to know and trying her best to supplement what he learned in school.

While the other master parents we describe focused less on the quantity of activities their children participated in, instead allowing or encouraging their children to focus on what they naturally had a penchant for, Elaine tried to emulate what she thought middle-class families did: loading their children up with things to do.

In addition to enrolling him in free afterschool activities during the school year, she spent the winters and springs sitting for hours on the internet, finding scholarships and filling out applications, to plot out his summers. While most of our master parents let their children select their extracurricular activities, Elaine could be "pushy," Chuck said, in setting the agenda, though Chuck understood why. Elaine was determined to keep her son so busy that he wouldn't get involved with wayward children in the neighborhood or end up in prison like her older son.

"It was a safety issue," Chuck said.

He took swimming lessons at six years old. Later, there were saxophone classes. While Chuck said he enjoyed most of it, there were missteps along the way. "For example, she put me in Boy Scouts briefly, and I quit. I just didn't like it, so I think it was too much time for me. She did allow me to quit things."

However, by a certain point, Elaine had arranged all the supplemental education activities she possibly could. It was time to get help. When Chuck was eleven, two things happened. First, Elaine connected him to Terri Chapman, who agreed to take the then-fourth-grader into her "CEO Academy" for children from Nashville's inner-city schools and neighborhoods.

Terri would become Chuck's mentor and Elaine's surrogate. The two became a Revealer team, whose shared mission was to expose Chuck to the broader world, and the broader world to Chuck. It was Terri who took preteen Chuck to fancy cocktail parties, introducing him to politicians, and when Terri took CEO Academy children on trips out of town without their parents, even if the group was only two or three kids, Chuck was always one of them.

Elaine says, "Terri has been instrumental because I really didn't know much about politics and plus I didn't have a car. She knew about those things so she took him where he needed to go and introduced him and showed him how to dress."

Terri was able to connect young Chuck to the right people, but his networking skills soon surpassed her own. She remembers eleven-year-old Chuck calling her to take him to a cocktail party for Senator William H. Frist at a farm near Nashville. Chuck secured the invitation himself. Terri felt out of place at the party, but young Chuck looked perfectly comfortable surrounded by seasoned elected officials and holding his own in political discussions.

With Terri's help, Chuck began to see who he could become. Terri introduced Chuck to the first politician who really mentored him, Ed Sanders.

"To an eleven-year-old, he was physically a giant. He had a Baptist preacher's booming sort of voice that just filled the room and a big laugh," Chuck said.

Sanders, who was also a pastor with a big church in Nashville, was very involved with the AIDS epidemic in Africa and was an advisor to President George W. Bush. Sanders was also running for Tennessee governor. Chuck recalls, "I volunteered and answered the phones, putting together the archives, that kind of thing. I put in the inquiries and that's what I did around the office."

What happened next, Chuck says, helped him see who he could someday become. "Ed just took a liking to me. He started taking me around with him, so I was like in the car with him, and he would just go around, and I remember everywhere we went, everyone thought I was his son. People always asked, 'Is this your son?'"

Sanders was usually a Republican, "but ran as an Independent that year because he had a disagreement with the party," Chuck said. "He was an imposing figure, and was an extremely eloquent speaker, and I just remember being dazzled by him, and it was probably that summer that I decided that that's what I wanted to do: 'I want to be like him.'"

The second thing that happened that summer when Chuck was eleven was that Elaine got him into a boarding school in Mississippi, which he'd attend until high school. Attending boarding school was one of Chuck Badger's dreams, and despite Elaine's financial and physical hardships, she found scholarships for Chuck that made it possible for him to attend. In Elaine's mind, she was exposing him to middle-class schooling. But by sending him there, she did more than that. Boarding school allowed Chuck to hone his communication skills and his newfound passion for government and politics. And even more importantly, he began to see more possibilities for his life.

While there, he became obsessed with the writings of Thomas Sowell, a black man like himself with conservative leanings. Chuck still calls the Harlem-born conservative economist "the most brilliant of conservative minds."

He also loved conservative writer George Will and is a great fan of former secretary of state Condoleezza Rice. "Reading their writings had a substantial effect on my political development," he said.

There was something else that lit the political fire within Chuck. From age twelve until his senior year in high school, he became preoccupied with the Iraq War. That example of life's harsher realities not only became a focus for Chuck, but also an intense topic of debate between Chuck and his peers, especially his classmates in boarding school.

"We were all on the cusp of going into the military." It was the central galvanizing political controversy of his generation, he said, and the crucible in which everyone's politics was formed. "It was for us what Vietnam was for boomers. You were either for or against. It became very much digging in the heels. Your ideology was fused by the fire of constantly being goaded into debates. There were arguments all the time about Bush and Iraq."

Chuck became captivated by school and by serious topics that mostly interested adults, like politics. And he was comfortable in the leadership roles he was increasingly called to take among his classmates. "I sensed some difference between me and my classmates. With group projects, I was constantly being voted group leader. All of my life, from young as ever, I was pretty much the person who was voted by all the other kids in the group as a leader. That happened a lot."

Chuck was in his mid-teens when his mother first saw him speak to an audience of hundreds. "I think maybe there were 500 people at that particular event. I was in awe," said Elaine. "I said, 'These people are standing up and clapping for my son.' I turned around and looked at the stage and I'm like, 'That's my baby.' I was so proud, but I was like, 'Wow.' Flabbergasted."

Chuck ultimately secured admission to the prestigious, tuition-free Berea College, where his story unfolded as if the life his mother had imagined for him was playing in a video, in real time. Elected to student body president, he was also a young leader in the Republican Party and among the 1 percent of national applicants to secure a summer internship in George W. Bush's White House. As the contentious 2008 election year rolled around, Chuck, a rising young political voice, made appearances on local television and National Public Radio, and was featured in the college newspaper.

As a result of Elaine's hard work as Revealer in encouraging Chuck's passion for public speaking and exposing him to mentors, like-minded peers, and the world outside their home in the projects, Chuck was evolving into not only the person his mother prepared him to be, but, more importantly, the person he believed he was meant to be.

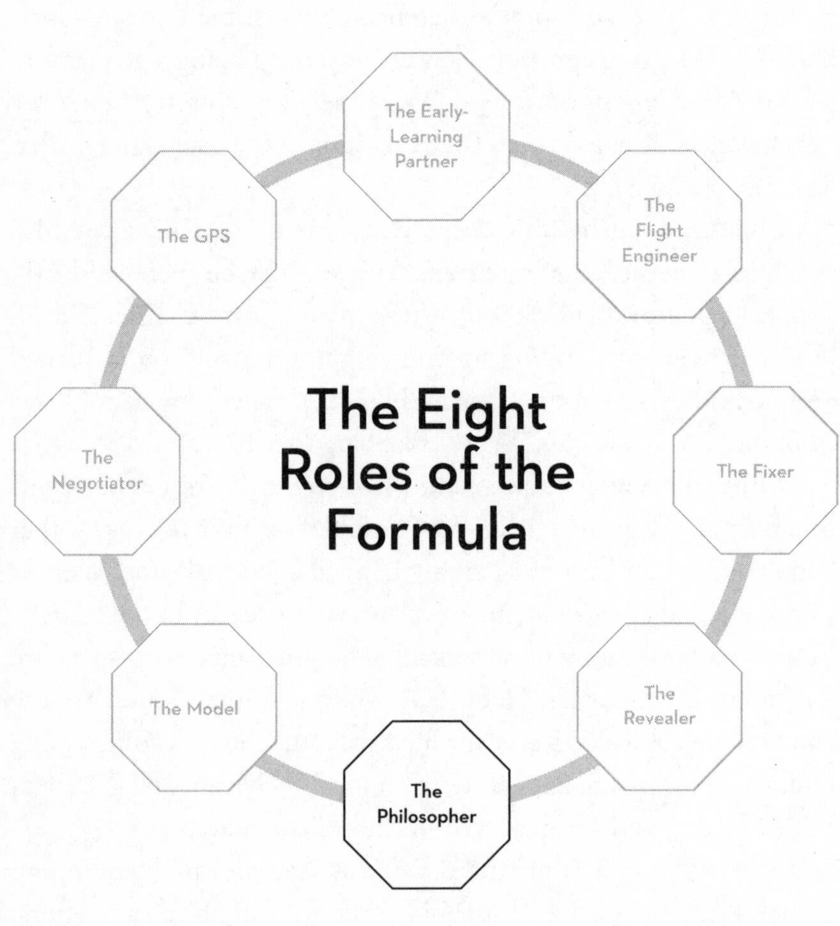
The Early-Learning Partner
The Flight Engineer
The Fixer
The Revealer
The Philosopher
The Model
The Negotiator
The GPS
The Eight Roles of the Formula

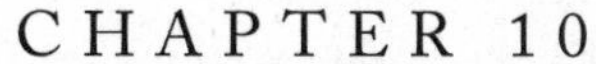

CHAPTER 10

The Philosopher (Role #5)

THE PRESCHOOLER WHO DEBATED ARISTOTLE IN THE BATHTUB

When entrepreneur and philanthropist Sangu Delle was five years old in Ghana, he and his physician father would get into deep debates about Aristotle, Socrates, and the Bible. Dr. Delle was often away from home making medical calls in outlying villages, but as Sangu recalls, “During those times he was around, I would always be with him in the mornings.”

While his father bathed, Sangu scrubbed his back and peppered him with probing questions. The time with his father only lasted ten minutes, but the length of these talks mattered less than their depth.

“He wanted to know why he was born, and when he was going to die, and what happens after death,” recalled Dr. Delle. “He would question certain elements of Christianity and ask hard, thoughtful questions.”

Once, after studying his picture Bible, little Sangu wanted to discuss a question that had occurred to him while reading about Jesus. “I asked him, ‘What is the most important virtue?’ and he said, ‘That’s a heavy question.’”

Two days later his father returned with an answer. "Humility," he said. But young Sangu pushed him. "Why humility?"

Dr. Delle wanted his kindergarten-age son to share his sense of duty to alleviate suffering, so one reason for telling Sangu that humility was the most important virtue was to teach his intelligent son not to feel superior to those less fortunate than he was, and especially the refugees who visited their home at night.

But there was another reason for his answer. Dr. Delle believed humility is what leads people to continue striving to achieve. A person "should never believe he has reached his maximum," he says. "That's why I never praised Sangu much. There are no limits to success and intellectual achievement."

Even today, Sangu says, with all he has accomplished, "I choose to be critiqued rather than be praised. I'm uncomfortable with flattery. And I fear hubris because I think it will seed demise."

THE THREE THEMES OF THE PHILOSOPHER

Dr. Delle was an excellent and strategic Philosopher—the role that helps a child find purpose and meaning in life. Through give-and-take discussions about ethics, human nature, and existence, the Philosopher helps the child shape their beliefs and choose a direction for their work.

"We would hotly debate topics, even topics that were far advanced for Sangu's age," Dr. Delle said. "Despite his age, I thought that it was important for him to develop a worldview."

As we heard from so many of our achievers, Sangu said, "My father always talked to me and treated me like an adult. I think it started with those morning debates."

Perhaps the adult talk happens because the master parent as Philosopher speaks to the child strategically, with the holographic ideal—that vision of the adult they hope the child will become, firmly in mind.

Of course, not every child is equally receptive. And like the Early-Learning Partner who spends more time with the child who responds enthusiastically when presented with new ideas or challenges, the Philosopher gives the most attention to the child who, like Sangu, asks lots of questions, thinks deeply about the parent's answers, and then comes back for more.

"Sangu wanted to know the purpose of life," Dr. Delle said. "That's why I introduced him to philosophy," from ancient oral traditions to the writings of Greek philosophers.

He also encouraged his little boy to develop his own interpretations of those age-old ideas. He knew that supporting Sangu in forming his own take on the Bible and the wisdom of ancient Greece, and treating Sangu with respect in the conversations and debates the two of them had, would build Sangu's confidence and prepare him to change the world.

The grounding Dr. Delle gave Sangu in scholarly philosophy reflects a long tradition of ancient thinkers influencing history's most impactful people. Take, for example, the Bhagavad Gita, also called "the Gita," reputedly the oldest philosophical text in the world. Mahatma Gandhi once said that he always felt great comfort after every read. And Albert Einstein said, when he read the Gita, "everything else seems so superfluous."

The Gita's power can be found within the framework of its narrative, an epic dialogue between two close friends—Prince Arjuna and Lord Krishna, his charioteer—in which they discuss the eternal principles that lead to a fulfilled life. And it's no coincidence that their conclusions, like those of philosophers and ancient texts the world over, highlight three consistent themes regarding the purpose of life: (1) the quest for insight, (2) the pursuit of prosperity, and (3) the duty to be compassionate.

These three fundamental ideas also permeated the life philosophies our master parents imparted to their children: seek deep understanding, avoid poverty, and help improve others' lives.

Philosophy #1: Seeking Deep Understanding

The parents in this book and others we interviewed who focused most sharply on the search for deep understanding tended to be intellectually astute individuals whose aspirations had been blocked or frustrated by circumstances beyond their control, by their own questionable decisions, or by a combination of the two. They were often immigrant parents, mostly but not exclusively men, who lacked enough experience in America to gauge how realistic it was for their children to succeed professionally on a high level—and who, even if they believed such success was possible, had very little idea how to assist their children in achieving it, aside from teaching them the pleasure of mastery. To these parents, the most valuable thing they could offer their children was an appreciation of intellect—the sheer satisfaction of using their brains to experience discovery, whether in the car, at the library, or anywhere else they found themselves.

Lisa Son's father was one such parent.

Lisa's parents both attended college in South Korea, but when they immigrated to the United States, they had to start over. Money was so tight that they lost their home several times. Her father, though he had majored in political science and received a journalism degree, was not proficient enough in English to work as a reporter in the United States. Instead, he drove a taxi, and worked in a series of warehouses, shoe stores, and gas stations. Her mother eventually secured a job as a nurse and became the main breadwinner. "It was the typical immigrant story—they both worked until 10 PM," Lisa said.

The only times her parents visited her school was when they were called to the principal's office, where her brother spent a lot of time.

"They didn't go to our schools very much because they were living more like it was in Korea, where the parents have no power," she said.

Her mother focused on her grades, because she wanted Lisa to grow up and have better things in life, but her father couldn't have cared less about material possessions or even school lessons. After all, his own education in Korea was not paying off, so pressing his children to get high grades and aspire to seemingly unobtainable possessions likely seemed pointless.

However, he was a master at preparing his children to be thinkers and to experience the world in an intellectual way.

To young Lisa, her father was "the smartest man in the world." He was a "true intellectual," who taught his shy, quiet daughter about Korean history and the Korean War and told her stories of his own life.

Recall Lisa's unusual parenting strategy of never telling her children an answer—letting her daughter figure out whether the word "crazy" looked right with a *-y* or an *-ie*, and standing in the dark and shining a flashlight on a ball to help her daughter figure out for herself why it was morning in Korea when it was night back home in Jersey. She didn't learn that at Columbia University or Barnard College, though she studied the psychology of learning at those two great institutions. Instead, she got the idea from her father. As he drove her around town in the family car, her father would ask questions to stimulate her thinking but never tell her whether she was right or wrong.

"He started very early with me, asking lots of questions about arithmetic and physics. He'd say, 'Okay, if we are going to start slowing down . . . we're starting at fifty miles per hour and we start slowing down at this distance, how slow do you think we'd be going? How much time would it take to slow down to this speed?' And then I would kind of think about it. I was really young, so I had no idea how to figure it out, but I would just say something like, 'Twenty miles an hour?' And he would say, 'All right. Keep thinking.' And that was it. It was always these open-ended questions."

Lisa's father believed children should come to know new things by figuring them out rather than being told. And he was able to teach his own children to think and remember because he was brilliant at making them believe they were playing when they were really learning.

"Before my brother and I could start eating, we actually had to say our multiplication tables. This was before kindergarten. That was normal in Korea. So we stood up, and we would go, '2 times 1 is 2. 2 times 2 is 4. 2 times 3 is 6. 2 times 4 is 8. 2 times 5 is 10.' And then the next week or so, we would do the three-times tables, and then we went all the way up to twelve in this fashion. And the funny thing is, I did that with my kids. So, they're a little ahead. Still, we thought of it as a game of memory. My parents weren't really forcing us because we thought it was interesting and fun!"

His goal, like Lisa's for her own children, was to raise insightful, enlightened humans who could reason and think for themselves.

He was also deliberate, devoting three years to helping Lisa learn that disciplined persistence produces mastery—another way of describing deep understanding.

"I was a real jock," Lisa said. "It was my father who first gave me tennis lessons when I was eight years old."

He bought her a wooden racket, and they'd play tennis two hours every day during the entire summer. "And I think from then, up until middle school, during the summers, we'd play, my dad and me, and he was there the first moment I got that perfect form. I got that perfect feeling of knowing how I had to move my body to get that rocket ball to shoot out right over the net."

That moment on the court was the culmination of a long process of encouragement designed to teach her the payoff of not giving up. "He told me many times before, 'You'll get it. You'll get it.'" She knew she wasn't getting it, yet, but she *was* enjoying the process. "He was infinitely patient. I started when I was eight, and it wasn't until I was twelve that I got it. I was like, 'Okay, I now know how to play tennis, and I'll never lose that swing.'" Young Lisa learned she could, through persistence, reach a place of crystal clarity, the perfect *ping* when the racquet hit the ball in exactly the right way.

Teaching persistence was a big component of her father's strategic philosophy. "Dad always used to say, 'You just keep going until it comes to you.'" He would tell Lisa that people are all born knowing everything, and that "when you study, you're just reminding yourself." He would say, "'Everyone can do it, but it takes different times because everyone's brains are different, but it's still all in there. You just keep going.' I remember thinking, 'Oh, okay, I know everything. It's just a matter of organizing it to be able to get it out.' So I never gave up."

Philosophy #2: Avoiding Poverty

This second philosophy as imparted by many of our master parents could be more colloquially summed up with three words: *Don't be poor.*

This philosophy is not just for underprivileged kids. According to Annette Lareau, who studies low-income as well as middle-class families, there's a long list of behaviors that middle-class parents teach their kids, like managing a checking account and choosing extracurricular activities that will look good on college applications, that are geared toward preserving their social status.

Because those skills are baked into a middle-class upbringing, middle-class parents never need to have a "don't be poor" talk with their children. Poor parents like Jarell's mother, however, directly told their children, "You don't want to live like this"—because "this," their life, represented the negative future they wanted their child to avoid.

A philosophy that centers around the denigration of the child's current life circumstances may feel offensive to some, but it's not meant to make the child feel bad or put down others in the same situation. Rather, it's strategic. Poverty is a substantial barrier to opportunity. For a child to experience the type of self-realization that master parents want for their children, they must first believe they can and should escape the limitations poverty imposes on them.

Children like Pam, Jarrell, and Gabby easily could have become resigned to the idea that poverty was inescapable had their parents (or, in Pam's case, her grandmother) not worked hard to convince them otherwise. For master parents struggling through day-to-day uncertainties about money while facing the constant, stressful indignities that come from living in poverty, the possibility that their children might also grow up poor was a hazard they were determined to avoid. Learning just for the sake of learning was a luxury; the more pressing purpose of mastering lessons was to improve one's lot in life, and avoid ever being poor again.

Jarell Lee's mother Elizabeth, in the role of Philosopher, taught Jarell that he had an obligation to do as well as he possibly could in school in order to escape poverty. She spoke of it often and directly, and her single-minded perseverance in selecting the right schools and shelters, always staying in touch with his teachers while organizing learning at home and around Cleveland, further impressed upon him the importance of doing well, so that he might someday live in the middle-class world she envisioned in her holographic ideal.

Lisa Son's mother likewise wanted to prevent her child from struggling financially as she had. While Lisa's father valued learning for its own sake, her mother's focus was on learning as a path to a better life—perhaps because it was she who managed the family's money.

Lisa's mother always tried to find money for the enrichment activities the kids asked to join. On one occasion during high school,

Lisa wanted to join the lacrosse team, and so mother and daughter trekked to the sporting goods store to buy the gear. But when they reached the cash register, one credit card after the other was declined. "My mother cried, and I cried." This experience impressed upon Lisa how much she never wanted to be in that situation again.

Eventually, Lisa determined that doing well academically was her best path to financial security. Her mother, in contrast, focused on how her education, together with social graces, could help Lisa attract a financially secure husband. According to Lisa, "My mom was an extreme perfectionist and expected perfection of us, too, especially of me as the oldest daughter . . . I guess as a measure of how good a daughter-in-law you'd be."

Though Lisa's route to solvency ended up being different than the one her mother had intended for her, the same underlying philosophy remains: *Financial security matters.*

Pamela Rosario's grandmother also valued financial security, but the strategy she had in mind for Pam was the exact opposite of the one Lisa's mom taught her. Pamela grew up in a family and culture where the women depended on men to support them financially and, because of that dependency, she often felt trapped. Being independent, as her grandmother always preached, was Pam's greatest dream.

"All I ever wanted was my own apartment," she said. That modest goal was what kept her focused.

Pam's grandmother, Abuelita, assured her that she didn't need to worry about much of anything if she became financially independent. "She would say, 'Make marriage be your choice. I don't ever want you to feel like you were forced into getting married because you had to be stable for your kids, or whatever the case may be. I want you to make enough money so you can choose who you want to be with.' I know that may not sound super empowering to a lot of people, but in our culture it's huge."

Philosophy #3: Helping Improve Others' Lives

The third philosophical theme our achievers' parents imparted was that the purpose of life was to make things better for others. Many of the parents who espoused this philosophy had succeeded in life despite coming from less-privileged backgrounds. Because they were now financially stable as adults, they knew their children would have the opportunities they needed to become financially successful, too. They were more concerned with ensuring their children understood that those opportunities weren't currently available to everyone—and that they had a duty to help change that, or at least do something to make the world a better place.

Diplomat David Martinez's parents—Lou, his mother, and Lee, his father—were both successful in their legal careers. But they both grew up under less-than-perfect circumstances: Lou came from a poor New Mexican community, while Lee was raised in and fled from an affluent but abusive Anglo family in Odessa, Texas. It was important to them that their sons knew what hardship looked like.

"We always told them when the gifts given are plentiful, you have a lot of responsibility," Lee said. "We tried to instill in them a responsibility for doing what's right for your whole community. For everyone. I think they both have done that in their own way."

Lee and Lou, along with David and his brother Daniel, volunteered as a family to work at the local soup kitchen and stayed active in church.

"I was an altar boy, a server at communion; I became a lector," David said. "And then I taught vacation Bible school to younger kids when I was in high school. I coached soccer because that was my big passion, and it was just a natural connection for me."

That commitment to helping others that David got from his parents is why he did so much volunteer work in college, even starting, at the University of Arizona business college, a "Make a Difference Day," which today gets 1,400 volunteers each year. His motivation "went back to a sense of responsibility and wanting to give back as a meaningful contributor—to helping others as my parents and my faith would tell me was my obligation," David said.

He remembers completing an internship with a Fortune 500 company during college, and realizing that, though it was an enjoyable experience, he didn't feel fulfilled. "I lay in bed every night and wondered if this was the sum total of what I was meant to do in life." He joined the Peace Corps six months later and then applied and was admitted to graduate school at Harvard "to get smart on foreign policy."

One of his Harvard professors, who had been an esteemed ambassador, "told me my most important efforts wouldn't be in an office, but in service to the American people as a diplomat, where I should, in his words, go where the fires are."

And that's exactly what David did. At the time a thirty-year-old diplomat, he was sent to Baghdad between 2013 and 2014, where he was one of several US foreign service officers responsible for screening and issuing visas to Iraqi citizens who helped the United States during the Iraq War. It was his job to decide who would be allowed to immigrate and who would not. And the philosophy his parents had taught him was on his mind during one of the most trying situations in his life.

"They would bring in photos of their family members who had been beaten, or stabbed, or graffiti sprayed on their homes that warned them that American traitors would die," David said. "Or they would pull up their shirts and show me knife wounds, gunshot wounds that they said Islamic terrorists, people who hated the Americans, had foisted on them. I still think about them."

As David explained, "It comes full circle, because that's the lesson that my mother and father always instilled in me. 'With great power comes great responsibility.' It sounded trite when I was young, but when you're sitting there and you're looking at someone, and you're looking at their children and they're crying . . . and they're telling you, 'I don't know how long it is before they kill me, and they take my children.' The weight of that responsibility is no longer this kind of ephemeral concept. It's there. It's in your hand. And you have to make a choice."

Like David's parents, Sangu's father had also risen to great heights from hard times. One of eighty-six children—not a typo!—Dr. Delle grew up in a poor village called Nadom, located in the northern part of Ghana. "In those days polygamy was the norm," Dr. Delle said. After his father's death, Dr. Delle's teachers adopted him. "They recognized my potential and nurtured me; they supported me and encouraged me. I owe it to them."

He went from selling *chichinga* (meat kebab) on the streets as a little boy to studying medicine in Italy. He was a doctor to European ambassadors. A cardinal, who'd later become Pope John Paul II, became Dr. Delle's mentor. Mother Teresa was another mentor and friend, and it was she who encouraged him to leave Italy and return to Africa to become a human rights activist. And while his medical work in Ghana earned him only $12,000 annually on average, that was a good salary there, much more than most people made in his country.

Parents like Dr. Delle who were able to improve their lot in life took pride in sharing their hard-won advantages with their children, but did not allow their children to take those advantages for granted.

"I was very frank with Sangu about life and realities of the world," Dr. Delle said. Doing so imparted to Sangu the feeling that the condition of the world wasn't right and that he had some responsibility to help fix it. When Dr. Delle spent late nights trying to help refugees, the idea that all lives were important was a sentiment and a philosophy he passed on to his own son.

These service-oriented parents were often so dedicated to their own life missions that they were sometimes either physically or emotionally unavailable to their children.

This lack of availability might seem to undermine the Formula, but how strategic a master parent is with the time they have with their child—how intentionally they use that time—is more important than the amount. The Philosopher is intentional about sharing their thoughts and giving the child questions to ponder, thinking through future conversations or past questions the child asked in anticipation of what time they do have for talking with their child.

For some achievers in the book, especially the men, a mission-centered parent's lack of time is nonetheless a sore spot. Several of the Harvard project's participants said they were heavily influenced by one particular parent who was often away for work, but they also longed to spend more time with that parent. For example, one young man, the son of a well-known political figure in South Korea, said he was greatly influenced by his father's dedication to work, his intelligence, and the thoughts and worldview his father had shared with him, but he had longed as a child for more time together. Now a parent himself and living in South Korea, the young man said he better understands why his father was so busy, though he plans to be closer to his own children.

Ryan wished that his father, the brilliant farmer, was more expressive, while Sangu wanted his busy father to be home more often. Sangu has said it was his mother who spent countless hours teaching him to read and count at a very early age, not his father; when his parents divorced, Sangu chose to live with her. His relationship with his father was fractured for a time, though later in life they became close again, and Sangu doesn't deny his father's strong influence on his success. His father's absence indicated to Sangu the seriousness with which his Philosopher parent took his mission. And that alone was a source of inspiration. Remove the Philosopher parent from the child's life, replace them with someone who is always there but less committed to their work and less fascinating because of it, and people like Ryan and Sangu would not likely be so dynamic or relevant.

The same applies for the Malveaux sisters. While CNN journalist Suzanne Malveaux's mother kept close tabs on Suzanne and her twin sister and their two younger brothers, their father often worked long hours. Suzanne and her twin Suzette understood why their father, a physician and former college dean of medicine, worked so much. He had a bigger purpose than just making a good living for their family.

"We understood it was about my father helping his extended family, and helping the black community," Suzanne said. "He grew up where it was poor. People died because they didn't have good health care. It was segregated, so my parents both saw firsthand that what they had in their lives was inferior in some ways. When he became a doctor, he was always being asked by all of the relatives and cousins and friends, 'Oh, can you see so-and-so,' and 'Can you fix this?'" And he did.

WHAT THE PHILOSOPHER CREATES, PART 1: BREE NEWSOME'S MISSION

A master parent's worldview is the soil from which a high achiever's own philosophy grows. Ideas and values from countless conversations infuse the child's thinking, similar to how minerals become the building blocks of a growing tree. While the achiever's own adult philosophy may differ from their parents', the Philosopher's worldview is foundational in the achiever's thinking and is reflected in their sense of purpose and chosen actions in life.

Which is what is so puzzling, at first, about the Newsome family. On the surface, it's hard to fathom how Lynne and Clarence Newsome, two mild-mannered educators, could have contributed to their youngest daughter's actions, which made world news.

"We were terrified," Lynne recalled.

On the early morning of June 27, 2015, Lynne and Clarence received a phone call from their older daughter, Gina: "Turn on the television." In shock, they watched as thirty-year-old Bree, who they still call "Brittany," scaled a thirty-foot flagpole before illegally taking down the Confederate flag that flew above the grounds of South Carolina's statehouse.

"Lynne, my wife, almost fell out of the bed," Clarence said. "My immediate reaction was to huff and puff because I knew Brittany was capable of doing something like this. I was concerned about her being in danger, of all places, in the capital of the state that first seceded from the Union. I know South Carolina well enough to know that was a very dangerous move."

From the top of the pole, Bree could hear the police officers who had gathered at the bottom calling for her to come down—"Now!" According to Bree, one officer, a supervisor, told the others to tase her.

It was about 6 AM, a typical muggy southern morning. "I can't imagine how much adrenaline was pumping in me, but I was focused only on the task at hand," Bree said.

Her co-conspirator, a thirty-year-old white man named James, stood below. He held on to the pole, daring the Capitol police to tase her. "If you electrocute her, you'll have to electrocute me."

Bree had already come to terms with several possible outcomes. "There was a process I had gone through, making peace with God and making peace with the possibility that I might lose my life that day."

Her parents, however, hardly had any time for such processing. And fear for their daughter made it even harder for them to see how they had contributed to her actions. Lynne especially was concerned that Bree had put herself at great risk. Clarence now laughs at his wife's first reaction. "It was evident in your expression," he recalled. "'Just wait till I get my hands on that . . .'"

"I was going to spank her," Lynne said half-jokingly.

But as they watched Bree climb the flagpole, they noticed something: Bree was wearing gear—a helmet and harness. There was someone at the bottom of the pole who seemed to be watching out for her. It all signaled Bree was not acting rashly or alone, but intentionally and as part of a group. Slowly, things started making more sense. "It reflected the conversations we've had over the years and the conversations she and her mother had," Clarence said. "We talked about social responsibility in ways that reflect and demonstrate integrity. She was a part of a group of people who had thought about this thing through and through."

This raised Clarence's curiosity. How had she pulled this off? he wondered. How did she keep it from them? How did she keep it from others? And who was her friend at the bottom of the pole?

Bree and about nine other activists who had initially met online gathered in person several days earlier to plan. Bree had grown up in Maryland but at the time lived in Charlotte, North Carolina, where her parents were born and reared and where she had spent her summers as a child. Clarence and Lynne had often discussed their family history, so Bree knew she was a descendant of slaves who lived and died in the Carolinas. Being African American and having ties to the Carolinas were just two reasons Bree accepted the group's nomination to be the one to climb the flagpole. James Tyson, the man at the bottom of the pole—who Bree had only just met—was chosen to be her lookout.

Bree and the rest had strategized to fulfill a purpose, and the purpose was to take down that flag. They believed that no one, especially not the descendants of former slaves, should ever have to look at that symbol of white supremacy flying on the statehouse again.

Both Lynne and Clarence had a strong sense of social responsibility and had always been clear-minded about the qualities they wanted their children to have. More than smart children, the Newsomes wanted to raise children who had purpose and meaning in life. Their daughters, in their vision, would use their talents to help others and continue the struggle for social justice.

When their oldest daughter Gina was an infant, Clarence took her in his arms and walked with her in the backyard. There, he introduced her to the world, pointing to trees, the sky, and the birds. He'd whisper in the ear of his baby girl, who'd grow up to be a psychiatrist, all the good qualities she was going to have and all the amazing things she'd do. Even when the girls were small, they'd talk to them about black history, about their volunteer work and Clarence's ministry, and about the importance of social justice.

In many ways, Bree's apple wasn't falling far from the tree, philosophically. Clarence Newsome was a historian by trade, and Lynne was an amateur historian herself. They both loved learning about their family stories and Black American history more generally, especially what happened in the Carolinas, since that was where they were both from. "Some people are embarrassed to say they were descendants of slaves. I find it a mark of pride that I came from such strong people," Lynne said. The two met and married while at Duke University. It was the 1970s, and they were both very much part of protest movements at school.

Clarence eventually found his calling as a minister and divinity school professor. Perhaps it was partly what he had taught his daughters growing up that led Bree—who had mildly punctured her hand on the way to the statehouse that morning as James helped her over a fence—to feel as if the piercing was somehow symbolic, a link back to her spiritual rededication to Christ in 2012. She took it also as a sign that what she was doing, while dangerous, had the potential to inspire great change.

Aside from James, who remained at the base of the pole, other activists were nearby, pretending to be joggers. Still, Bree couldn't suppress a wave of fear as she climbed. She knew if she made it back down, she'd surely be arrested, but that didn't scare her. She had been arrested before for protesting. "My greatest concern was someone coming by with a gun, a vigilante. The peace that I had was a spiritual peace. I believed that God would deliver me from this situation, but even if he didn't, I trusted God no matter what."

There was another reason for her unease. Ten days earlier, a twenty-one-year-old white man, Dylann Storm Roof, had fatally shot nine black church parishioners in Charleston. When authorities discovered his website, it included a photograph of him with a handgun and the rebel flag. The photograph and the killings reignited a fierce debate on whether the Confederate flag should be taken down from the Capitol. When the flag stayed up and the state refused to fly it at half-staff even on the day of the victims' funerals, Bree and her group of activists resolved to take it down themselves.

Sweat-drenched and resembling a tree cutter or utility worker, with a harness covering her chest and a helmet hiding her long dreadlocks, Bree climbed the flagpole as the world watched. When Bree reached the top, unhooking the flag and holding it in her two hands, she shouted, "In the name of Jesus, this flag has to come down. You come against me with hatred and oppression and violence. I come against you in the name of God. This flag comes down today."

She descended into the arms of police, who immediately arrested her and James for defacing a monument on the Capitol grounds. As she was led away in handcuffs, a television crew peppered her with questions. Bree recited the Twenty-Third Psalm before calmly answering them.

Less than an hour later, a security guard put the flag up again, and pro-rally supporters carrying rebel flags had packed the site where Bree had just stood. But Bree's actions had made a bigger impact, going viral and turning Bree, an activist, musician, and filmmaker, into an international superstar. Within an hour of her being arrested, $60,000 had been raised for her bail and legal fees; within twenty-four hours, $100,000. A famous film director called to negotiate the rights to her life story. One month after Bree had removed the flag temporarily, the South Carolina House of Representatives voted to do what the state had refused to do for many years: remove the flag permanently.

Once Clarence and Lynne finally were able to speak to Bree on the phone, while she was still in jail, Bree immediately disarmed them: "First of all," she politely said to them, "if I did worry you, and I probably did, I want you to know that I apologize." Before Clarence could say even a word, she said, "Daddy, before you ask me any questions or say anything, there is something I want you to know."

"I said, 'Well, what is it, Brittany?'" Clarence recalled. "She said, 'I have listened to you all my life teaching and preaching about freedom and justice, and that God will protect you, and I want you to know that I believed every word that you said.'"

WHAT THE PHILOSOPHER CREATES, PART 2: JARELL LEE'S PURPOSE

Just as Bree carried what she learned from her parents and applied it in a way they never could have imagined, Jarell took what he'd learned from his mother Elizabeth and built on it. Elizabeth focused on one primary message: that Jarrell needed to excel in school and escape poverty. And indeed, Jarell did excel. But, he knew, there were lots of other disadvantaged children who needed chances, too. He wanted to get the best education he could, not only to show other poor black children they deserved the same, but also to directly help them achieve it—something that became his purpose in life.

This life goal first began to percolate at fifteen, when he was accepted to Hawken High School, a suburban, mostly white, elite prep school. The teachers and other adults who knew something about the school had all been telling him the same thing: that attending Hawken meant being around all the "best and the brightest minds." There, he could sharpen his own mind.

"I looked forward to that, because I'd always been at the top. So I said, 'All right, I'm going to go there and see something different. I don't know what it's going to look like, but it's going to be great.' So, I get to Hawken, and I realize these kids weren't any smarter than the kids that I knew at East Tech. They just had tutors and all these different opportunities."

After an orientation visit at Hawken, he returned to his old high school, East Tech, a mostly black magnet school.

"Sitting in my English class, my teacher Mrs. Colper saw me, and I guess she read my face. And she said, 'Jarell, don't be sad, it's not that bad here.' But in reality, I wasn't sad at all. I was furious, because all my life I felt like I had to work hard for something, and I had the experience of not getting something not because I didn't work hard enough, but because I didn't have enough money. And then I went and I saw all these kids that people told me were greater than me, and they weren't. They just had more money.

"So now sitting there in Mrs. Colper's class, I was back with the type of people I grew up with who would never have that opportunity, and watching my teachers bust their butts and still never be able to give us what those kids had. Because of money. And I just didn't think that was fair at all, and we were all black kids, and they were all white kids. It's since been fifteen years and that fury I felt still hasn't gone anywhere."

But, he says, it really wasn't about race—"In my life white people have been helpful to me"—rather, it was about class and inequality. The few middle-class black kids at Hawken could be just as arrogant in the way they perceived kids like him, or even more so, as the rich white kids.

What he saw on that first visit to Hawken is still vivid. The wealth, the entitlement. There was something wrong with the world, and, he said, "I felt like I had to fix it."

Jarell believes his experience growing up in the inner city, but also attending prep school and later Harvard University, where he cleaned toilet stalls for extra money while a student, afforded him a unique experience that allowed him to see the world "from multiple people's different points of view; people who never interact. So, it is my job to do what I can to make those two worlds interact. The point of view I've taken is, from the position of the underdog, how can I make life better, livable even, for the underclass in our society?"

As a young principal in Chicago, Jarell's philosophy is that he has an obligation to teach other poor children how to get themselves out of poverty. He is doing the same thing for his students that his mother did for him: discouraging any doubt as to whether they deserve to be successful in whatever fashion they might decide, while building their skills and confidence to ensure they can pursue and achieve that success.

THE PHILOSOPHER'S GIFT

If the ultimate goal of the master parent is to raise a fully realized adult, then the Philosopher role is one of the most important in the Formula, on par with the Early-Learning Partner in terms of the extent to which it shapes a child. Without a Philosopher to help them develop an internal compass pointing them toward their personal north star, even the most brilliant child is unlikely to make a significant impact on others' lives.

Recall that *Fully Realized* = *Purpose* + *Agency* + *Smarts.* The Philosopher guides the child toward a meaningful mission in life that, together with smarts and a sense of agency, is key to shaping the achiever's accomplishments, and foreshadows their ultimate legacy.

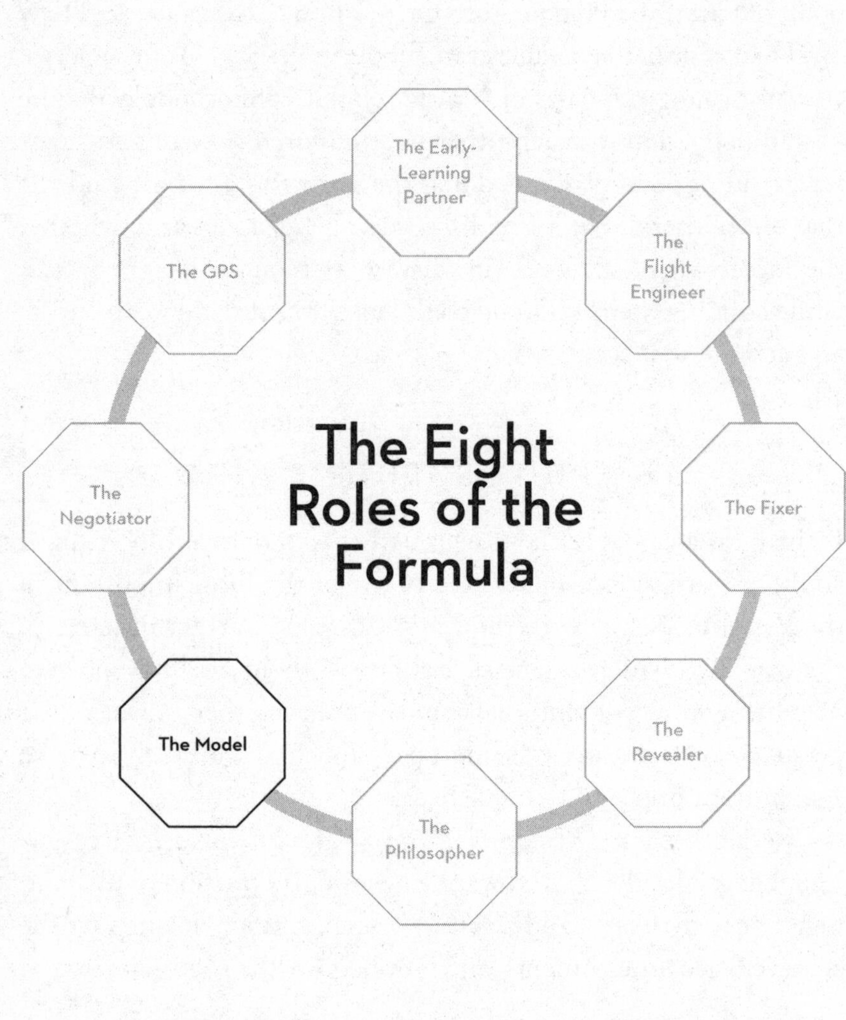
The Early-Learning Partner
The Flight Engineer
The Fixer
The Revealer
The Philosopher
The Model
The Negotiator
The GPS
The Eight Roles of the Formula

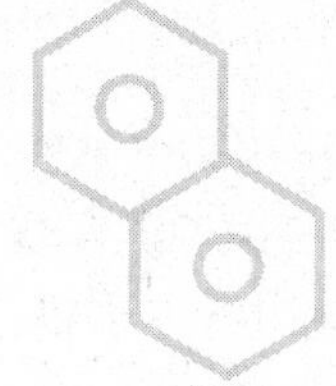

CHAPTER 11

The Model (Role #6)

A RIPPLE EFFECT

The 4-H tractor-driving contest is the most intense and anticipated event at the annual Kentucky State Fair, at least for the Quarles family. An entire wall of Ryan's paternal grandmother's living room is dedicated to relatives who have won the competition. In this family, there's no substitute for that trophy. Ryan's father, both uncles, and several cousins were previous victors. If he has a son one day, Ryan knows for sure he'll encourage his child "to go for it when he comes of age."

Everything Ryan needed to know to win the contest he learned on the farm from observing his father. Roger Quarles wasn't just a good farmer; he was the best. Born into a rural community, in a family of farmers stretching back two centuries, he studied agriculture in college and to this day is still a passionate champion of people who live off the land. And like many of them, Mr. Quarles himself had overcome great challenges.

Ryan's parents met at the University of Kentucky at the end of the 1960s. They were each the first in their families to attend college, and had experienced periods of poverty growing up, at times lacking indoor plumbing in their homes. Even at college, Mr. Quarles was too poor to afford a dorm room. He just scraped by, living in a greenhouse at the College of Agriculture.

Once he finished his bachelor's degree, he stayed on and earned a master's degree in agronomy, researching soybeans during the early days of the crop's commercialization in the United States. But there was another reason he remained: his future wife was two years behind him, studying for a nursing degree.

Later, once the couple had bought their own farm and had two sons, Mr. Quarles modeled for Ryan and his older brother Clint what it looked like to be meticulous and hardworking—qualities that were key in young Ryan's preparation for the tractor contest. The competition included not only an obstacle course, but also a written test that stressed safety and engine-maintenance know-how. Mr. Quarles, a shining example of what a tractor champion looks like, knew from personal experience there was no reason Ryan shouldn't get a perfect score on the test, and told Ryan so. Eventually Ryan did, but it took years of work.

Training specifically for the driving part, however, was even tougher. To get good at it, you needed to start preparing very early. "I remember driving a vehicle on the road at eight years old. Most farm kids will tell you that they learn to drive a tractor at nine or ten years old," Ryan said.

To increase the challenge, the rules of the competition required maneuvering a trailer hitched up behind the tractor, a John Deere forty-horsepower—a feat Ryan's father showed his sons how to do when they were just beginning elementary school. But the tractor contest was so competitive, officials would also put holes in the ground with golf balls on top of the holes. "If you rubbed a hole with your trailer or your tractor and the golf ball fell off, so many points were deducted. If you just ran over it, even more points were deducted. It was so cutthroat that you were given an inch of clearance to back up a ten-foot wagon into a fictional shed," Ryan said. To prepare, Ryan and his brother would set up an obstacle course on the farm each day when they finished working in the fields. They would practice using tobacco sticks as the obstacles.

At six foot four, quiet but demanding, Mr. Quarles was the very model of a serious farmer. Regular days on the farm were all about work, but the times Ryan spent with his father preparing for the competition were special. "There were lots of good memories," Ryan said.

Mr. Quarles made sure his son had the tools he needed for the competition, which meant that John Deere tractor. "My dad took time out of his day to go pick up a loaner tractor at the dealer. He took time out of his day to help me with a pursuit. It sounds silly, but I guess it was really no different than a parent taking their child to a band recital or a competition or tryout."

But Mr. Quarles knew the competition was more than kid's play; getting ready for it taught patience, mastery, and the care needed when driving farm machinery.

He was there every time Ryan competed, and when Ryan lost, Mr. Quarles provided criticism. There were no kid gloves. Ryan understood that, though he never liked it. He preferred more sensitive feedback and specific, detailed explanations, as his mother would give.

Though Ryan eventually won the competition, "it took me several years," he said.

The first time he did so was in 1997, when he was fourteen; he won it again four years later, in 2001. After the second state win, he went on to win the National Tractor Competition at Purdue University. "My brother never won. Even today I bring it up. Not only was it bragging rights, but it was also about doing something that my dad had done."

THE MASTERFUL MODEL

The master parent in the sixth role of the Formula, the Model, exemplifies qualities the child can aspire to. Mr. Quarles modeled self-reliance, tenacity, and intelligence, all of which Ryan mirrored in his several runs for elective office. Esther Wojcicki modeled fearlessness, which all three of her daughters have demonstrated in spades as they've worked their way to the top of the tech and medical professions. Sangu Delle's father, a man personally mentored by Mother Teresa, modeled spiritually grounded work for social justice, which Sangu is continuing in his own way, through business and philanthropy.

Interestingly, modeling in families can come in very unexpected forms. As we'll see, the most significant exemplar is not always a parent; sometimes it is a sibling, a grandparent, a never-before-met uncle, or even a long-dead ancestor. And sometimes our achievers were most inspired by a familial characteristic modeled across multiple generations: a mastery of farming skills, a legacy of resilience during hard times, or a commitment to fighting for social justice.

Still, the most influential of all Models is more often than not a mother, a father, or both.

A body of research called *social learning theory* argues that much of what we learn comes from observation—watching and listening to other peoples' words and behaviors, then imitating them, which a child has their first opportunity to do with their parents. Social learning gives the child a basis from which to form hypotheses about their own potential and decisions. The master parent models ways of being that the child, either purposefully or unintentionally, emulates. For example, a father loves baseball so much that he becomes a weekend warrior or a coach, modeling the emotional investment and hard work that can lead his son or daughter to become a standout player in high school.

A cynic might say, "What's the big deal? After all, a lot of fathers take their kids to the baseball field to practice." And every farm boy learns to drive a tractor. But what was different about Ryan's father is that he, like the other master parents in this book, modeled the highest of high standards. Ryan saw in his father's day-to-day actions, and in the stories his father told about his own experiences as a competitor, the dedication it took not just to enter and win the state tractor championship, but also to become a first-rate farmer.

Mr. Quarles had a Burn to pass on a family legacy of hard work and frugality. He modeled what it took to be a great farmer, from managing the ins and outs of the family business, to mastering the economics of the farming industry, to showing how to dominate a big-wheeled machine. In business discussions, Ryan noticed how other farmers admired his father's intelligence, and he pictured himself in his father's place. Today, his influence stretches further than his father or Ryan, back then, could have ever imagined.

Ryan could be considered the farm equivalent to baseball's Derek Jeter: both young men spent a great deal of time with their fathers while growing up, developing the skills their fathers modeled, which made the sons the very best among their peers.

Like Mr. Quarles, Charles Jeter, father of the famed former Yankee, was passionate about the interests he shared with his son. Charles was also a shortstop, at Fisk University, and when Derek was around eight, he was shown his father's scrapbook. Charles told Derek he too could build a baseball scrapbook if he worked hard.

Derek, who also became a shortstop, has publicly said, "I wanted to be just like him."

Although Charles Jeter worked as a substance abuse counselor, he was also a Little League parent, coaching Derek in baseball and Derek's sister in softball. He played a foundational role in shaping Derek as a top-notch athlete and high academic achiever.

Charles never pushed Derek to play baseball, but he realized when Derek was very young that he had a passion for it and some talent. That's when Charles dedicated himself to helping Derek succeed at reaching whatever baseball aspirations he had the ability to achieve. Plus, Derek's commitment to baseball provided Charles with the child's full attention as, during their time working together on hitting and catching, he modeled other qualities he wanted Derek to embrace.

Derek has said he learned qualities like good sportsmanship, kindness, discipline, and fairness on and off the field by watching his father not only coach baseball but also just be a great dad.

When a child holds a parent in high regard, as the child of a master parent does, they form a vision of their future self that mirrors much of what they most admire in that parent. Ultimately, this reflection of the parent in the child results from the choices the parent made during countless moments when the child observed them, together with thoughts the parent shared in moments of contemplation or feedback as the child's sounding board. The child's aspirations come to resemble the parent's hopes for them, not because the parent has required it, but through the child's admiration for the parent.

It is through influence, not coercion, that the master parent as Model transmits their qualities to a new generation, as Ryan's and Derek's fathers did with them.

SHOW RATHER THAN TELL

Floyd Malveaux, former dean of Howard University Medical School and the father of CNN journalist Suzanne and law professor Suzette Malveaux, was studying at Michigan State University to earn a PhD in microbiology in December 1966 when his twin daughters were born. While his wife, Myrna, would become the girls' primary caregiver and learning partner, Floyd provided a model of diligence and commitment, qualities he would pass along to his four children.

He did this by showing them these qualities firsthand. Suzette and Suzanne watched his rise to prominence in medicine from the time they were very small. Whether leaving home in a suit, or sitting in his study, buried behind books and working in a lab coat, Floyd was the epitome of commitment, a true professional and hard worker.

Though they were still very young when the family left Michigan so that Floyd could attend medical school at Howard University in Washington, DC, the twins observed how difficult change was for their family. They also understood that the changes were necessary if their father was going to be a doctor. And later it would be their own education that necessitated a change for their family, as Floyd resigned his position at the medical school to start a private practice in order to generate the income to afford the girls' upcoming college tuitions.

"They had to understand that there were sacrifices that had to be made in order to get an education," Floyd said.

The girls also witnessed Floyd's commitment to service, not only through what they saw of his career and the way he lived, but also in the conversations they witnessed him having with other black doctors that came to see him at the house—and through their annual trips to Floyd's and Myrna's hometowns.

Nearly every year while the kids were growing up, the family went on a long car trip to visit family members in Louisiana. Floyd wanted to make sure his children experienced the people, places, and stories that gave him such a strong sense of responsibility to help further the struggle for racial equality.

Floyd explained, "I wanted them to get to know their family, to know their relatives, because we didn't really have any relatives up here [in the Washington, DC, area]. I wanted them to know their culture, and I wanted them to get a flavor of how my wife and I grew up in Louisiana under different conditions. I wanted them to recognize that what we were doing, of course, was trying not only to live our lives, but to somehow contribute to better the lives of people who were still in Louisiana and were struggling with many of the things in Louisiana and the South is in general."

As Floyd pursued his professional dreams, he was always well aware his children were watching, which made him work even harder. He also included them in the private medical practice he began when he left Howard's medical school. All the children helped out: the girls were receptionists and the boys were part of the janitorial staff. And what they saw him do there—from envisioning an idea and seeing it through, to leading a team and earning his employees' respect—guided what they, too, could one day do. Floyd was passing on to his children how to set their sights on a goal and then fulfill it.

Children learn best how to do things by seeing others do them. A parent as Philosopher, who communicates what is good and worthy to do, gives the child a reason for choosing a particular goal in life, but provides little if any guidance about how to actually achieve it. Even the best description is a poor substitute for a good demonstration. Imagine Ryan's dad trying to explain to him how to avoid running over those golf balls in the 4-H competition, versus getting on the tractor and actually showing him.

WHEN THE PAST PROVIDES THE MODEL

Although we tend to focus on what children see in the here and now when we think about modeling, stories about ancestors can have a similar impact. The high achievers we interviewed often knew their family histories in detail, and in more than one case had reached back across generations to find inspirational models.

Diplomat David Martinez grew up carrying his father's surname, Peters, but he was more drawn to the Martinez side of his family. "We only used my father's last name, but I grew up hearing from people on my mother's side, especially my aunt, telling us these stories about the history of the Martinez family and New Mexico and how our ancestors had come from southern Spain in the 1590s. And how we had this long unbroken chain of presence in northern New Mexico where I grew up and how they lamented that now it came down to this branch of the family, these four sisters, only two of them had kids, and no one was going to be there to carry on the family name."

When David was in middle school, he had an idea. "I said I want to go by Martinez so one of us will carry the Martinez line and the other one, my brother, will carry the Peters name. My father, in typically supportive fashion, said, 'You know, it sounds like you thought a lot about this and if this is what you want to do, well, do it.'"

David was in seventh grade at the time.

He was also inspired by his maternal grandmother, who died before he was born. "My mother is my archetype for service, and she'll be the first one to tell you that her own mother, my grandmother, is her archetype," David said.

David's grandmother, while not around anymore, was still modeling indirectly through her daughter. Growing up, David watched his mother serve food to the homeless who came to the church, witnessed her run and win a political campaign to become a judge, and saw the effort she devoted to ensuring he and his brother Daniel had opportunities as teenagers to serve the poor. Observing his mother in these roles was like seeing his grandmother in action, doing what she would have done in the same situation. It was as if his mother had taken the handoff, as though in a relay race, and was now continuing her own mother's mission.

Everyone who has ever told David about his grandmother "starts to tear up and then goes on to tell me why she was the most amazing person they ever knew," he said. "She never had any education. She was a lunch lady at the high school; she ironed clothes and cleaned people's houses for extra money."

But his grandmother had this way about her, that when she knew someone in the neighborhood was going through a divorce, or having problems with their children, or whatever, she would bake empanadas, take them to the person's house, and stay as long as they needed to talk. She saw the food and her presence as a way of giving back to people—of taking care of her community.

To David, it was almost like his mother and grandmother had the same spirit.

"My mom's view of service has always resonated with me," David said. "It's really a lodestar that I look to. You know, people like my grandmother could have done so much for so many more people if they had just had the opportunity," he said. "If their lives had not been consumed with raising children, with dealing with the difficulty and doubts, with never having any money or any access or struggling with English as a second language as she did, think of what they could have done."

His mother would say, "Now you have those opportunities, David—we have worked to give you those. Don't waste them."

Rather than hearing his mother's words as a compulsion or an order, as in, "You must do this," he heard her saying, "Think about those people" like his grandmother "who came before you to get you to where you are. And if that has value, what are you doing to give back to others?"

David said his mother "never let me forget that any worldly success would be hollow unless at the end of our lives those who knew us could say that we had done right by our fellow men and made amends when we had not."

Sarah Richlin, another participant from the Harvard project back in 2009, was also inspired by a grandparent. In fact, she told of how several generations of relatives were influenced by a story her grandfather often told.

One of nine children raised by a poor Jewish single mom, Sarah's grandfather eventually worked his way through medical school picking up odd jobs, like selling shoes. His siblings each chipped in to help him continue on in school to become a doctor once they had jobs of their own. But prior to being accepted to a medical school, Sarah's grandfather's future was unclear. How he, a young Jewish man lacking financial means or influential connections, climbed out of poverty is a story of serendipity—and pluck.

One evening, Sarah's grandfather found himself having dinner in the home of a stranger who happened to be a successful doctor. He saw it as an opportunity for a free meal, but he also knew getting a recommendation from the doctor would give him the leg up he sorely needed to get into college. Before leaving dinner, he made a bold move. He asked the doctor, whom he had just met, to provide him with a college admissions recommendation.

"The doctor said, 'You seem like a fine young man and very motivated—unfortunately I just don't know you well enough.' My grandpa said, 'That's perfectly fine, and I completely understand,'" Sarah recalled.

He rose to leave and walked slowly toward the door. But as he placed his hand on the knob, the doctor stood up and said, "Wait! Let me sign that piece of paper."

Sarah's extended family is packed with high achievers. She strongly believes her grandfather's story of hard work and pluck is what inspired the whole lot of them to succeed. On the surface, the story is simply about the kind of pivotal moment in time that can affect the course of a life. "But I think the lesson that stuck with me was just his own sense of gratitude [toward the stranger] and his ability to reflect and look at the bigger picture," Sarah said.

What also tugs at the hearts of Sarah and her relatives is how one person's actions, whether an ambitious young man's decision to take a risk or a doctor's act of kindness, can beget so much else. The story modeled not only for Sarah, but the rest of her large extended family of high achievers as well, how a little thing like asking a stranger for a favor could open the floodgates to a cascade of opportunity across several successful generations of a family.

Honoring a Birthright

While Sarah's grandfather became a financially successful doctor, other intergenerational Models, like David's grandmother, were individuals who never had the opportunity to reach their potential, but whose struggles still inspired.

One Harvard project interviewee told of a grandmother who could speak Chinese, but not English; she never learned to read, either. But she survived famine and war and built a successful retail business. Her work ethic and perseverance, true survival stories, business success, and encouragement to study hard stuck with him and stirred him more than the stories of his own parents, who were both college graduates.

Yet another achiever was inspired by an uncle he never met who, at a young age, became the CEO of a Fortune 500 company. The young man, who often heard his mother talk about her brother, intentionally modeled himself after his uncle, following a similar track. He recently became CEO of a major company before the age of thirty.

Of all the places where achievers heard about their families' great accomplishments, the most special was often at the dinner table.

Bree Newsome's parents spent much of their dinnertime talking about current events and history—their community's, and their own. And Bree's young age didn't stop the Newsomes from carrying on with their mealtime discussions. "When Bree came along, she just fit right in," Lynne said. They'd pull up her baby chair to the table and include her in the conversation.

These dinnertime conversations continued throughout Gina and Bree's childhood.

"They heard us talking about ancestors and praising relatives as examples. All of that conveyed the values that we regard as important to our lives and our worldviews," said Clarence, whose ancestors' civil rights activism in South Carolina was echoed in Bree climbing that flagpole.

But it was more than talk. The Newsome parents modeled actions they wanted their children to emulate.

Both parents were involved in Helping Hands, a food pantry. "We talked about it in terms of what we were doing to help other people and to make sure other children had the same kinds of advantages and experiences Bree and Gina had," she said.

The girls watched Lynne create afterschool programs for children from underserved communities. And Clarence became a leader and voice in the community, as well as a minister and, later, dean of the Divinity School at Howard University.

"We wanted them to be good people. We didn't want to create prodigies," Lynne said. For Lynne, a good person meant someone who was kind, and who cared for others. It meant someone who was similar to her own family members, people who loved history and were proud of their racial identity. Lynne's mother worked in the registrar's office at Johnson C. Smith, a historically black college. When Lynne was a little girl, she spent hours in the school library reading up on history. She also had a favorite aunt who often talked about family history and lore. More than anything else, Lynne and Clarence wanted children who'd stand up for others and help uplift the race.

With ancestors who'd survived so much, from famine in China to slavery in America, from poverty in the Jewish ghettos of Brooklyn to hardship in the Spanish-speaking communities of New Mexico, these achievers had a sense that if they were not successful, they would fail to honor their birthrights—that they had an obligation to carry on, to continue their family's journey.

Building upon a proud legacy is a lot like continuing a successful family business. Historically, family businesses have ensured the survival of not only their owners' families, but also the communities the businesses served. As values and know-how are passed on through generations, along with the family's legacy, each new generation models how to walk in the footsteps of predecessors, harvesting fruits from seeds their ancestors planted, and planting seeds for future generations to cultivate.

TRACING FAMILY MINDSET

Every family faces challenges, and the work of overcoming those challenges, especially when they threaten the family's survival, can become a family project that cuts across generations and decades. While one family's intergenerational project might be to accumulate enough savings to protect their land against drought, another's might be to accumulate enough education to avoid economic exploitation, or enough influence to affect which financial and material interests elected politicians serve.

The result of this kind of intergenerational project is a shared family mindset. Through dedication to the project, each generation develops skills and attitudes they then model for their children, helping equip them for survival.

The Quarles family passed down a culture of self-reliance in farming—a way of life upon which past generations had depended for their very survival.

For as long as Ryan can remember, his family lived by these rules: "You have to earn what you want in life," "Life is not fair," "It doesn't matter what possessions our neighbors may have . . . You play with the hand you're dealt." And that's what they did.

Ryan's earliest pre-school memories are of work. "It was every activity you can think of that is related to farm work. Manual labor. We were out in the field working on various crops, baling hay." It was all hands on deck. A failed crop could mean missing

Christmas. Not even five years old, Ryan was right there planting seeds and feeding the farm animals next to his father; his mother Bonnie Quarles (who has since passed away); and his brother Clint.

From the time he was six years old, Ryan earned $1 per hour for the work he did on the farm. During the summer months, that work was constant, day in and day out, seven days a week. During the school months, he worked when he got home, sometimes until the sun went down. Mr. Quarles had a journal where he kept track of the hours. Once a year he went through and added up the hours each son had worked, and subtracted any deductions—for example, if they had broken or torn something, he would deduct the replacement cost. And then each son got a check. Like his father, Ryan kept his own records, just to be sure the numbers were right. If there was a discrepancy, they reconciled.

When Ryan and his brother Clint turned eighteen, they were told they were on their own. "We were cut off. If we ever got into a pinch, we got a loan and paid them back with interest. We did that a few times."

Ryan's father not helping with his kids' college expenses may seem harsh, but financial discipline was a lesson he was constantly teaching. Over the years, Ryan had observed his father's money handling, noticing how his father carefully saved up for the down payment on the next bank loan or to pay off another piece of machinery.

It's a tradition in rural America for families to pass farms down through the generations. But despite the Quarleses having lived and worked in the area for 200 years, there was no land for Ryan's parents, because of a family misunderstanding. That meant Mr. and Mrs. Quarles had to start from scratch. All they had was know-how, a willingness to work and save, and a habit, passed down over generations, of self-reliance. And gradually, from nothing, they built an economic foundation, a livelihood that allowed Ryan's father to become progressively more prosperous and independent, and to diversify the way he used his time for leadership and service.

In his own way, young Ryan was just as frugal and disciplined as his father. He graduated from high school as class valedictorian and class president, with $20,000 saved from working on the farm and buying himself only an occasional CD through the years.

However, his bounty wasn't enough for college. With no help coming from home, Ryan had to find scholarship money to supplement his savings. "I took a typewriter home—those ancient machines—every day for a period of three months my senior year." He ended up filling out seventy-five scholarship applications and developing what he calls "a piecemeal scholarship package."

The biggest scholarship Ryan was offered was from the prestigious Washington University in St. Louis. Ryan tracked down his parents in the greenhouse and shared the news. "The first words out of [my father's] mouth were, 'Well, how are you going to pay for the rest of it?' It wasn't, 'Congratulations!' It was, 'You got to work hard.' He always basically conveyed if you want something you got to go out and earn it." Ryan ended up attending the University of Kentucky, where his parents and older brother had also gone, and where the cost of attending was lower than many of the other colleges he applied to. "I eventually got a full ride after we patched together all the different scholarships . . . I also lived at home for two years to save money." And of course the $20,000 he'd been saving from work on the farm also helped out.

The frugality Ryan learned on the farm, passed along by previous generations and modeled for Ryan by his father, formed the foundation of an almost superhuman level of self-discipline, which in turn became the basis for Ryan's future success as a student, political candidate, and elected official.

Instead of the unpredictable weather that challenged Ryan's Kentucky farmer forebears, it was the all-too-predictable racial caste system in Louisiana and the poor Black Creole culture of the 1940s that set the stage for the Malveaux family's mindset. Floyd attributes his journey from a small Louisiana town to the deanship of

Howard University Medical School, and his own medical practice, to a prideful ambitiousness that threads through four generations on both sides of the Malveaux family—a "think big" mindset that rejected the view among southern whites that black Americans were inferior. Instead, Floyd embraced the perspective that no person should allow others to trample their aspirations.

"I was always interested in education, but it went further back," Floyd said. "My mother was really the motivating force for me. She was one of six children, and lived in rural Louisiana, where most kids didn't go to high school—they were working outdoors in the fields."

In keeping with the times, his mother was expected to care for her younger siblings rather than attend high school, but she recruited one of the priests in the parish to help change her father's mind. "She really fought for it and went through high school and became a teacher and got her bachelor's degree by going to school on weekends and at night."

Blacks in the rural South when Floyd was growing up were viewed as farmhands who had no particular need for education. Social relations between the races were strictly regulated by the "separate but equal" Jim Crow doctrine enshrined fifty years earlier, in 1896, by the *Plessy v. Ferguson* ruling that separate facilities were not inherently unequal.

Despite being raised under these conditions in the small town of Opelousas, Louisiana, twelve-year-old Floyd began planning for his own education just as his mother had. "Her encouragement was through example. She was ambitious. She wanted to do a number of things, and I saw that. I think both my wife and I probably passed along some of those traits to our children just by being examples."

Like his mother, young Floyd made a mature decision about his future at a young age. At thirteen, he entered the seminary. "I had been thinking about being a priest at age twelve or so," wondering if he might have a calling. "I also recognized that the educational system in Louisiana, and especially in a small town in Louisiana, was not very good. It was a segregated system, so clearly, I didn't have choices in terms of what schools I went to. Even at that age, I recognized that if I wanted a good education, I couldn't stay down here and get the type of education I really wanted and needed. So my decision to go to the seminary at that age was twofold. I did want to know if I had a vocation, and I thought about it. But I also wanted to get a better education. The seminary, I thought at that time, was really the solution in terms of fulfilling both of those elements."

It turned out he didn't have a calling. After three years in the seminary, "I came back into the lay community, so to speak, and pursued my studies there. But even my studies and my commitment to university teaching and being a physician, of course, are all about service, actually, and advancing your own intellect at the same time."

And a father who modeled the courage to set high goals for learning and service produced children who've done the same.

NEGATIVE POSSIBLE SELVES AS REVERSE MODELS

Not all master parents are heirs to a family story they want to continue. Sometimes they are aiming explicitly to rewrite it.

Chuck's mother Elaine had parents who didn't think children should talk in front of adults; she raised a son who'd talk before large audiences when he was only an adolescent. Esther Wojcicki grew up in an orthodox Jewish community where she was disregarded because she was a girl; she raised three of the world's most powerful female innovators.

In their own ways, parents like Elaine, Esther, and Jarell's mother, Elizabeth (who grew up in a foster home and regretted dropping out of high school), were motivated to create fresh chapters in their family stories, and they aimed to raise successful people who'd one day, like Sarah Richlin's grandfather, be paragons of inspiration for later generations. And they did this through modeling behavior that was very different than what they'd grown up with.

Esther's daughters are known for the fearlessness they learned growing up near the campus of Stanford University with parents who modeled what it looked like to "make waves." While Stan pushed the boundaries on understanding the origins of the universe, Esther, the high school journalism teacher, challenged public policies using what she calls "life's two most important questions: 'Why?' and 'Why not?'" ("The trick," she says, "is knowing which one to ask.")

It was not unusual to see Esther pushing a stroller door to door in the neighborhood protesting one thing or another. "They were building a housing project right near where I was living and the housing project was too dense and inappropriate, and I decided that I didn't like it. I had to convince all the people in this community, I had to fight the university, I had to fight the city, I had to fight the federal FHA, I had to fight all these different levels, and I won."

The girls were right there watching everything. "They thought it was fun," she said.

In the way she carried herself and the challenges she took on with the girls there watching, Esther imbued her daughters with a sense of responsibility, taught the value of prudent risk taking, and demonstrated that people have the power to change their own and others' circumstances. To Esther, teaching her children to be independent was practical. For instance, she wanted the girls to learn to swim so they could play without her supervision. If they could read, they could follow signs and get home if they got lost. Counting meant no one could cheat them out of their money. But it was also a way of ensuring her daughters learned a different way of interacting with the world than the one her own parents had tried to teach her.

By the time the family moved to Europe for Stan's work, Esther had her hands full with three girls under five. "There was no phone, no electricity; we were out in the middle of a gigantic farm. My number one neighbors were cows that you would see out the window."

Demonstrating take-charge assertiveness, "I had to make the girls be more independent," Esther said. "They were running all over the place; I didn't know where they were."

Her answer was the very model of risk taking, when she taught the toddlers, then ages three and five, how to ride a bike without training wheels. "I taught them so they wouldn't get in the way of the cows. You don't see kids that age riding bikes like that by themselves, without training wheels these days. If you use training wheels, they will get used to the training wheels. But if you teach them how to ride a bike without the training wheels, they will learn to ride right away. You just hold the kids and you run."

ABUELITA'S LESSONS ON WHAT NOT TO BE

Negative role models can be as important as positive ones because they provide ample justification for not following that negative model's path, as well as guidance on what not to do. Social psychologist Daphna Oyserman calls this the "negative possible self." This self is the person you don't want to become: the drunk uncle, the unemployed cousin, the deadbeat neighbor, the submissive spouse.

Being raised by "a village of kids" until she was five meant Pam had numerous Models available to her, and she mimicked many of their interests.

A favorite teenage "uncle," Tio Franklyn, worked at a car shop, so she became obsessed with racing Mitsubishi Eclipses. Another uncle, Tio Gardel, loved American football. "So I started learning about it." At the age of four, she proclaimed her favorite team to be the Broncos. "Had I ever seen them play? Not at all. But I said, 'Okay, I'm going to pick a team, too.'"

She noticed two of her aunts were avid readers, "so I would pick up a book and say, 'Oh, yes, I do not agree with this.' I did not know what I was reading but I knew that I wanted to model that behavior that looked cool and sophisticated."

She admired Mami Anny, the one who loved listening to eighties music, for being so expressive and independent, "in that eighties wild-child way," though "I would think, 'That's cool, too, but I'm going to tone it down a little bit.'" Pam's goal was to one day get a job, and move into her own apartment, "so I thought, let me model these other behaviors."

Even her young parents served as positive Models. Although they were not around much when she was a very little girl in the Dominican Republic, her mother later became a journalist and her father a professional baseball player in America. "I'd tell myself, 'Wow! I have that kind of DNA. I can do it,'" she recalled.

But while watching her many teen "parents" provided her with some things to copy, it also showed her some things to reject. Before she reached her own teen years, by then living in the United States, she had developed a sense of where each path she had seen the teens traveling could take them, and she knew which ones she didn't want to follow. "I feel like I didn't really make a lot of the mistakes that they did, especially in terms of being pregnant from a very early age, or whatever the case may be . . . I felt like I already lived that through each of them, because I followed them."

Once Pam's grandmother had all the papers ready to start bringing her family over to the United States, five-year-old Pam was the first to join her. Abuelita became Pam's first adult guardian, and Pam saw her as very powerful. She brought the family to a new country, and Pam wanted to be like her. "My grandmother, she was the mover. She was the power player. She was the indispensable person in the family. She was the sun that everyone else revolved around. So, any command, any movement, any action, it was all coming from her. She was the mastermind."

Abuelita, or "*Abuita,*" as little Pam called her, noticed the streak of independence that had developed within the child during the years she spent with Abuelita's teen daughters in the Dominican Republic. She wanted Pam to keep that independence and strengthen it, but also to channel it.

She did this by telling Pam a story, an old tale concerning a girl who didn't know how to cook and clean. She got married, and when her new husband discovered she didn't know how to do housework, he "returned" her to her family. It was a tale of family shame.

"I just didn't want somebody to return me," Pam said. "In my culture you're rewarded and seen as an amazing person when you can do the dishes and cook and be a great wife and have lots of kids. And I just thought, 'Wow, I am going to fail at that because that's not me.'"

Abuelita told Pam that if she were financially independent, she wouldn't need to worry about being returned.

Pam's response was to learn as much as she could, graduating high school as valedictorian, winning a scholarship to an Ivy League university, and finally getting her own apartment—her symbol of independence. The cultural model of the girl who was returned was a negative possible self that Pam made sure would never apply to her.

Pam is a perfect example of how master parents act as Models in ways that do not always look the way we expect. Her grandmother might have followed the norms of her culture, but she taught Pam to reject them. Pam did just that, while also embodying her grandmother's strength. She took on the lessons learned from her many teenage "mothers," both positive and negative. And like all of our achievers in the book, she used what she gleaned from those Models, however unorthodox, to thrive in a complex world.

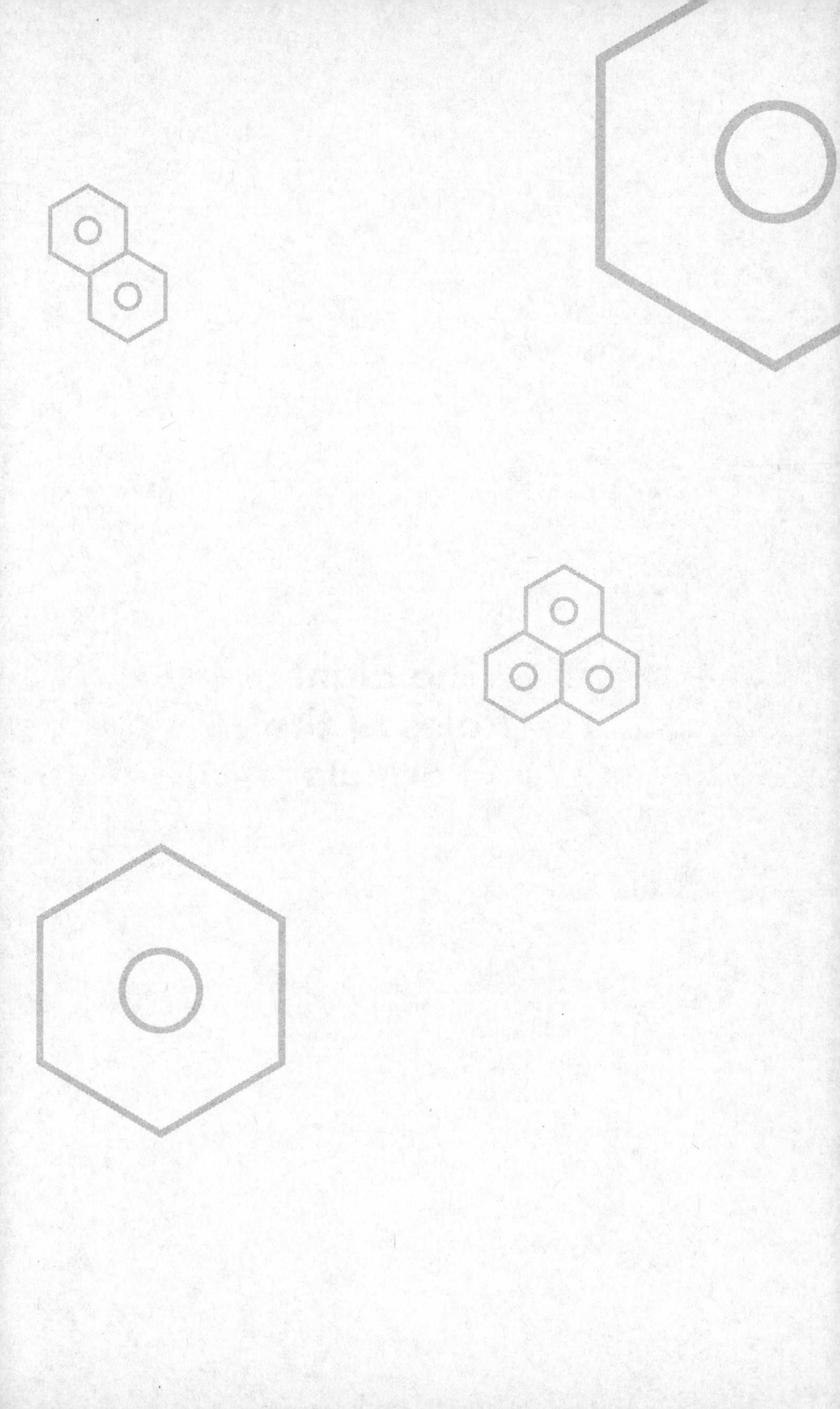

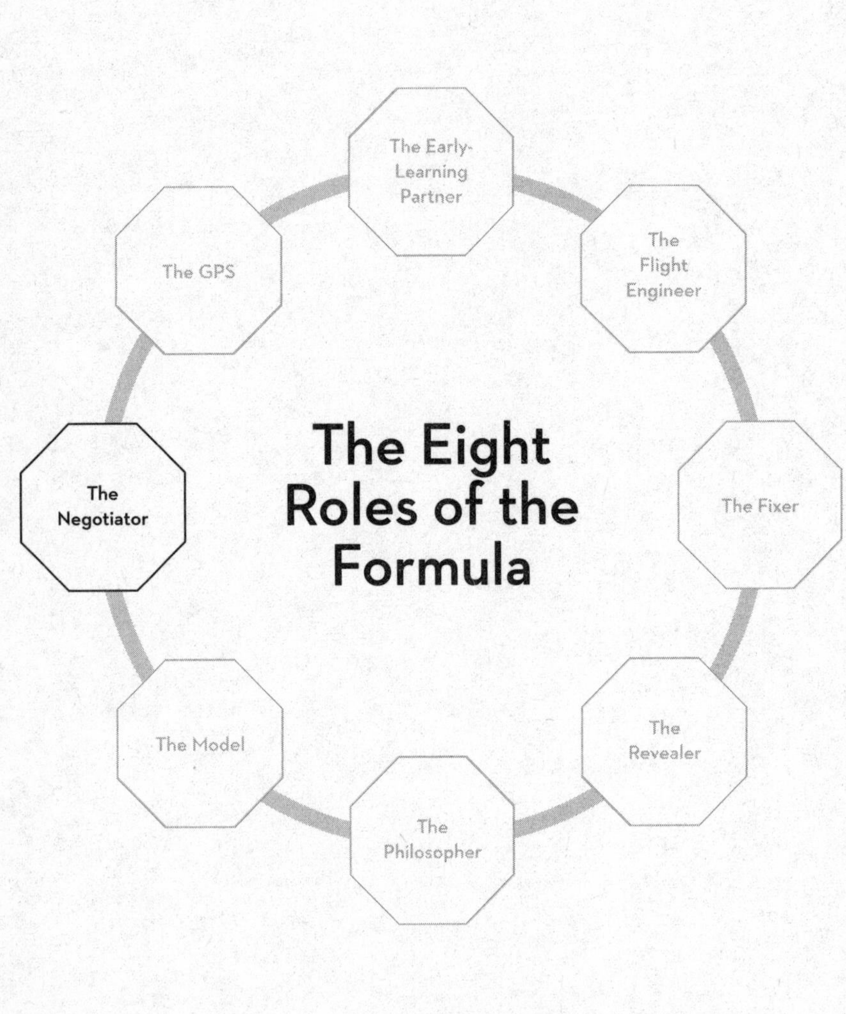
The Early-Learning Partner
The Flight Engineer
The Fixer
The Revealer
The Philosopher
The Model
The Negotiator
The GPS
The Eight Roles of the Formula

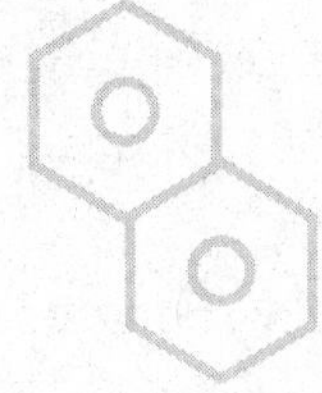

CHAPTER 12

The Negotiator (Role #7)

LITTLE MAYA LEARNS TO ADVOCATE FOR HERSELF

Maya Martin, a Dartmouth graduate who earned a master's degree from the Harvard Kennedy School, was only seven years old when she went head-to-head with her teacher. She'd been disappointed with the young woman's instruction for weeks, but this particular day, the teacher had crossed a line. Maya could hardly wait for the day to end so that she could tell her mother, who would make things right. When she finished recounting the story about her confrontation with the teacher, she asked her mother, Michelle, "What are you going to do about it?"

Her mother's response was unexpected: "What am I gonna do about it? No, what are *you* gonna do about it?"

"What do you mean?" Maya asked, aghast. "I'm only seven!"

Michelle, a college administrator, had a quick answer. "Maya, I'm not always going to be here to help you, and you've got to learn how to advocate for yourself."

But her mother did help Maya come up with a plan to execute.

The year before, Maya had been at the top of her first-grade class. She was so advanced, she skipped second grade and went directly into the third grade at the beginning of the new school year. Skipping a grade was welcome news to Maya and her family, since she could read at age four and much of what was taught in first grade she had known prior to kindergarten.

Finally, she'd be challenged. At least that's what they thought.

Instead, the teacher was young and green. "Some of the kids liked her because she didn't really do a lot of teaching," Maya said. "She did a lot of playing around. She would teach us how to do cartwheels during class or tell jokes. But if it was math or science or social studies or English, it was very limited because she didn't have a lot of control over the classroom."

Maya disengaged from all that waste of time. "If I wanted to play, I could do that on the playground," she remembers thinking.

As the children learned recreational skills, Maya camped out at the back of the class and read. She endured the situation for weeks, but after one too many lessons on the proper technique for somersaults, she was fed up.

"Why don't you join the group?" the teacher asked.

"Because I would rather read," Maya responded.

The teacher continued to press her to come and join in the fun, but Maya answered, "When you decide to teach something like science or math or reading or social studies, I will join. But in the meantime, I'm going to read my book."

Maya's parents had always taught her that it was okay to question adults, if she did it in a respectful way. Her parents, she said, were "system questioners," who never just accepted things the way they were.

She believed that if she followed the rules her parents laid out, disagreeing politely, her teacher couldn't do anything to her. "I never got loud. I always used my words and not negative words. I just expressed myself."

The next day, however, the teacher demoted Maya from the advanced reading group to a lower-level group, which had only flimsy pamphlets for readings. She thought to herself, "What's this? It's not even a book!"

That was the day she went to Michelle for help. And with her mother's coaching, Maya confidently marched into the principal's office, where she requested a meeting.

The principal's assistant giggled, seeing the tiny girl stride in with such maturity, but she still made the appointment for Maya. Later that day, "I went in for my meeting and told the principal what happened and that she needed to come see it for herself."

The principal took the little girl's complaints seriously and began observing the classroom. Sometimes, she would take over and model good instruction, but the teacher never got better. Then, one day, she was gone.

"I don't really know what happened," Maya said. "All I know is we went away for break and when we came back we had a new teacher."

Learning How to Challenge Authority

Although she was only seven, Maya had grown accustomed to being taking seriously by adults. "Anything I asked my mother about race, any type of inequality that I noticed, she would be very honest with me about all of that. She would never hide any information. She thought it was more important for me to have it than not to have it. My father was a lawyer. He taught me that if I could make an intelligent argument for something, I could get it."

Maya was also parented to have a strong love of learning, fed by exposure to museums and libraries and interesting people and places. At home, books were as common as kitchenware and got just as much use. But school, more than any place, was where Maya expected to immerse herself in learning.

The confluence of that parenting and a poorly prepared teacher resulted in a power struggle, one in which Maya would come out the victor and gain lifelong lessons. The first: *If you don't like the way things are, but you don't say or do anything, nothing is likely to change.* Then, when Maya spoke truth to power, she learned a second: *When you challenge authority, there may be a heavy price to pay—even if you're right.*

The third lesson came from her mother: *If you have an opponent who ranks higher than you, you may have to go over their head, to someone higher in the food chain.* But the final lesson was the most important. Maya learned she could be her own advocate, which was good preparation for her later career as the founder of an education organization based in Washington, DC.

BRINGING A CHILD TO THE BARGAINING TABLE

Maya's parents were fine Negotiators, the seventh role in the Formula, educating Maya from a young age in how to deal astutely with adults who wield power.

The Negotiator's role has a dual purpose: First, the master parent teaches the child a certain relationship with authority in the home. The master parent administers rules in ways that respect the child's intelligence, and encourages adult-like discussions about those rules to refine the child's reasoning skills and steer them away from bad choices. Even as they set boundaries, they're careful not to be dictators, encouraging their child to advocate for themselves and offering them choices.

Second, the master parent teaches the child how to apply negotiation skills in dealing with adults outside the home, as when Michelle helped Maya choose the best tactics for going on the offensive against her vindictive teacher. Building on what a child has learned already through dealing with parents at home—for example, the importance of speaking respectfully when stating their perspective—the Negotiator prepares the child to advocate successfully to get what they want from others, especially those in positions of power. When the child is young, this might just mean, for example, making the case to a teacher to allow more options on a class project. But each new instance gives the child essential practice for their adult future, when millions of dollars or thousands of lives might hang in the balance.

One of the concepts children learn from the master parent as Negotiator, either implicitly or explicitly, comes from negotiation theory and is called the Best Alternative to a Negotiated Agreement, or BATNA. A person's BATNA is the best course of action available to them if their negotiations with another party fail because an agreement cannot be reached—it's the best option they're left with if they refuse to take the most favorable deal the other side is willing to offer.

Let's say a parent wants their thirteen-year-old child to come with them to visit the child's uncle, but the child doesn't want to go. The parent might say to them, "If you go, I will give you $30." The child may choose to do what the parent wants and receive the $30, and both parties are happy. But if the uncle is boring or unpleasant enough, the child might just decide to take the BATNA, which in this example is to stay home with empty pockets.

The art of master parenting during parent-child bargaining is making sure the child gives careful consideration to all of their options, rather than settling too quickly on one or the other. To make sure the child thinks hard about whether the decision to stay home is really the superior choice, the parent might point out that they will pass the mall on the way back home, where the child could use the $30 to buy those jeans they've been wanting.

Astute negotiation with the child also teaches them the difference between their *position* and their *interest*: the position is what they say they want, while the interest is their underlying reason for wanting it.

A savvy master parent in the above example might then ask the child, "Exactly what *interest* makes you take the *position* that staying home broke is better than visiting your uncle?" The child might respond, "There's nothing interesting to do at Uncle George's house," leading the parent to realize that the child's interest is in avoiding boredom and to propose, "You could bring your favorite book or play video games on your phone!"

This type of back and forth helps a child develop the habit of weighing their options thoroughly, and investigating the possibility they overlooked a potential solution.

The parent as Negotiator helps the child develop a maturity that lets them prevail when there's a lot at stake. The child becomes articulate and confident, which makes a strong positive impression on potential allies. They grow into disciplined deliberators with the skill to step back and size up situations. They also develop the ability to empathetically imagine themselves in others' positions, allowing them to anticipate others' desires and next moves. And they use these skills to advocate not only for themselves, but on behalf of others, too.

NEGOTIATORS, NOT PUSHOVERS

Our high achievers shared several amusing and clever examples in which their parents rewarded them for self-advocacy. "I made an argument with my father that because I did not have a toy for show-and-tell, that was going to cause negative effects on me later," Maya recalled. "I was going to be the child that would be ostracized and would have no one to talk to. We went to Toys "R" Us on the way to school and he let me pick out a new toy. Which my mother thought was ridiculous, but my father said I made a really good argument."

In another case, Suzanne and Suzette Malveaux wanted to join the Boy Scouts. Their mother in particular did not think it was a good idea because she thought that being the only girls in a group with all those boys would be "torture." But the girls marshalled a good argument: the Girls Scouts wasn't enough for them. The boys, Suzanne recalls, got to do "camping, and the hiking, and the canoeing, and the swimming, and the rappelling." Their parents were convinced. The twins became little trailblazers: their Boy Scout troop became the first and, at the time, the only one in the country to allow girls.

However, being open to negotiation doesn't mean granting every wish. There was probably no deal the Malveaux sisters could have brokered, short of having their parents be chaperones, that would have resulted in permission to attend a potentially out-of-control party at the seashore. (And if their parents *had* offered that deal, the daughters would surely have chosen their BATNA, and skipped the party.) And some things just weren't up for discussion. When it came to R-rated movies, their parents simply said no.

Master parents give their children lots of practice at making choices. They are clear about the boundaries they're setting. But within those boundaries, they are willing to bargain and compromise to find solutions that satisfy both the parent and the child—as long as the child makes a good argument.

"No Quitting."

There is, however, one particular rule that Negotiators all enforced. Their children were not permitted to just stop once they started something. Once the child began a hobby or interest, they had to stick with it, at least for a while. Master parents usually allow the child to make the initial choice, guiding and encouraging them to explore and find their passions. But once the choice is made, sticking with it for a while becomes a nonnegotiable requirement. The child isn't allowed to go back on an agreement.

In Lisa Son's case, she allowed her daughter to pick an extracurricular activity every semester and quit only after the semester was done. "I never want her to say to me, 'I don't want to do this anymore,' because once she says that and I let her stop, she knows she can quit everything for the rest of her life. I want to decrease the chance of that. So she has to stick with one activity for only a semester."

Rob Humble was seven when he begged his father to allow him to take piano lessons.

"No," said Bob Senior. "I'm not sure you're ready."

Rob continued to insist that he was. Eventually, Bob Senior gave in—but not without a catch. "I will not let you quit until you take it for five years."

Rob eagerly agreed. "I'll do it. I'll never get tired of it."

After a few lessons, the piano teacher noticed Rob hadn't practiced that week and told him so. "That burned him up," Bob Senior said.

"That's it," Rob had said. "I don't want to take any more lessons."

But Bob Senior wasn't about to let Rob break their contract. "In four years and nine months and two weeks you can quit," he told him.

A few years later, a musician friend of Bob Senior noticed Rob was good at reading music. She told him that he didn't have to practice as much as he was—just enough to fool his piano teacher—which Rob recalled "breathed new life" into him. Instead of fretting over practicing, Rob began to enjoy the piano and kept taking lessons—for a total of nine years.

Bob Senior designed their agreement for piano lessons based on a solid understanding of his child. He knew young Rob would soon want to quit, but he also knew that if Rob stuck it out, he'd gain not just musical skills, but also a valuable life experience. "Having him stick to something, I believe is one of the best lessons I've ever given him."

Albert Einstein was about five when his mother Pauline discovered that he often struggled to concentrate. An accomplished pianist who knew how instrumental learning music could be in developing discipline and focus, she hired a tutor to teach her son the violin.

Albert threw a tantrum and then a chair at his violin teacher, but Pauline was not having it. She put her foot down and hired a new tutor. Albert's concentration improved.

There are times when negotiating with a child is appropriate, but there are also times when the parent simply knows what's best and has to impose their will.

NEGOTIATING A PRESCHOOLER'S BEHAVIOR

Part of the Negotiator's job is also to select disciplinary approaches that best fit their child. The master parent weighs various courses of action they could take and chooses the one most likely to result in the outcome they desire. If Pauline Einstein had been a permissive parent and given in to her son's refusal to practice the violin, would Albert have achieved the history-making breakthroughs he did? Einstein himself called the theory of relativity "a musical thought," which he said came to him intuitively. Hans, his first-born child, once said: "Whenever he felt that he had come to the end of a road or into a difficult situation in his work, he would take refuge in music, and that would usually resolve all his difficulties."

The high achievers in the book rarely displayed behavioral problems by the time they reached kindergarten, but before that it could be a different story. Some, especially Bree Newsome and David Martinez, were quite strong-willed. Their parents had to figure out how to strike the right balance between setting boundaries and not crushing the child's will.

Lynne and Clarence learned early that molding the qualities they wanted Bree to have would take insight and patience. On one occasion, Clarence noticed two-year-old Bree was eating too much popcorn. "I admonished her to stop. But she paid me no attention at all. I said, 'Daddy said you have eaten enough popcorn. You need to stop.' She didn't miss a beat. She took a kernel up to her mouth."

He stood up tall and strong and walked in a slightly threatening way toward her, but he didn't scare little Bree. The toddler stood up too, charging forward.

Clarence was taken aback. "A lot of children would have retreated but she came to meet me as if to say, 'You want to square off?' I realized I had a challenge on my hands."

He lifted her up—but not to spank her into obedience.

"I had to win her confidence but do it in a way where she respected my authority. I was dealing with someone that was daring and bold. I decided instinctively to wrap my arms around her, holding tight but without harming her."

She had to work to break her father's grip, which she could not do. Her strong will dissolved into tears. "I walked around the room still holding her firmly and said, 'Now, Daddy loves you but you will obey Daddy. That began our bonding. I sensed early on that this was not a person you could easily bond with without gaining her respect."

Starting when the child is an infant, the master parent becomes a student of the child and learns to tailor their parenting and style of communication to the child's personality, interests, and proclivities, as Clarence did. They reject blatant misbehavior, but otherwise avoid imposing ideas or behaviors inconsistent with the child's individual tendencies.

David Martinez was a much harder child to handle than even Bree, though you might not guess it today. He became a US diplomat at the age of twenty-seven, holding top-level assignments in the Middle East and Latin America. In 2015, he received the State Department's Superior Honor Award for outstanding intelligence support to the Secretary of State, and he is a two-time recipient of the department's Meritorious Honor Award. As a diplomat, David is calm, verbally fluent, self-reflective, and a thoughtful negotiator, but it took two talented Negotiator-master parents to help shape him that way.

The first-born of two boys in the Martinez-Peters family, he was a handful at the age of four and, as we saw in the Flight Engineer chapter, struggled with "disruptive" behavior in kindergarten. "We had to harvest his energy and keep it moving in a positive direction in terms of staying busy and learning something or doing something productive and not getting distracted or into trouble," says his father, Lee Peters.

Lou, David's mother, said, "I felt like a fish out of water. My whole life, I always wanted a child. I love children. I never had any trouble interacting with my nephews and my niece, but with David I really felt inadequate. He was difficult on a lot of different levels that I just did not understand."

David was even a tough baby.

"I had trouble soothing him," Lou said. "I realize now that it's probably because he was reacting to my anxiety, and being an active gifted child, he was probably feeling my sense of insecurity."

Daniel, who was only a year younger than David, was almost too easy to control, Lou recalled. "Even raising my voice to Daniel was enough to make him never do whatever he did to incur that loud voice for months. He did not like to have his parents upset with him, so he was very different," she said. "It was hard for me to find a way to discipline David . . . I would put him on time-out. I'd send him to his room. He would sit there and play, but it didn't change his behavior."

David was about four when Lou finally figured out the answer was putting him alone in the bathroom for a bit, where there was nothing to do but be alone and bored. Their bathroom had doors separating the toilet, the tub, and the sink.

"I'd close that door and then he would be in the part that had the sink," where he couldn't hurt anything or himself, says Lou. "I had a little stool in there and he had to sit in there. Separated from the adults and the conversation. I finally succeeded with this punishment."

David's strongest desire was to be engaged—in learning, in play, or with other people. If isolation was the BATNA for doing what his parents wanted, then doing what they wanted was his preferred alternative.

Master parents as Negotiators must strike a balance between enforcing firm limits and providing the child with space to develop the judgment needed to regulate their own behavior. Recall Diana Baumrind's concept of authoritative parenting: the parenting style that results in the most desirable academic and behavioral outcomes is one that expresses loving responsiveness while also setting consistent boundaries.

As Negotiators, David's parents harnessed their son's high energy, sometimes bargaining with him and other times making decisions for him in order to keep David moving in a positive direction.

MASTER PARENT VERSUS TIGER PARENT

The Negotiator is the role that most sharply highlights the contrast between the Formula and another parenting method recently touted (and often debated) as producing successful children: tiger parenting, as we first discussed in chapter three. The tiger parent takes the highly authoritarian point of view that their perspective should dominate their child's in virtually every case. If what the child wants to do doesn't match what the tiger parent believes is best, the child is summarily overruled. The master parent, in contrast, respects the child's point of view, listening to their child and letting them make a case for what they want before rendering a final decision. The master parent also takes into account the child as an individual, rather than imposing one-size-fits-all conceptions of success or the specific path to it.

Tiger parents and master parents both focus intensely on early childhood and preschool learning and actively support their child's education. Both negotiate with others outside the family to protect their child's interests, and both value high achievement. However, the tiger parent allows their child significantly less discretion in decision making, especially when it comes to how the child spends their time.

Tiger parents are strict. They prohibit activities that most Americans think are normal. In *Battle Hymn of the Tiger Mother*, author Amy Chua writes, "Here are some things my daughters were never allowed to do." She goes on to list sleepovers, playdates, complaining about not being in a school play—and more.

For the child of a master parent, sleepovers and playdates are fine. So are TV and computer games, as long as homework is done first. There's no right type of instrument or extracurricular, or required grade or class rank. What's important to the master parent is that their child develop and pursue their own vision for who they want to be. The child may need to negotiate regarding how or when to pursue that vision, but the vision itself is their own—and the parent's support of that vision is seldom if ever in doubt.

In other words, the difference between tiger and master parenting here is more than whether a parent allows time for socialization with peers through sleepovers and playdates, or permits the child to pursue nonacademic passions like drama or drums or video games. It's who is in the driver's seat when it comes to determining the child's interests and setting standards for performance.

Maggie Young's home on the North Shore of Long Island, in a small town less than two hours outside of Manhattan, was a musical home. Her mother played the violin and viola, and her father, a double bass player, was also a music teacher at the violin school her parents owned and operated. All four of her siblings—one older, three younger—played string instruments.

It was also a home of discipline and routine. "My mom would get up first, around 5:15 AM. She'd take out the dogs and then shower. She would wake all of us up, then we all had an order that we took a shower in. My brother was quick, so he was first, but I was last because I had long hair. Then we'd all get dressed and stumble downstairs and talk to our mom in the kitchen and have a fast breakfast."

Tiger Parent vs. Master Parent

What Chua prohibited:	What our master parents did or allowed:
• Not being the #1 student in every subject (except gym and drama)	• Encouraged high achievers to compete, especially with their own past performance, but to be their own absolute best, not necessarily #1.
• Choice of their own extracurricular activities	• Encouraged passion projects of the child's choosing.
• Watching TV and playing computer games	• Although our master parents limited television watching, they did not prohibit it completely: television after homework was okay.
• Getting any grade less than an A	• Nearly all of our high achievers were straight-A students, but their master parents were okay with a less-than-perfect grade as long as they believed the child did their best.

By 6 AM, the four children began morning practice.

"We'd do scales and the foundation stuff, like an athlete stretching. We all had our rooms that we practiced in. It's a very small, old house and we all had our corners. It didn't matter if you were in your room and my mom was downstairs in the computer room, or at the dining room table or in the kitchen—she could hear all of us. So when sounds stopped, she would yell, 'I can't hear you!'"

Maggie practiced before school every day until she graduated. "My mom would say things like, 'For every time you do it wrong, you have to un-train the muscle memory and then retrain it correctly. So for every time you do it wrong, you have to do it ten times correctly.' I remember putting pennies on the music stand. Ten pennies on this side, and if you do it correctly, then a penny goes over there. If you miss or do it incorrectly, a penny goes back; then you have to do it correctly and nothing moves; then you do it correctly again, and you move the penny over."

That routine may sound as strict as any tiger parent's, but it wasn't. Maggie and her siblings had choices.

At a certain point, the siblings wanted a change in routine. "I remember in high school just being tired all the time and wanting to sleep late. My mom would frame the choice: 'Okay, you want to sleep, come home and you can do your first note on the violin at 3 PM and see how that feels, but you know the amount of work doesn't change. It just moves to a different portion of the day.'"

They switched practice to after school, but "we hated it," Maggie said.

They discovered their mother was right. Getting it done in the morning was much better.

This ability to choose didn't just cover when to practice. It also extended to whether to play at all. Maggie said her parents would have allowed any of the children to stop instrumental music altogether if that had been what they wanted. That's different from imposing decisions by nonnegotiable decree. Maggie's older brother actually did quit for a while when he got older, though after working at coffee shops for a few years, he eventually returned to music and got a master's degree.

The outcomes Maggie's parents produced are the same ones that tiger parents often seek, but anyone who looked inside the Youngs' home would have seen that it was neither a dictatorship nor a production factory for prodigies. To the contrary, it was a home filled with as much freedom as routine—with books, conversation, and TV watching, and with music literally bouncing off the walls. Dinnertime discussions were lively and reading was a beloved hobby.

"I would say in our dining room we have easily two hundred to three hundred books," Maggie said. "Some great literature, some not great literature, but a great mix. I wouldn't say my parents were reading Melville or Faulkner. But they were reading. My parents always read before bed and they always took us to the library. My mom said, 'You can have as many books as you can carry from the library.' I was a book hoarder, so they all stayed on my bed with me. It wasn't uncommon for me to have ten to twelve books under my pillow. I would just stockpile them, and my parents, both of them, I remember seeing them from my bedroom at night, they were both always sitting in their beds reading."

And when it came to the early music lessons and the discipline required, Maggie's mother didn't just think up these structures for her four children. She was a violin teacher trained in the Suzuki methodology, a way of teaching young children how to play stringed instruments in which proper posture and standing are taught in a non-coercive way. Its founder, Japanese violinist Dr. Shinichi Suzuki, believed the method's philosophical and humanistic underpinnings also inspired children to follow and choose righteous moral codes in life. Maggie's early music lessons weren't about being perfect; they were about learning discipline and experiencing the "I got it!" moment that teaches the value and payoff of hard work, especially in pursuit of something you love.

Could it be that tiger parenting is more like master parenting than expected, and that cultural background has little to do with what parenting style works best? Some might assume that Maggie, who was raised by a very attentive mother to be a meticulously disciplined violinist from the age of two, is Asian American, but she's not—she's white.

Could it be that the most essential features of parenting high achievers are the ones tiger parenting and master parenting have in common?

Is the Tiger Really Necessary?

A fundamental distinction between master parents and their tiger counterparts seems to be that master parents deeply inspire their children toward excellence, while tiger parents more aggressively require it. Still, an intriguing possibility is that tiger parents inspire as well and don't actually need to be so coercive.

The way that tiger mom Amy Chua describes her daughter's preschool years is a match for our master parents' examples. For example, Chua was a strong learning partner who used games to teach letter recognition before her daughter turned two, and she describes her child as a sponge for early learning. A pediatrician who asserted it wasn't possible for an eighteen-month-old to recognize letters had to eat crow when Chua's daughter proved him wrong.

In a letter that appears in Chua's book, that same daughter attested to the strictness in some aspects of the parenting she experienced. Chua's tiger mom practices were real. They happened. But Chua's daughter also describes a father who taught her to think for herself and be her own person and a mother who was fun to be around. It makes one wonder whether the key ingredients in Amy Chua's parenting really were the ones that she says came from China—in other words, the tiger parent aspects—*or* instead the practices consistent with the Formula for master parenting.

IS THE FORMULA *THE* SUPERIOR AMERICAN STYLE OF PARENTING?

Generalizing about a culture makes everyone squeamish, says Amy Chua, but she does it, and so do a growing number of studies that compare American parents to Asian parents. The consensus is that so-called tiger parents—stereotypically Asian parents—are basically family dictators, who do not allow their children to question or challenge the parents' perspectives.

In order to change the world, a child needs to develop the power of persuasion. Children who begin early, like those raised with the Formula, learn with a Negotiator parent how to listen well and defend a viewpoint. As a result, they become skilled at the most important tool for exercising influence. Yet traditional Asian parents are less likely to encourage their children to negotiate with them as authority figures.

Amy Chua, whose family comes from southern China, says in her book, "My parents didn't give me any choices, and never asked for my opinion on anything," in contrast to her Jewish American husband's parents, who, like many other Americans, "believed in individual choice and valued independence, creativity, and questioning authority." His parents and other Americans that Chua criticizes for allowing so much freedom of choice sound like master parents in the Negotiator role. So might this role, and the Formula overall, be rooted in a specifically American ideology?

A number of other nations rank higher than America when it comes to scores on standardized tests, so these days the world looks elsewhere for the best examples of how to raise successful children. But standardized tests aren't full measures of success; they only cover cognitive skills, when, as we've seen, full self-realization requires so much more.

Further, we'd argue that *even in those nations the Formula would produce the superior outcomes.* Could the reason be its grounding in America's culture of individuality and free thought? Is the Formula, which develops self-expression and negotiation skills, a distinctively American parenting style?

Our answer is yes.

To be effective in the role of Negotiator, a parent needs to welcome their child's effort to respectfully express a contrary point of view. Culturally, this may feel more natural for the American parent, compared to those from other regions of the world, especially Asia or the Middle East. Here's why: independent thought and free speech and the open exchange of ideas are engrained in the United States' political DNA, starting with the First Amendment to the US Constitution, which guarantees the freedom of speech.

One of the mothers we interviewed for the book, Mahru, had all the qualities of a master parent. An Iranian nurse who has lived for decades in the United States, she was strategic, smart, opinionated, and brave. She had three sons, the oldest of whom, Troy, is a neuroscientist in the United States. Despite Troy's scientific prowess, he was neither a product of the Formula nor as fully realized as the achievers in this book.

Recall that being fully realized results from having smarts, agency, and purpose. When we asked Troy whether he was raised to have a sense of purpose, he repeatedly insisted that the answer was no, saying, "I don't think about life as me having a purpose."

He explained that he would describe himself as curious, yes, but purposeful, no. But how could a young man raised by such smart and purposeful parents not have developed a drive to make some change in the world? In all other respects, he seemed so much like the other people we had interviewed.

Troy's father was in the middle of getting a degree from MIT in 1979, when he and Mahru chose to leave America and return to their native Iran, to join the resistance movement there. Troy was just entering grammar school. As a result, from the ages of seven through thirteen, during Troy's most formative years, when he might otherwise have been learning self-advocacy and finding a sense of purpose, he was living in Islamic Iran under strict theocratic rule.

The answer was riveting. He said, "I can tell you right now that the notion of a personal philosophy did not exist in my culture . . . The elites that would express one were very far and few in between. If they said it out loud, they would be imprisoned or shot."

Troy was a natural leader, even in Iran's religious schools, but the parental discussions out of which negotiation skills or a life mission might have grown did not and could not happen for Troy—it was too dangerous. Highly educated and politically savvy, his parents knew that helping Troy develop a sense of purpose or negotiation skills might embolden him to speak out, and thus gravely endanger him and the family.

A number of the other achievers we studied were not American born either, but like Troy's father, one or both of their parents, including Sangu's and Alfonso's fathers, spent time studying in America. Even those who did not study there had admired the American ideology of free thought and independent thinking, and had parented their children accordingly.

The stories of Asian achievers, however, varied from this pattern. Parents who played the Negotiator role were hard to find among them, but for totally different reasons.

From the outside looking in, Asian American families (Chinese, Japanese, and Korean) appear to restrict their children's right of self-expression. However, what Americans interpret as prohibiting challenges to authority, Chinese call *chiao shun,* meaning "training" the child in the appropriate or expected behaviors. According to researcher Ruth Chao, the reason for imposing standards is "not to dominate the child, but rather to assure the familial and societal goals of harmonious relations with others and the integrity of the family."

These harmonious relations include the child's compliance with adult dictates. The Chinese word *guan*, which means *to govern* and has greatest relevance in Chinese culture during the school years, applies both to a teacher's control of children in a classroom and the parent's control at home. It connotes care and concern simultaneously with firm control. In return for the care, concern, and dedication of their elders, Confucian thought requires that the young must show obedience, respect, and loyalty to their elders, or *filial piety*. This tradition of extreme respect for adults is believed to lead to good behavior and high levels of effort and performance in school.

However, there's some evidence that Chinese Americans lean more toward master parenting and are less tigers than we have been led to believe. That 2013 study of 444 Chinese American children and their parents we cited in the section on tiger parenting in chapter three confirmed that tiger parenting is a real thing. However, it also found that tiger parenting ranked second in parental effectiveness behind what the authors called "supportive parenting," which involved more warmth and reasoning during parent–child interactions. Supportive parenting's principles are very closely related to the principles of the Formula.

The authors of the study wrote: "It is actually supportive parenting, not tiger parenting, which is associated with the best developmental outcomes: low academic pressure, high GPA, high educational attainment, low depressive symptoms, low parent-child alienation, and high family obligation."

Lisa Son is Korean American and hardly a tiger mom, though there are things about Amy Chua, and even more about an Asian style of parenting, that she admires. For example, she likes the idea of insisting that children persist through difficulty when learning a musical instrument or mastering a skill, because it makes the child think, "Oh, my parents believe that I can actually achieve better" (something tiger parenting and master parenting share).

But what many Americans do not know, she says, is how much Korean Americans, especially those who either are born or have lived in the United States, are pushing for a more American style of parenting—one that aligns more closely with the principles of the Formula.

Lisa visits Korea every summer, where a few years ago she was in a two-part documentary created for a major Korean television station talking about her research specialty, metacognition, or how to think about thinking. A central purpose of the documentary was to influence Korean ideas on parenting and teaching, to get them to be more supportive of creativity and open expression of ideas. "They named the show *How Do You Make Your Kid Number One* or something like that," Lisa said, "in order to get a lot of people to watch."

The show was very popular and viewed by three million people.

"I told a lot of the people that I knew to watch, and they all watched and thought it was interesting," she says. "Afterward, people would say, 'Oh, yeah, happiness. We need to get the kids to learn in a certain way and to think about their own thinking instead of just obeying what the teacher says.'"

However, Lisa believes the change is going to be slow. It has to be led, she says, by the growing number of Korean Americans like herself who may have been born in Korea, but have lived in America and "have experienced a different type of education," in which parents and teachers, like the master parents in this book, encourage creativity and self-advocacy.

WHAT THE NEGOTIATOR ACCOMPLISHES

It's easier to assume that parents of children like Maggie and her siblings, and like the other children in this book, are heavy-handed dictators—"Those poor children!" Thinking this way takes the pressure off of us, because we can say, "I want my kid to succeed, but not at the cost of their happiness or well-being." The problem with that perspective is that it doesn't ring true for Maggie or our other achievers, who not only excelled, but also enjoyed doing so.

Little Sangu craved those informal lessons and conversations with his father. Lisa Son and her brother could barely contain their glee every day before dinner when they got to recite their math tables. And Maggie can't remember a time she didn't love playing the violin. Our achievers accomplished so much not because they were coerced into doing so, but because their master parents hooked them on learning, and then gave them the resources they needed to keep doing it.

Excellence requires a balance of passion and self-regulation. By providing their child with room to pursue their interests as well as practice making decisions about their own time and behavior (but without abdicating the parental responsibility to provide guidance), the master parent as Negotiator both nurtures that passion and gives their child the tools with which to shape that passion into success. An astute decision maker, shrewd in advocating for the attention and resources required to make their dreams a reality, the Negotiator's child is well equipped to make their way in the world, while moving ever closer to their best self.

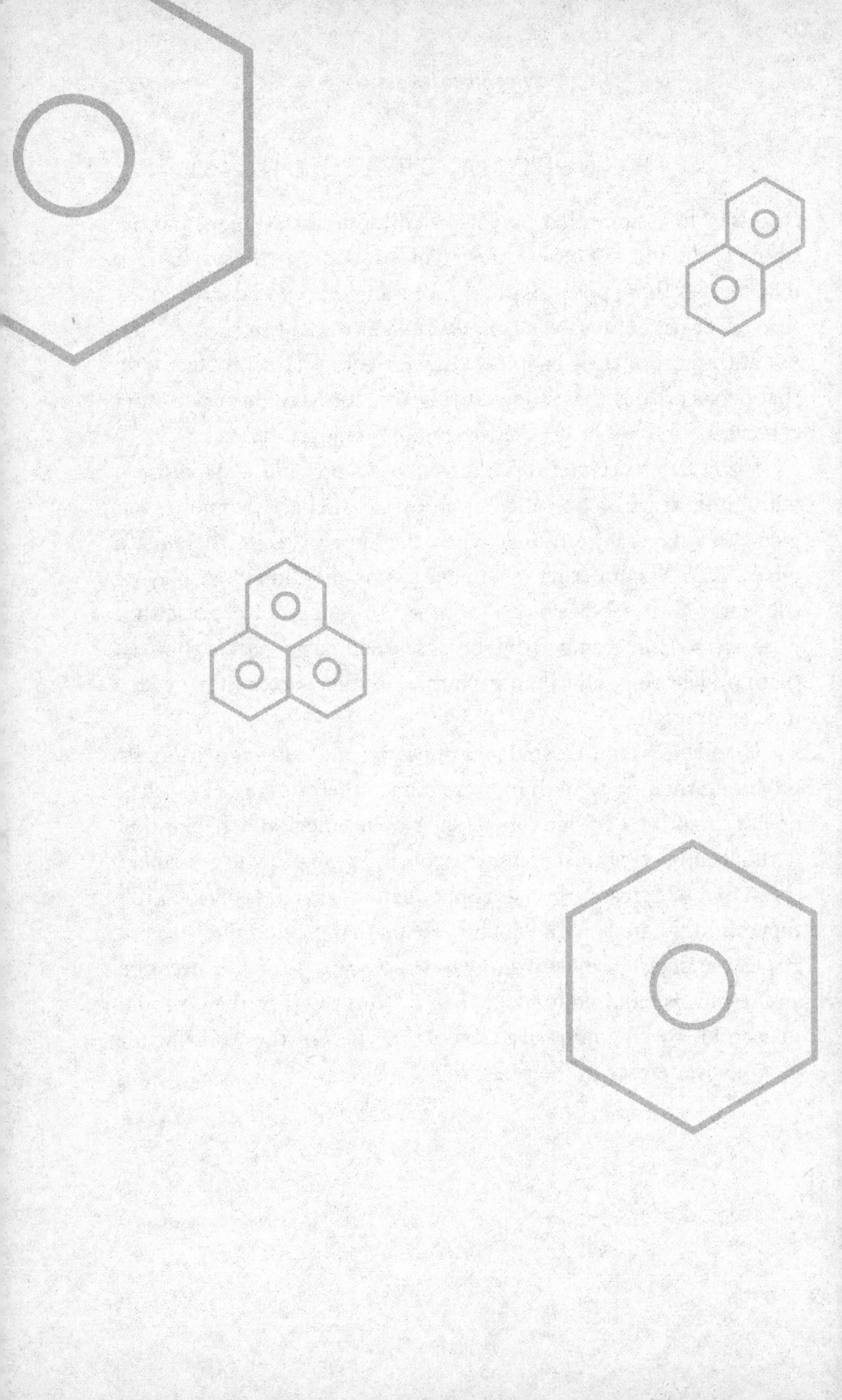

CHAPTER 13

Mastering Hurdles

SUCCESS MINDSET

The German philosopher Friedrich Nietzsche wrote the famous line, "That which does not kill us makes us stronger," more than a hundred years ago. Inspiring words, but not entirely true ones. Tragic things can be and many times are permanently debilitating. But when bad things happen to us, if we have a sense of agency and self-efficacy, and a compelling mission, the process of surviving them can build skills and fortify attitudes for overcoming future struggles—and that really does make us stronger.

The children of master parents are fierce, serial problem solvers. And a child taught to confront challenges, one who is determined to figure them out rather than surrender to them, has a better shot at overcoming them.

The key is the way we view the challenges that we face. In the world of sports, the iron will to confront and surmount obstacles is nurtured deep in the elite athlete's psyche. And nowhere are these obstacles more literal than in the track-and-field sport of hurdling. To be a good hurdler requires the courage to rush full speed over a series of three-and-a-half-foot steel obstacles.

The secret to the hurdler's bravery is that they embrace rather than fear the crash. Understanding that a momentary lapse in performance is less important than overall growth, the experienced hurdler extracts from each fall whatever lessons there are to be gleaned.

In our rush to admire and celebrate an academically capable child's accomplishments, we sometimes fail to appreciate their fortitude and determination. Like hurdlers, high achievers learn, by working through setbacks, how to stay the course and emerge victorious with equanimity from adversity.

A person driven to excel but unafraid to fail possesses what experts in the field of achievement psychology call a *success mindset.* A mindset is any attitude or set of attitudes that affects perceptions and decisions. There are a number of different mindsets that contribute to positive outcomes in life, but the following seven are most consistently related to success:

- **Growth:** *Hard work will improve my technique and make me better.*
- **Resilience:** *If I stumble, I'll keep moving. I won't give up.*
- **Sense of Belonging:** *I fit in here; this is where I'm supposed to be.*
- **Grit:** *I'm going to stick with this and not give up.*
- **Mastery Orientation:** *I set my own standards. My goal is to be the best I can be.*
- **Confidence:** *I can do this.*
- **Sense of Duty:** *I have an obligation to myself and others to succeed.*

These are exactly the kinds of mindsets the Formula helps produce. Recall how the Early-Learning Partner prepares the achiever to be persistent through working on little projects. The child learns that effort produces new abilities, which fosters a growth mindset. Or, think of the parent in the role of Philosopher, cultivating a sense-of-duty mindset by helping the achiever find purpose.

Despite their prior accomplishments, our achievers sometimes had to overcome certain hurdles to strengthen or sustain a success mindset. A few found themselves in places where they didn't fit in; others put too much pressure on themselves academically. Several faced mild learning difficulties early on and more than one struggled with discipline issues (mostly talking too much due to boredom) during their earliest school years. Some of these obstacles were external and potentially life-shattering: two high achievers in this book had their fathers die tragically right as they were entering college. Others were more internal, or less visible to other people, but struck right at the heart of who the achievers were: Rob, the smartest boy in his hometown, for example, was terrified that he might not be as smart as people thought.

HOW ROB HUMBLE MANAGED SELF-DOUBT

If there is one thing Rob Humble could change about his childhood, it's the amount of praise he received. He wishes he hadn't been given so much. "That made me risk averse," Rob said.

The well-meaning people in his hometown of Collinsville who talked about how smart he was when he was a boy had no idea that expounding on his brilliance wasn't good for his health or mindset.

In fact, self-doubt became one of the biggest hurdles in Rob's life. "I spent my entire life in absolute fear of failure, in literally every transition."

His parents, he says, are not to blame. They encouraged him and supported him. They emphasized effort, not his smarts. In fact, Bob Senior says he learned of Rob's high IQ in early elementary school, but has never told him, even to this day.

The problem for Rob started outside the home. From elementary to middle school to high school and beyond, anxiety asserted its ugly grip every time someone marveled at how smart Rob was. When he started his first job at a large business, where he successfully supervised much older and experienced workers, "I was in a catatonic state for about a week." After graduating from Harvard Business School, "I had the closest thing that I ever had to an emotional breakdown." And despite his continued success, "I had severe anxiety that actually, over time, morphed into depression."

Luckily for Rob, his father had taught him to be a problem solver. What Rob needed was to change his internal dialogue—how mindset often plays out—from *They'll think I'm a failure* to *I know I can figure this out, as I always do.* In other words, he needed to remind himself of all the other times he'd used hard work and his problem-solving skills to rise to the occasion.

A problem-solving orientation predisposes a child to see obstacles as puzzles that can be solved by deconstructing them into smaller tasks. Remember Bob Senior always challenging four-year-old Rob to build something new with Legos, and then challenging him to do it again but bigger or with awkwardly shaped blocks? Rob had to wrap his mind around the problem or challenge, envision the solution in his head, and then execute what he pictured in his mind's eye. Doing this over and over in a low-pressure environment—with a father who loved him—was a good exercise for someone anxiety-prone like Rob: when he felt anxious about a difficult new task, he had lots of memories of having previously figured out how to complete a tough task successfully to help reassure him he could succeed this time, too.

Among the things Rob read to seek answers on how to quiet his fear of failure was Carol Dweck's well-known work on mindset, which distinguishes between people with a "growth" mindset, who believe they can get smarter through effort, and those who believe their intelligence is predetermined or "fixed."

"I was a case study for that research," Rob said.

Rob believes he has a predominantly fixed mindset, though he thinks that, at least some of the time, he can shift into a growth mindset—for example, when he ended up victorious in the robot-building contest in college at Washington U, after almost dropping out of the engineering program because he started out so far behind.

According to Dweck, Rob's belief that he goes back and forth between a fixed mindset and a growth mindset is correct.

"Nobody has a growth mindset in everything all the time. Everyone is a mixture of fixed and growth mindsets," Dweck has said. "You could have a predominant growth mindset in an area, but there can still be things that trigger you into a fixed mindset trait. Something really challenging and outside your comfort zone can trigger it, or, if you encounter someone who is much better than you at something you pride yourself on, you can think, 'Oh, that person has ability, not me.'"

Unsurprisingly, parents can have a big influence on mindset. Dweck and her Stanford University colleague Kyla Haimovitz recently discovered that parents can foster a rigid or fixed mindset in a child based on their reaction to the child's failures! If a parent appears alarmed by their child's poor performance, the child may become afraid and worry that they lack the ability to do better, encouraging a fixed rather than a growth mindset. Instead, Dweck and Haimovitz propose teaching parents how to focus on failures as interesting lessons that offer ripe opportunities for learning, the way that Bob Senior and other master parents did.

Now a successful businessman based in Austin and a picture of confidence, Rob remains on medications to help control his anxiety. He doesn't hide it. He's quite open about it, encouraging people to seek help for emotional issues. He watched his mother refuse to take her medicine because of stigma, and he believes there are many successful people like himself who are also struggling with anxiety issues but are ashamed to admit it.

While some of his anxiety may be hereditary—as mentioned, his mother is bipolar—Rob believes that it started with him constantly being told he was smart as a child. And though he still experiences the same self-doubt, the problem-solving skills he learned from his master parent father early on have made it easier for him to focus on the impact of his efforts and on growth, things he now emphasizes with his own two small children.

HOW DO MASTER PARENTS CREATE HIGH EXPECTATIONS? NO PRAISE

As praising a child's effort over their intelligence, and its positive impact on mindset, shows, what a parent praises, and what they don't praise, can make a big difference in their child.

Many of the achievers we talked to told us their parents rarely praised them for their academic achievements. Deciding not to consistently praise a smart child might seem harsh, even cruel, but we've all known smart kids who, because of the attention and praise they received for being brilliant, became arrogant or superior and wasted their talents. What our master parents chose to celebrate, and therefore encourage, instead was their child's character: the moments in which they used their sense of purpose and agency, paired with their considerable talents, to make the world a better place.

Having just learned he was going to be featured in *Forbes* magazine, Sangu Delle "called my mom, super excited," but her response was underwhelming. "That's nice," she said, "but have you called your grandmother? And did you buy her fiber and vitamins?"

It was just one example of the ways his parents and siblings kept him grounded.

While our master parents would do anything to help their children, they also put their focus on character over external measures of success. They openly celebrated the type of person the child was becoming rather than grades, test scores, or awards.

"I had to reach a high, near-perfect bar to get positive feedback from my parents on my intellectual pursuits," said David. "But they were much more ebullient with praise for good conduct, such as sharing, compassion, empathy, and bravery. My mom wouldn't even tell my brother and me our IQ scores because she feared it would inflate our egos and give us the wrong sense about what was most important. I still don't know mine."

And yet, master parents let the child know they expected great things from them academically, which was in its own way a kind of silent praise—a wink and a nod that the child was capable of that level of achievement.

"No one jumped for joy when I brought home a great report card," recalled Maya. "They would say 'good job' but act as if it was not a surprise, because it wasn't. However, I was praised a lot when I stood up for something that I thought was right, when I took a leadership role, or when I had any kind of performance or artwork in an art show. All of those were areas that my parents really heaped praise on me."

Maya recalls her mother being extremely proud when, in preschool, she befriended a classmate who was dying of cancer. "All of the other kids wouldn't talk to him because they thought he looked sad," Maya recalled. "All of those types of things my mother shared with everyone else in our extended family, and they all shared in the celebration. There was this silent belief across everything that 'Maya is smart and hardworking and that is to be expected.' But I learned from my parents and my extended family that what really mattered was what kind of person I was and how I showed up in every space, even nonacademic ones, and put forward my best or made things better."

Even though praise was rare, encouragement was common. Lisa Son recalled, "If I was struggling or stressed about something, my parents might have said something very small, in passing even, or under their breath, just loud enough for me to hear forever, like, 'Of course you'll get it. It takes time.'"

The encouragement was a confidence boost, because it let her know her parents believed she could succeed, "whether it was math or tennis or piano or applying for something. It's different from the typical 'positive feedback' people talk about, when kids do something well, for instance."

It is the type of positive feedback she now gives her own young children. "When my son was frustrated learning to tie his shoes on day one, minute one, literally, I would sort of smile with an expression of acted disbelief on my face saying, 'Hey, it's been one minute. This kind of thing could take a year.' And not so surprisingly, his frustration dissipated immediately."

Praising a child can be powerful. However, the key to using praise productively is to be strategic in what you applaud.

MAYA CONQUERS AN UNEXPECTED TRAGEDY

Maya, the seven-year-old girl who outmaneuvered her teacher in the Negotiator chapter, grew up to be a social entrepreneur in Washington, DC, the founder of an organization named PAVE that teaches advocacy skills to help more parents be what this book calls Flight Engineers for their children in public school systems.

By the time she reached high school, Maya was an exceptional student, with an extraordinary success mindset. But in her senior year of high school, she needed a push to keep going. She had started applying to colleges. Everything was organized. She even gave her teachers all the recommendation forms ahead of time.

Then tragedy struck. That autumn, her father, a lawyer who had previously fallen into DC's drug scene, became fatally ill.

"My father had been sober for quite a few years but had wrecked his body with drugs and alcohol. He had a stroke and went brain dead in the middle of presenting in court. That was my senior year in high school. In October, we had to decide to take him off life support. I was out of school from the time we put him in the hospital and after his funeral. I went back to school two weeks later just because school is a very comfortable place for me. It was a place I was always very successful, and I felt good, and I would rather be there than to be at home moping."

Several other deaths of close relatives happened around the same time, including the passing of her beloved great-grandfather, and of her grandfather, who had hidden he was dying from lung cancer.

"That was hard on my mother's mother, my grandmother, and that was hard on all of us. He passed away at the beginning of December, so I really wasn't focused on college." She stopped applying.

To get back on track, she needed a shot of resilience—to somehow summon the internal voice that always said, "I can do this," that had been with her for most of her childhood.

Fortunately, Maya's mother Michelle was such a student of her child that she knew exactly what to say to trigger the attitude of determination that Maya needed to get through.

"Two days before we were supposed to go on Christmas break, December 22, my mother said to me, 'Maya, I know you haven't focused on college at all, and that's fine, but there are two options. You either apply to school and you go to college or you're going to wind up staying here with me and having to get a job.'"

Michelle had the quiet confidence of a master parent. She didn't get upset or overly worried about Maya's stumbling on this hurdle. She knew Maya loved school, that it was comforting to her. She also knew that Maya was a practical child, used to making good decisions when facing trade-offs.

Their conversation forced Maya to envision a negative possible self: working or sitting at home when she should have been in college. And that wasn't what she wanted for herself. "I'd worked too hard," Maya said.

She was able to set aside her grief long enough to make her dream of one day attending an Ivy League school come true. Fortunately, many colleges at the time were accepting a single, common application, so Maya could kill lots of birds with a single stone.

"I hustled. I took the common application to my mother and we sat down at the table and I told her, 'Tell me whatever you know about each of these schools.' Some of them I had done some research on but I'd paused all of my research because I had been going through all of this stuff."

But lack of knowledge about some of the schools wasn't the only problem to solve. "We had no money . . . My mom said, 'Just write a letter,' so we wrote a letter saying, 'Here's how much my mother makes. I can't afford these applications, my father just passed away. I'd appreciate it if you accept this application—and waive the fee.'"

Not only did all the schools waive the fee, but Maya also got into every school she applied to but one: Harvard, where she was waitlisted, and where she later attended graduate school. And the moment Maya stepped on campus at one of the schools that accepted her, Dartmouth, she fell in love with it—so much so that she chose to attend there despite having to forfeit a full scholarship at another college.

JARELL ENTERS AN ALIEN WORLD

Jarell Lee had both smarts and social skills—but that didn't make it any easier going from home in the most decayed part of Cleveland, to a school where more than a few classmates hailed from multimillion-dollar mansions in the rich suburbs. Each day was like stepping across a social Grand Canyon.

His hurdle was feeling like a misfit—and not only at school, but also back in his neighborhood, where "nerds" like himself who kept to themselves were easy prey for gangs.

When he was thirteen, he was invited to a party for the first time ever. A studious boy trying to make it in a rough-and-tumble neighborhood, he often felt out of place, but he was as spiffy as anyone else that day, in a do-rag headband and baggy pants—which sagged only at the hip, since of course Elizabeth Lee was not having his underwear showing. But as he left the party that night, he was attacked by a gang of six or seven boys. They stomped and kicked Jarell, who curled up in a fetal position. Fortunately, a neighborhood drug dealer walked out on his porch and shot a gun in the air several times, sending the gang of boys on their way, likely saving Jarell's life. He woke up in the middle of the next afternoon at the hospital with a concussion, his head swollen and gashes webbed all across his forehead. "I think I had bruised ribs, a big gash across my finger. I was out of school for a week, but by the grace of God, I have no scars."

Instead of letting him hide out in the house reading and playing video games after that, his mother coached him not to be afraid to go out. That was the beginning of his journey to achieve a sense of belonging: to not just conform in his speech or dress to blend in with different types of people, but also insist that people accept him as he was.

By the time he started high school, Jarell had set his sights on Hawken School, the elite prep academy. He wanted to attend the very best high school he possibly could, and Hawken was it. But since he didn't initially get the scholarship he needed, he spent his freshman year at an inner-city school, where he learned to survive by befriending different groups of students. By sophomore year, he'd secured the scholarship he needed and transferred to Hawken.

But Jarell was one of very few black students in the school, and one of the even rarer poor black kids. He was as much a fish out of water there as he had been back in his home neighborhood. Fortunately, he already had plenty of experience with being different.

Social scientists like David Yeager at the University of Texas at Austin study the impact of feeling like an outsider. In his research on both high school and college students, Yeager learned that those who feel out of place get lower grades and drop out more often than students with the same skills and talents who feel like they belong. However, students who are not surprised by feeling like they don't belong, but instead expect it and regard that feeling as normal, are able to work their way through the problem. Like leaning into a stiff wind and moving forward, the person cannot stop the wind, but neither do they allow the wind to stop them.

Jarell also coped another way: by actively pushing back against the things that made him feel like he didn't belong. As he settled in at Hawken and grew convinced he could succeed there, he felt like he was having to adapt too much. He started to think that maybe the school needed to also do some adapting. "I didn't really have the words for this in high school," he recalls, "but I remember getting into Hawken, and in tenth grade English class reading *The Scarlet Letter*. I remember the teacher—he was like really renowned as a great teacher; everybody said, 'He's so great, he's so great.' I remember sitting in class and thinking, 'What's so great about this?' He goes on a long lecture monologue about how the book is so great because of this tragedy. Tragedy this, tragedy that. We had all read the book, and I'm way confused. I raised my hand and I said, 'Hey, um, I just don't understand. You keep calling this a tragedy and I don't understand why it's a tragedy.'"

The teacher started to explain but Jarell interrupted. "Yeah, I get it. She had a baby out of wedlock. People do that every day. It's not a tragedy."

Of that Jarell was sure, because that's how he himself came into the world. Though he understood the tragedy was less about the female protagonist being unwed and pregnant by a priest than about how the Puritans ostracized her because of it, he found the story out of date, with no cultural relevance. Jarell told his teacher, "'I don't see why this book is so great or why any of the other books we're reading are so great.' I didn't really have words for it then, but I realize now that I was rejecting the ideals that the literary canon was putting out. There were no black authors, no authors of color, no authors that wrote about my experience or came from my experience. So I was being taught that this set of experiences was much more valuable than mine. And when I think about the standards that we hold people to or the standards that we say are important, I keep asking the question, 'Whose standards are those? Who says that that's important? Where did that come from?'"

Today, Jarell believes his obstacle "was more about me thinking I needed to fit in. Instead of fitting in, I wanted them to come into my world. Now I understand what I was doing. I was pushing back against the paternalistic cultural norms that had become standard."

He became a leader at the school, starting "spirit week" and coordinating diversity programs. But most of the time he felt like no one cared to understand where he came from or knew what he really thought.

One day during his junior year in high school, he stood in front of a microphone and spoke words that caused the audience to react in a big way—words that were memorable even a decade later not so much for their eloquence but because of what happened months after those words were spoken.

That day in 2006, Jarell was wearing his usual baggy khakis, sneakers, and big T-shirt with the word "Facilitator" written on it. He had organized the school pep rally to discuss race and class.

Anyone could have the mic. Now, he could give them a peek into who he really was. Still, he prepared to keep things light, to be the person they all expected him to be: the funny black dude.

But as he stood there, "I felt a shift," Jarell recalled. It was like after that gang attack when he was thirteen, when his mother told him to get out of the house, and not be afraid. "That's when I said to them, 'I feel a lot of you count me out because of the way I look, the way I dress, where I am from and the things I like to do. You think I am a joke.'"

In a deadpan tone and voice, he finished his statement with a bang.

"But you know what, I'm probably smarter than all of y'all."

The entire room erupted in laughter.

His teachers didn't laugh, but to everyone else, it was Jarell being Jarell, making a joke.

He stood there thinking that nothing he had just said was funny. He had taken off his mask, revealing himself to them for the first time. But they didn't know what they were seeing and his words, it seemed, had gone unheard.

"I was thinking, 'Obviously you don't believe who I really am, but I'm going to show you.'"

Months later, he did.

A great school Jarell had first heard about back when he was a little boy living in homeless shelters accepted him: Harvard University. No longer did he feel like the poor kid who was out of place in a prep school; now he knew he had belonged there just as much or more than anyone else.

And today, Jarell believes living in two worlds, one poor and the other affluent, helped him become someone who can bridge those worlds for younger generations in his career as an educator—to become a beacon for kids like the one he used to be, kids who also might fear they don't truly belong.

HOW "GRITTY" RYAN QUARLES FOUND A WAY TO WIN

To become Kentucky's state agriculture commissioner, Ryan Quarles faced huge barriers. First, he was much younger than the normal candidate for statewide office; second, he was not well known. He had to learn quickly how to conduct a statewide campaign, overcome his anonymity, and convince people he was ready for the job.

But his campaign to get elected commissioner was just the latest step in a much longer journey toward the vision for his life he had embraced as a child. And to be able to work toward the same vision for so long, Ryan needed what psychologist Angela Duckworth calls *grit*, which your grandmother may have called *stick-to-itiveness*. In her 2016 book, *Grit: The Power of Passion and Perseverance,* Duckworth presents research on what distinguishes people who stick with the same goals over long periods of time. Grit is about having stamina, she says: "It's a marathon rather than a sprint." It's working toward the same goals in a way that over time builds the skills required for achieving big things—the types of things that most folks don't have the discipline to do, like finish medical school, write a book, rebuild a car, or, like Ryan, work for years to become an expert farmer and state policy maker.

Duckworth developed a twelve-item inventory to measure grit, which includes statements like the following:

- Setbacks don't discourage me. I don't give up easily.
- I finish whatever I begin.
- I have difficulty maintaining my focus on projects that take more than a few months to complete.

If a person agrees rather strongly that the first two statements remind them of themselves, but the third does not, then they've got grit.

Success, Duckworth found, had as much to do with grit as intelligence, if not more. While there are people who possess both intelligence and grit, the two are not highly correlated. In fact, in a study Duckworth conducted on Ivy League undergraduates, the students with higher IQ scores rated slightly lower on grit. And in study after study, students of roughly equal intelligence who rate higher on grit do better than their equally smart peers.

As Duckworth puts it, grit is seeing the future you want and not stopping until you make that future real. Since grade school, Ryan had been passionate about two things: farming and politics. And ever since he became a page at the state capitol, he began to consider how he could use politics to help the farmers in his community—the men who used to sit with his father at the local diner at lunch every day and discuss the latest issues. The combination of his ability to imagine his possible self at the state house, thanks to his page position, and his hard work at home on the farm, where he'd cultivated discipline, helped make him the gritty candidate he needed to be to win the commissioner's seat.

Ryan approached the challenge of beating a veteran by working harder than everyone else. In the space of a few months, he drove a total of 65,000 miles (without leaving the state!) and knocked on 9,000 doors. He became the youngest statewide elected official in the nation at the age of thirty-two through dogged determination, explaining to thousands of people, one at a time, why a vote for him was a way to help Kentucky's small farmers.

MAGGIE MASTERS A MEMORY SLIP

No achiever we profiled is more mastery oriented than violinist Maggie Young, or more highly accomplished at their craft, which makes it hard to imagine her struggling at anything. Still, there were times that she failed to meet her own high standards. And in response, rather than get discouraged, she chose instead to double down on her efforts to become an even better musician. In one instance, she had also fallen short of what her mentor and favorite teacher, Mrs. Rosenberg, expected.

At the end of her first year of graduate school, Maggie experienced the one thing she most feared: a memory slip. There are monsters every musician needs to avoid onstage, but the memory slip was one demon even the most accomplished musicians dread more than anything. The memory slip, Maggie explains, "can happen in so many different ways. You can have a muscle memory slip with your hands—that's when the action is not engrained deeply enough in the muscles—or you can have a structural memory slip where you forget what's next."

Maggie's slip that day, in front of her eight-faculty-member panel, was small and understandable. "There was a passage that was very twisty," she recalled. "It's very easy to stumble. It was the Bartók Second Violin Concerto."

The problem was, she had made the same slip four days earlier in front of her private teacher Mrs. Rosenberg, who was also on the panel, observing her every move. "I knew she knew. The minute it happened, I looked at her."

Nothing's wrong with having a slip, but it was obvious to Maggie and Mrs. Rosenberg that Maggie hadn't taken care of it during the previous four days.

"I waited three days and I called her when I knew she would be out, and I left a message. I didn't know what to say but you have to call her because you're at the end of the year, and you need to have a good summer.

"She called me back and said, 'Well, Maggie, darling, you're a very talented girl but I'm not interested in talented people. You're not a little girl anymore. You're not cute. I'm not interested in someone like you, and I was really proud of you, and you've done so well with me . . . you won all the competitions, and you performed with the orchestra, but I know the real you because I see you every week.

And everyone loves you, and thinks you're really great, and I think you're not.' And we're on the phone. And she goes, 'Are you crying?' and I said, 'No, I agree with everything you said.'"

Rosenberg's comments were harsh, but Maggie knew they were right, and that she needed to hear them. Rosenberg was saying that Maggie needed to change her thinking, to focus less on being the cute, talented girl everyone was so impressed by, and instead become the musician who desires to be competent at her craft—but not for external reasons like grades or a teacher's approval. That desire needed to be internally driven.

What Maggie needed to develop was an even stronger mastery orientation than she already had.

Maggie got an A on her panel performance, but perceived that she had failed herself. That memory slip was a huge turning point in her life. She returned to Juilliard at the beginning of the next year, the second year of her master's program, with a certain mindset.

"I was like, 'Okay, everything is going to be different.'"

It was, eventually—but not until she conquered her fear of slipping again. And Maggie knew there was only one way to get over that fear: practice. She recalled the pennies she used to keep on her music stand, and her mother saying, "For every time you do it wrong, you have to un-train the muscle memory and then retrain it correctly."

"The muscle memory that you set when you're very young has ramifications for your whole life," Maggie said. Just like early development of a mastery orientation.

When Maggie's parents scrimped and saved to keep their children at Juilliard, they knew she and her siblings would not only gain friendships, but meet people who'd push them to stretch their skills and have the courage to compete. That exposure came in handy when Maggie needed it the most.

That same year, as, at twenty-three, Maggie was struggling to put her memory slip behind her, she decided to enter a competition she had previously lost. The last time, she hadn't tried very hard, but this time, she gritted her teeth. "I put my foot down and I really worked incredibly hard and still lost. And I lost to a girl in my studio who I thought wasn't nearly as good. I remember I went home and I cried and I called my mom and for two days I didn't get out of bed. Because it's one thing to lose when you're not trying, and it's another thing to lose when you really tried. I looked at this girl who won. We were kind of at the same point in our careers and doing the same things and the same auditions, and I said, 'I will be damned if she ever beats me at anything ever again.' I would be in a room, and it would be a very tangible thought: 'I bet Stephanie's practicing right now.'"

Maggie had picked her rival, a habit of high achievers in this book. While they judged their progress based first and foremost on their own past performance, many of our high achievers also liked to measure themselves against one or two worthy competitors (who sometimes had no idea they were the achiever's rival) because it encouraged them to work harder and to do better.

"I looked at her very ruthlessly in my analysis: What does she have that I don't have? And I went, okay, it's her work ethic. I said, 'Fine, I can do that. I have the stuff she doesn't have so I need to adjust.'"

The next year, her hard work paid off. She won the biggest competition of all: the one that came with that solo onstage at Carnegie Hall with Alan Gilbert, the conductor at the New York Philharmonic.

THE FUTURE NEWS ANCHOR WHO STUTTERED

Suzanne Malveaux, now a celebrated CNN journalist, was not even aware she had a speech problem. She loved school as a little girl, "but early on, I was marked as remedial. I used to stutter. I didn't really realize a lot of this was going on at the time, because I think I was shielded from it."

The reason she believes her parents protected her from that knowledge? To get past her obstacles, Suzanne needed confidence—which wasn't so hard to garner in a family with the Malveauxes "can-do" spirit.

Suzanne recalled an old report card from kindergarten. "It read: 'The class just made butter. We asked Suzanne, "How do you make butter?" and she could not tell us how to make butter.' So, there was something that was going on with my attention or something else that was happening. They kept testing me year after year, so I ended up going to a special speech class."

Suzanne was taken out of her regular class for a few hours every week to spend time in another classroom with two troublemakers. "I'll never forget them because they used to disrupt class all the time." In that separate classroom, "I would have my headset on repeating the words."

She knew something was wrong—that she didn't belong there—but just didn't know how to express it.

"My feeling was, 'What am I doing here? Why am I here? This doesn't feel right to me, because I can read all those books over there on that shelf.' The good thing was I didn't know that I was stuttering. I didn't even know that I was having a hard time with the instructions about making butter, because that wasn't revealed to me. I discovered it much later in life when I opened the file."

Suzanne's sister Suzette believes their parents were determined to make sure Suzanne didn't get pigeonholed, or pigeonhole herself. As they progressed through elementary school, neither sister felt like an academic star. Suzanne was in gifted and talented for a short time, but then returned to a regular class. Suzanne struggled with multiplication tables; Suzette struggled to learn to tell time. Suzette says, "My dad discovered it, because he asked me the time.

I looked to Suzanne, and he said, 'No, Suzette, I want *you* to tell me what time it is,' and I couldn't."

Each of these challenges became a family project with flash cards and practice—no shock or panic, just a steady approach to solving the problem and overcoming the barrier. Suzanne's parents never told her that anything was wrong, only encouraged her to work harder, which helped sustain her confidence.

She recalls, "I paced back and forth in my room for hours trying to get the multiplication tables to stick. I would say just about everybody in the family was involved. It was important. There was a lot of encouragement. But, also, there was a sense of, 'Okay, you've got to focus.' Mom and Dad were not punitive in any way. It was a lot of encouragement, maybe a little concern too. I think by fifth grade I was kind of stressed."

But she overcame it all. By middle school, both girls were academic standouts, getting all As while participating in band and cheerleading and Boy Scouts and student government and honor society and theater, and doing it all with unflinching confidence.

PAM ROSARIO DISCOVERS HER PURPOSE

During her first few years in Miami, Pam learned English from a combination of schools, where "everyone was an immigrant, teachers weren't invested, and schools weren't that good," and her grandfather. "He spent so much time trying to help me with pronunciation."

Her elementary school in Miami was a magnet school located in a bad neighborhood, with an unusually high number of sexual predators. By fifth grade, some of her friends were smoking and drinking, but not Pam, whose family members were devout Christians and who had vicariously observed teenage angst during her very early life in the Dominican Republic and knew how to dodge those adolescent mines. She studied just enough, finishing her work thirty minutes before class. “The material they were teaching us was great, but the teachers were not invested enough in our learning for us to understand what they were trying to teach.”

But Pam’s biggest hurdle in her early school years was to resist thinking of herself in the demeaning terms that some teachers used to described her.

“I had teachers who said things like, ‘She’s probably not going to make it to high school. Probably going to get pregnant’ by a certain age.” They would say, “‘Oh, you’re not doing this right. Dominicans this, Dominicans that, you’re not going to amount to anything.’ I don’t think I was mature enough to say, ‘They’re wrong, and I’m better than this.’”

Because of her teachers’ comments, she wondered whether her skin color and immigrant status would keep her from being who she really wanted to be.

“I remember deciding to be a fashion designer just because I didn’t feel there was a place in academia for me, like being a doctor or a lawyer, because of my complexion. I thought that in American culture, it was only cool to be Latino if you looked European like Sofía Vergara. Not if you looked more African, like me.”

By the time Pam entered sixth grade, Abuelita had moved everyone from Miami to a house in New Jersey. The home was now packed with family members and twelve younger siblings and grandchildren. “Moving to Jersey was a blessing in disguise,” Pamela said.

The cool friends who had sometimes been distractions in Miami were not there. All there was for her to do was study, and that’s what she did. If she had remained in Miami, Pam believes she might never have gone to college.

In Miami, she was always looked down on because she was a Dominican. In New Jersey, Pam wanted to prove a Latina could be an academic superstar. That idea grew out of her roots in the

Dominican Republic. "At home and in church," said Pamela, "once I started excelling in the US, I continued to hear that I should succeed to make the country proud."

The feeling that she was "carrying my entire country on my back" inspired in her a sense of duty that served as her motivator.

"I knew if people see you failing or doing something wrong, it's not like Pamela is this bad person. It's like Dominicans or the family is bad," she said.

She became a straight-A student, and a participant in numerous extracurricular activities, from French club to student government. When Pam, who became fluent in French by picking it up from a relative, didn't get into the AP French class, she asked the teacher to give her work after school to prep her for the AP exam anyway.

She studied hard, spending three hours a night on homework. School "was my thing," and she didn't want to share it with anyone, especially not her large, loving family. She negotiated with her grandmother to let her focus on her grades and less on chores, which her grandmother agreed to do.

That decision was likely one of the most important decisions in her young life. It allowed her the freedom to immerse herself in her studies and become a school leader. Pam quickly became one of the top eight students in her class and eventually number one—though her friends had no idea she was the top scholar in the school.

"They were like, 'So, you do your homework?'" she recalled, laughing.

More than anything, Pam was concerned about beating her academic rivals. "I started beating the other kids, who at that point were all white. And I was like, 'Okay, I can do this.'" Her confidence began to build. "After that, I saw a change in my goals. I started thinking maybe I could be a lawyer, maybe I can be a psychologist, maybe I can be a doctor or a philosopher. I could get all As, beat a lot of people, and get a lot of recognition."

That was her goal: to be the very best. "It's not even so much about beating people because of the color of their skin; I was beating these stereotypes. I made it my life's mission to beat this stereotype."

Still, when senior year arrived, she didn't have a clear plan for the future. She had a part-time job at TGI Fridays and didn't see a way up. "Until that point, my goal was never to go to college. I just wanted to be independent. Senior year, I realized I needed to re-strategize."

While Pam was smart and willing to work hard, her family was not in the same social circles as the other students' parents. Her school counselors never took a special interest in Pam, even though she was a high achiever.

She wondered, "How am I going to hit this goal of being an independent woman and having all these things?"

The answer came by chance.

"I overheard a teacher having a conversation with one of my peers, telling her about Ivy League schools," recalled Pam. "My classmate was a white girl whose parents were professors and held in very high esteem by the school."

Pam recalled the teacher was a man who "would often speak a lot about affirmative action" in a way that suggested minorities were getting an unfair advantage.

At that moment, none of that mattered. She had a whole country's reputation to think of, so when it came to getting the information she needed, there was no shame in her game. "Once people started hyping me up and saying that I had to do this [do well in school] for my country, my hustle went to another level and my mentality was, 'I need to do everything,'" to show Americans that she and other kids like her could be successful too.

She asked the teacher all about these Ivy League universities. "All I had heard about were state schools and they were all expensive. I wasn't going to any of those, because my family didn't have money for that. So I overheard their conversation," in which the teacher had also talked about financial aid, "and I was like . . . ha!"

The teacher may not have intended the advice to be for Pam, but she took it.

Now in her mid-twenties, several years after graduating from Harvard, Pam has her apartment, her symbol of independence, and is working in finance.

Like Jarell, Pam now feels a sense of duty to share the knowledge that's helped her succeed.

"I never was a person to say, 'I see myself as the next president.' I only ever wanted to achieve the goal of independence, and now I focus my energy on getting other people of color to achieve that financial independence and getting them into positions that weren't really made for us."

THE VOICE OF THE BEST SELF

In many cases in life, the only thing that truly holds us back is our own self-doubt. This is why the internal voice that master parents cultivate is so important; it is the voice of the achiever's best self. With each new barrier the achiever overcomes, that voice grows increasingly confident.

Learning from their master parents how to face challenges rather than shrink from them, and becoming stronger as a result of those battles, is what gives the child a success mindset. Whenever a new obstacle arises, they are able to say to themselves, "I've faced something difficult before, and I can do it again."

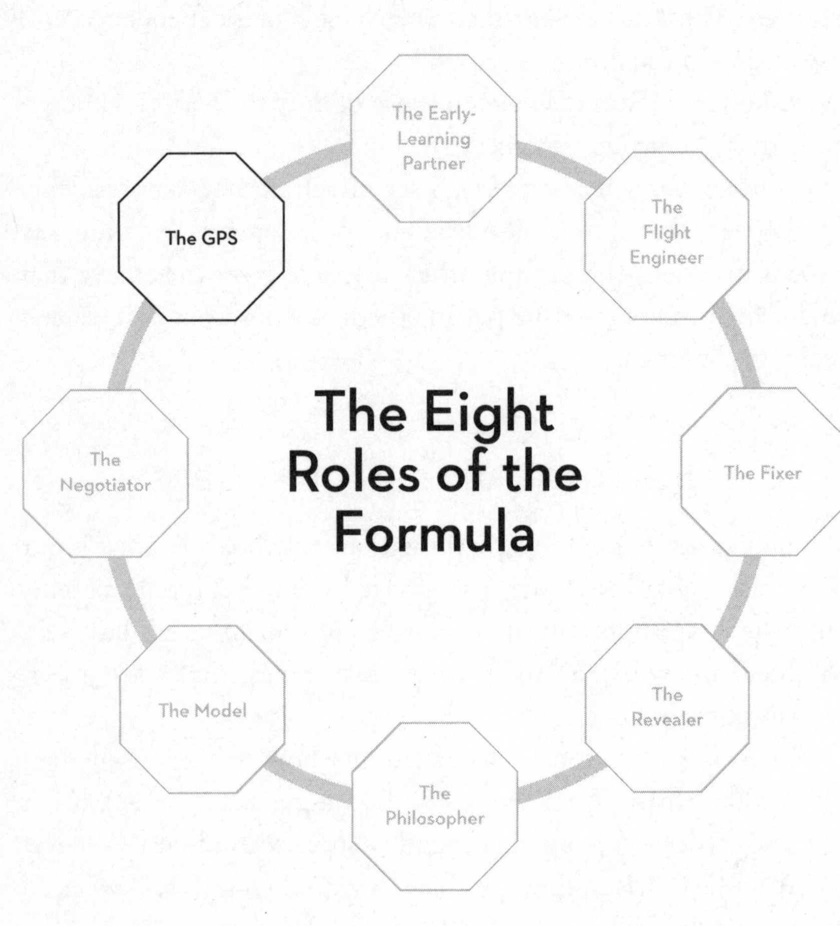
The Early-Learning Partner
The Flight Engineer
The Fixer
The Revealer
The Philosopher
The Model
The Negotiator
The GPS
The Eight Roles of the Formula

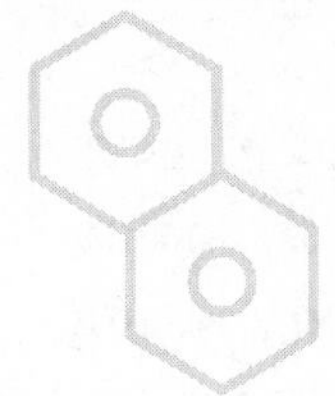

CHAPTER 14

The GPS (Role #8)

THE NAVIGATIONAL VOICE IN THEIR HEAD

When he turned five, Sangu began a strange nightly ritual based on something his mother would tell him: "Before you say your bedtime prayers, I want you to go and look in the mirror in the bathroom, and ask yourself: 'What have I accomplished today? Can I really feel confident that I've actually done something useful today?' And if you feel confident that you've actually done something today, say your bedtime prayers, and go to bed." Many nights, he'd need to head to the family's small home library to read or study "until I felt I had met the threshold" by learning something new.

Even when Sangu was off to college, his mother's words were always in his head, and to this day, they serve as a guiding force, an opportunity for personal growth not to be squandered.

"I've literally had days where I pray and I'm about to go to bed and I say, 'I didn't do anything productive today.' And I won't go to bed because I can't go to bed when I had a day when I didn't accomplish anything. So, I'll go back and read something."

That isn't to say he's always appreciated his mother's words. "At the time, I thought it was very bizarre. I remember thinking, 'Why am I doing this?' But, the older I got, the more I appreciated why she did it."

All of our master parents passed on distinctive nuggets of advice like Sangu's mother, which are echoed many years later by an internal voice in their grown child's head, providing wisdom and guidance when most needed.

Recall the internal voice that told Rob Humble he could build that robot his freshman year of college. Full of anxiety, feeling inadequate, Rob needed a reason to believe he could succeed in a challenge that seemed overwhelming. Bob Senior, his father, had been showing Rob his entire life that he could figure things out. In fact, Rob's favorite saying of his father's was, "If you can break it down, you can figure it out"—exactly what that internal voice reminded Rob to do that day in college.

The lesson Chuck Badger's mother Elaine instilled in her youngest son was the importance of self-presentation. As she always told him, "Appearance is everything. You get one chance to make a first impression." She understood that people would treat him with respect, or not, depending upon his appearance, and decided he needed to "appear middle class," which to her meant dressing a certain way. Chuck heard more times than he can count that "just because you live in the projects, the projects don't have to live in you."

As Elaine explained, "I just did not allow certain things, like low pants, untied shoes, and unkempt hair. I would just obsess with the way he looked when he walked out the door. He had to look presentable. I was raised that way so that's why I raised him that way."

That mantra, "be presentable," continues to guide Chuck as he walks with confidence among the giants of politics. From the colorful socks he wears to his signature bow tie, his cuff-link collection, and the seersucker suits he's known to don, Chuck still lives by his mother's belief that someone out there is always sizing you up.

The lessons Maggie's mother taught her on the physics of poise, back when she was a tiny violinist trying to stand on a foot chart, were with her more than two decades later as she stood proudly on the stage at Carnegie Hall. As Bree Newsome looked down on the police officers at the base of that flagpole on South Carolina's capitol grounds, she remembered everything her father had told her about taking a stand in life. And when David Martinez, the American diplomat, had to help decide which Iraqi citizens would be permitted to immigrate to the United States, he heard echoes of his parents' words imploring him to imagine himself in others' shoes, especially those less fortunate.

That parental voice that Rob, Chuck, Maggie, Bree, David, and others carried with them was the last and most unusual role in the Formula, the GPS. Through repetition and consistency over many years, the master parent's pearls of wisdom become permanently installed in the adult child's memory, like the navigational voice of a global positioning system device that helps prevent wrong turns.

This role is different from others within the Formula in that, rather than impacting the child in real time, the parent as GPS communicates *across* time, from the past, through what the child remembers them saying or doing. Those memories are the culmination of everything the parent has done in all the other roles of the Formula, and they return to the child in the form of an echo at moments when, as an adult, they have a decision to make or a challenge to overcome.

In the chapter about siblings, we talked about the importance of a child's receptivity in determining how much they learn from a parent, but it's in adulthood where this quality bears the greatest fruit. Master parents pass along wisdom to their children through many roles: the Philosopher (think of Sangu's father telling him to avoid sycophants), the Negotiator (recall the practical advice Michelle gave Maya about her teacher), and even the Model (think of Ryan's father *showing* him how to be a leader). But some children are more receptive to that knowledge than others. Our high achievers were very receptive. They not only heard the advice given to them by the master parents, they packed it away and carried it along with them. Their parents' wisdom stayed with them—in the form of the navigational voice.

But the parent as the navigational voice is more than a collection of aphorisms; these pithy expressions are just one form the role takes. More broadly, the parental GPS is a map of insights stitched together from lessons the child has learned from their parents about life. It provides a sense of direction that helps the adult achievers navigate their own lives and become fully realized human beings.

THE GPS AND THE FULLY REALIZED HUMAN BEING

Myrna Malveaux was full of sayings when her girls were growing up. If she wanted her girls to keep working on something that seemed impossible, she'd tell them, "You can do anything for . . ." three months or three years or fill in the blank.

But one maxim was most inspirational: "Mom used to have a saying: 'Feel the fear and do it anyway,'" recalled Suzette Malveaux. "That's the name of a book. She's read the book, and I've read the book. I read it multiple times actually. I remember that was really something that she emphasized very early on. Mom definitely would tell Suzanne and me that we can do anything we put our minds to."

And they did, from joining the Boy Scouts to traveling the world to taking on the most difficult challenge in their life: their mother's diagnosis with amyotrophic lateral sclerosis (ALS), a devastating, incurable disease. As they faced *that* major obstacle, the simple saying they learned from their mother, to feel the fear and do it anyway, helped them give her the best possible quality of care.

Suzette was with her parents when their mother got the diagnosis. She was also the person to call Suzanne.

"I remember when Suzette told me," Suzanne said. "I was driving home in the car. She told me what it was, ALS, and what that meant. I just pulled over in the car. I was just crying, just shocked by the news. It was devastating. I spent a lot of time on the floor that night and many nights just really mourning what was about to take place and what would happen."

Very soon after hearing about their mother's illness, the sisters and their two younger brothers reordered their priorities. The family was used to making sacrifices for one another, as their father Floyd had done when he left his university post to open several medical offices so he could afford the kids' expensive college tuitions. They remembered all the times that Floyd said, "Everyone has to pitch in" to make the medical practice successful. This new challenge was different, but the family ethos remained the same. That can-do spirit that Floyd possessed, and that his mother had before him, ran through them too.

Suzette, then a full-time lawyer, put her legal career on hold to become the boots-on-the-ground caregiver alongside their father. She spent the whole night after receiving Myrna's diagnosis learning about ALS. She pored over medical books just as she remembered her father doing over the years. And she found out that, one by one, over the course of a few years—usually three to five—all of a person's voluntary muscles stop working. They can't walk, then they can't talk, then eat, and finally breathe. After a while, Alzheimer's and dementia can also set in. Suzette learned basic medical procedures on the fly, watching her father care for her mother as he taught her in his characteristic style of showing more than telling. And over the next few months, she learned more advanced medical skills so that she could to do for their mother some of the things that nurses and doctors do, in order for her mother to remain living at home.

While Suzette cared for their mother, Suzanne took on the role of civil-defense squadron, reaching out to the world from her position at CNN. When the girls were young, they saw their mother use storytelling as a teacher to get her students' attention and inspire them. Suzanne would now use storytelling on an international scale to teach the world and inspire the search for an ALS cure.

"I was using my platform and getting the word out there—speaking and lending my voice telling stories," she said. "That was something I felt I could do. It made sense to me, especially because ALS was considered a rare disease."

She traveled across the nation listening to stories and talking to experts. "I created a CNN series on ALS, and a feature on my mother, and I told her story: the initial phases, the challenges and struggles. That's what kept me going—that one particular project. I still had my show, but the ALS work is what kept me engaged."

Video of the show is riveting and raw. "This is my family's story," Suzanne starts. Myrna is shown in an ambulance, her mouth filled with tubes. "She was struggling to take the next breath," Floyd says. The twins' brother Greg adds, "Mom was choking and couldn't swallow." Another video clip shows Myrna, who favors the late Hollywood legend Lena Horne, dancing just a few weeks before at Mardi Gras, surrounded by her family.

Suzanne did more than make that one video. "I became an advocate. I met many people and really kind of thrust myself into ALS organizations and started a website."

She also, at the age of forty-seven, became a mother, adopting a baby girl who she named Sayla.

"I'm the last one of my family to become a parent," Suzanne said. "I started to feel a longing."

She wanted to make sure Sayla would have a chance to know her grandmother. Sayla became a bright light for Suzanne as she helped care for her ailing mother, and a joy to Myrna, even as her situation deteriorated.

When Myrna's ability to speak diminished to nothing, Suzanne's sister Suzette and her father Floyd started using a pink board with letters on it. The navigational voice in Suzette's head echoed her mother's encouragement, saying, *Be patient, Suzette, you can do this!* Suzette taught Myrna how to spell with the board, with the same dedication she saw her mother use in teaching special education students.

Using her fingers, Myrna could point to letters on the board to spell the words she wanted to form. And she was very opinionated. Once, when listening to a TV discussion about the selection of a new pope, she spelled out that they should choose somebody black. She also told Suzette that her hair was too curly.

As the disease progressed, Myrna became completely paralyzed except for the movement of a single finger. The spelling board was no longer useful, so they had to go high tech. Suzette underwent extensive training on a DynaVox, familiar to many as the machine that the late scientist Stephen Hawking used to communicate. Myrna would put her hand on a clicker and click when the cursor, which continuously cycled through the letters, was over the letter she wanted to choose. When she lost the ability to move that finger, too, she instead used her eyes to blink or stare.

A few years into Myrna's illness, Floyd was diagnosed with stage IV brain cancer. Despite his illness, he still did as much as he could to help Suzette, but things were getting tougher. Myrna lost the ability to spell, as well, so Suzette, like a flexible learning partner, created pictures. The DynaVox allows for the creation of boxes, each corresponding to a different topic. Her mom could blink "into" a box, opening it up to reveal the picture inside and trigger the playing of a prerecorded phrase. If she was too warm, for example, she could blink at a box with a picture of fire and the computer would say, "I am too hot."

Suzette created different boxes representing her mother's favorite television shows. As Suzette explained, Myrna could click to say,

"I want 'TV' or '*Ellen*' or '*Wendy*, my favorite show.'" When Myrna first became sick, Suzette recorded her mother saying all of her favorite sayings and each of her children's names. "Now, when she blinks on a box, she hears her own voice, saying her own phrase. She can choose 'I love you,' or 'Thank you,' or 'Hey, puddin' pie,' or any of many other phrases, even 'Put your ass into it,'" which means "Try harder!"

Eventually dementia set in and the DynaVox was no longer useful.

Myrna died peacefully in April 2018. But her children still have their mother's wise voice in their heads. And they also have themselves—the remarkable people their parents raised them to be.

Floyd described the holographic ideal he and Myrna had for their children, that vision that they were always parenting toward: "We sought to instill in them, especially through example, how to love and respect yourselves and others, especially family and those close to you; treat everyone the same and show compassion, especially for those in need; establish moral and social values for your behavior and how you want to be treated; develop your skills and gifts to their maximum . . . or to the limit that is feasible for your gratification and to sustain your livelihood and that of your family and to assist those in need; become a positive role model for others; and enjoy life and good health . . . while you have it."

If the holographic ideal is the vision of the person the parent dreams the child could be, then the adult achiever who becomes a fully realized human being is its embodiment. While the hologram was an ephemeral image, the adult achiever is its personification.

But a fully realized human being doesn't mean a perfect person, or a static one. It means someone who is making the most of their abilities as they travel through life. And as they explore new routes, overcome hurdles, and press ahead, the master parent as GPS provides them the help of a virtuoso guide.

As the oldest achievers in the book, Suzanne and Suzette Malveaux are examples of what fully realized looks like. How they responded to their mother's illness highlighted something beautiful as they drew upon all of their skills and internal fortitude, all of the attention and advice their parents had invested in making them fearless, purposeful, and brilliant culminating in this one moment in time. Operating at the edge of their capabilities, they reached beyond what they believed they were capable of (Suzette performing medical procedures for her mother; Suzanne adopting and caring for a baby even as she also increased the nation's awareness of ALS).

And yet, even as skillful as they are today, they are still fortified by the wise words of the GPS's navigational voice, the advice from their childhood that carried them through the toughest times of their lives.

THE ACHIEVERS AS PARENTS

It's important to note that the GPS isn't operational only during the worst times of an adult achiever's life. It's equally key at what is often one of the happiest: when they become parents themselves. The parenting that the masters modeled is providing a veritable playbook our achievers frequently draw on as next-generation master parents.

Bob Senior's methods, for example, provide a map of good parenting that Rob, now raising two children with his wife, consults regularly.

Rob's son is very much the budding engineer, just as Rob was as a child. "He was doing basic addition before his fourth birthday. And he was doing basic multiplication by his fifth birthday. He's obsessed with Legos, *Minecraft*, origami, and anything that moves—remote-control cars, toy construction equipment, his drone, glider, parachute men." And like Rob, who learned to knit when he was a child, his son has learned to crochet.

Rob loves showing his son new tools and watching his creativity. "For example, I taught him how to make a pulley system with Legos and string and he built a three-story building with an elevator."

On top of the same types of resources his father, the ultimate learning partner, used, Rob's bag of tricks includes internet tutorials on YouTube, which ramp up play time to another level. Inspired by a particular tutorial, Rob and his son built a robotic arm out of cardboard and syringes. It moved remotely, reminiscent of the robot Rob built in college. Based on another YouTube example, they built a pneumatic rocket launcher.

And just as Rob eventually became obsessed with building bigger Lego bridges and taller buildings, his son eventually became preoccupied with making rockets out of various other kinds of materials. He also wanted to see how they performed differently.

Rob and his wife Anna place a lot of emphasis on supporting their children's imaginations—which, from his own childhood experience, Rob knows can build all kinds of cognitive abilities.

While his six-year-old son loves math and envisions things he wants to build with blocks, his three-year-old daughter imagines characters and stories.

"My daughter is very artistic and imaginative, constantly pretending she's someone or something else," says Rob, "crafting elaborate stories involving fairies, giant butterflies, princesses, and countless other characters. She will make two or three wardrobe changes in a typical day to complement her fantasies. She loves to put on puppet shows and she's always painting, drawing, or coloring. Supporting this type of play is right up my wife's alley so they are always dreaming something up.

"We don't try to be busybody parents that push stuff onto them. We just try to satiate all the interests that they have, though it's exhausting at times."

Fortunately, his still wise and attentive father is with him, and not just over the phone or via regular visits. He's there every day as an ever-present navigational voice. When asked about his purpose in life, Rob said it's just spending loads of time raising his son and daughter to be happy, smart, kind, well rounded, and unafraid of a challenge. "Parenting this way just feels natural because it's the way I was raised," Rob said.

N'Gai Croal remembers how, when he was boy, his father would say, "All learning doesn't happen at school." He'd do things like take N'Gai and twin sisters Aida and Nneka outside to talk to them about the cloud formations.

Having embraced his mathematician father's respect for science and technology, new father N'Gai, along with his wife Kyla, pays special attention to research on parenting and carefully applies what he learns. For example, N'Gai recalled reading about phonemes, the smallest units of sound that form words, and how children find it more difficult to learn words in other languages if they did not hear the phonemes used in those words at a very early age. He also learned that children can hear in utero. So, before their daughter was born, N'Gai and Kyla started reading to her in English and French and playing classical music. They also hired a nanny who speaks Spanish. Their toddler is now able to distinguish between all three languages, and speaks mainly Spanish to the nanny and English to her parents.

Their main goal, however? Kyla said it's "to make sure she enjoys learning"—the same goal N'Gai's father had for N'Gai and his sisters.

Familiarizing his two small children with Spanish is important to David Martinez, too. Having Spanish ancestry on his mother's side, and the effort his parents made when he was growing up to demonstrate the value of a multicultural upbringing, provided an extra reason to ensure his oldest son went to a Spanish-language day care while his family was living in Colombia, South America, where David was a diplomat.

"When we read with him at home," David said, "we point to words and say the English and the Spanish word. Even if he doesn't hold on to this, even if he loses it later, the research I've seen shows that using this verbal space in the first four years of life . . . to speak both languages, you are expanding the mind. You are giving them not only new words but a different way to view the world because they are viewing the world in a second culture."

David is also steered in his own parenting by remembering how much his parents supported his and his brother Daniel's passion projects, from combing the desert for lizards with David to accompanying Daniel to theme parks all over the country to ride new roller coasters. Like his parents, David and his wife are "finding those things that our children latch onto to empower them. Our oldest son's favorite toy is a bright pink squid my wife won at Coney Island. He takes this thing around and we had some comments about it when we lived in Colombia. Remarks like, 'Oh, he shouldn't have a pink toy, that's a girl's color.' They wanted us to take the pink squid away."

David and his wife had an unambiguous response: "Absolutely not! We want him to embrace it. If he loves it, we're gonna love it with him."

Whatever their son takes a liking to, "we're gonna roll with that. If he wants to play with Barbie dolls, we're gonna find a way for him to take that and make it his own. We don't want to stifle their creativity in any way."

THE GPS'S NAVIGATIONAL VOICE CROSSES GENERATIONS

Suzette Malveaux felt the same way about her daughter. Nailah Harper-Malveaux is the oldest of the achievers' children in the book, and an excellent representative of what these children are destined to become. A 2016 Yale graduate, Nailah has been raised similarly to the way Floyd and Myrna raised Suzette and Suzanne.

Like Myrna, Suzette helped her daughter create elaborate projects. "My mom would help me with these crazy big projects where we had poster boards and other things. When I was writing essays she would sit down and we would sometimes edit and she would point out little things that maybe could change, and from that I learned from her how to be really detail oriented. I think that hands-on involvement was helpful. But I also always felt like I had an inner drive to do well, and that may have been passed down from her."

That "can-do spirit" was passed down to Suzette from her father Floyd, who got it from his own mother. And although she didn't always realize it, Nailah's childhood rearing was also heavily influenced by her grandmother.

To help her daughter learn how to overcome her own hurdles, Suzette borrowed Myrna's favorite saying, the same one that helped Suzette and her siblings when Myrna became ill: "Feel the fear, and do it anyway."

"That saying has definitely been instrumental in my life," Nailah said, unaware it came originally from her grandmother. "I've had experiences with my mom when I've said, 'I can't do it' or 'I don't have the experience or credentials,' and she said, 'Feel the fear and do it anyway.'"

A freelance theater director, she finds herself directing actors much older than she is, which sparks moments of insecurity. But Nailah has come to believe fear is only a compass "with which to judge if you're going in the right direction," she said. "I often feel like the things that are the scariest to do are really important things to try; fear is something that tells you, 'This is the next step.' It's something you don't feel comfortable with, but that will broaden your horizons in a really important way."

Suzette followed her mother Myrna's master parenting playbook in other ways throughout Nailah's childhood, though with her own twist. For example, instead of teaching storytelling through paper dolls as Myrna did for her and Suzanne, Suzette did it during short commutes when Nailah was in elementary school. "My mom was always working really hard, so we would get to talk a lot in the car. We would make up huge stories that would continue every time we got into the car. She would tell a bit, and then I would tell a bit, and then we would end it for the next car ride. I loved doing that," recalled Nailah.

Like her mother and aunt, Nailah also chose a career as a storyteller, though Nailah's commitment to theater is a bit mysterious to her mother and other relatives. "There are different markers for success and theater is definitely not as clear of a pathway" as journalism or law, Nailah said. "So people have a hard time understanding how to help and how to measure how I'm doing."

But Nailah is just the latest Malveaux to reject the script that society had preordained for their life. Nailah's great-grandmother, Floyd's mother, rejected the idea that she should only work on the farm and care for her siblings, deciding instead to become a teacher. Floyd followed by rejecting the standard limitations imposed on young men like himself in the 1940s' caste system of the Jim Crow South, asserting his aspiration to be a scientist and doctor. Suzanne and Suzette rejected standard ideas about what girls could do, as well as their father's hopes that they would go into medicine, when they decided to enter journalism and law.

Each new generation of the Malveaux family has always found their own purpose in life and chosen their own professional journey—even as what they learned from their parents has guided their way.

So when Nailah made her own choice, the Malveauxes collectively provided her with a sound bite of encouragement and advice that only a family of high achievers would give—an exhortation that could have come from any of the master parents in the book: "Go for it, but be the best at it."

CONCLUSION

The Formula's Secret

Long before we began wondering if there was a Formula for extraordinary parenting, we noticed something intriguing about people who had raised exceptionally bright and purposeful individuals. These parents possessed a quiet confidence, as if they knew or could see something the rest of did not or could not.

What we learned through our conversations with them was that they'd had a clear vision of the type of adult they wanted their child to become, and a drive to make that vision a reality—a "Burn," which we eventually discovered came from their own backstories.

Each also had a plan. Strategically, day by day, they nurtured in their child the qualities they thought would best serve them as an adult. And that nurturing began as early as birth.

Childhood is not a waiting period for when real life begins. Every interaction a parent has with a child has the potential to be a meaningful, enriching moment in the journey. The master parents in the book knew this. They knew they could affect the courses that their children's lives took—and they did.

What set these parents apart from others who might have more education or resources wasn't any particular genius. Rather, it was that *strategic thinking* about how to achieve what they envisioned for their child, and that determination, that Burn, to follow through on doing what they thought would help the child become who they were meant to be.

Every one of us can be more strategic in how we approach parenting our children. And every one of us has a backstory that can inspire our parenting and motivate us to be more intentional and thoughtful in how we interact with them.

Some of our master parents' Burns were ignited from tragedy or struggle. What happened to her brother when their family tried to get him medical help drove Esther Wojcicki to make sure her daughters were fearless in questioning authority figures. Elizabeth Lee wanted to see her son Jarell live a better life than her own. But others, equally effective, grew out of what the master parents most valued or had learned from their own parents. Bob Senior's Burn was to pass down to Rob the problem-solving skills he'd received from his inventor grandfather and great-grandfather.

By committing to guide our children based on whatever we've learned through our own living, whatever that might be, we can give our kids a better shot at meaningful lives.

That does not mean every child will be a Sangu or a Maggie or Ryan. Not every child has to be or should be. But every child has the capacity to find purpose and achieve more than they or their parents could have imagined. By believing "This is who and what my child can be, and I am willing to sacrifice to see it through," and then acting on that belief, any parent can use the principles of the Formula to raise a child with agency, purpose, and intelligence.

Doing so does require time and sacrifice. Sometimes, as with Jarell and Chuck, it also requires resourcefulness. But what it *doesn't* require is special brilliance, or any particular set of family circumstances. As we saw, the Formula's efficacy doesn't discriminate based on race or class.

Some of the hurdles parents face, like homelessness and poverty, are certainly larger and longer-term than others, but we all face challenges that can make parenting harder. Our master parents experienced career highs and devastating lows, divorces, war, deaths, and illnesses. Because of his human rights work in Ghana,

Sangu recalled, Dr. Delle was once marked to be killed by firing squad. Several middle-class women among our master parents found themselves barely making it financially after divorce: Gabby's mother lived on $600 a month after becoming a single mother. One father had to juggle caring for his child with caring for his bipolar spouse, and more than one parent had to keep going after family members' tragic deaths. And yet these parents all still successfully raised a high achiever.

How did they do it? They were more strategic than the typical parent about the time they spent working with and for their achiever. They used whatever downtime they had to maximum effect, sometimes making great sacrifices to put their child's growth first.

After Sangu's nursery school teacher told his mother that Sangu had great potential, his mother quit her much-needed job to supplement his education. Elizabeth Lee was able to spend a lot of time working with Jarell in the homeless shelter before she found work, but she still continued to work with him after finding a job. Esther had her hands full with three young girls when their family moved overseas for her husband's job, but she still made the time to be an effective Early-Learning Partner while also doing some freelance writing.

Rob's father was a full-time teacher, but school finished at three, so he used afternoons and weekends as well as their shared summer vacation to play with Rob and his sister. David's mother and father were both lawyers but arranged their schedules so that they could be with the children when they got home from school, only finishing work from the office once the two boys went to bed. They made a conscious choice to spend time with their children.

They also made sure that time was *strategic* time. Our master parents spent lots of time contemplating how to challenge and inspire their child even when the child wasn't around. Dr. Delle only spent ten minutes or so every morning talking to his son about philosophy, but sometimes took days, as he traveled through remote villages, deciding how to answer Sangu's thoughtful questions in ways that would also stimulate the child's independent thinking. Parents also took advantage of more organic enrichment opportunities by including their children in meetings with other adults—like when Dr. Delle allowed Sangu to sit in on late-night refugee visits, and Ryan's father allowed him to attend lunches with all the farmers at the local diner. The meetings were going to happen anyway, but both fathers purposefully included their interested, attentive sons. Other parents spent strategic time with their children at the dinner table or in the car during long trips. Bob Senior and his wife knew that the songs and word and memory games they played with Rob and his sister during long road trips could improve their children's concentration and increase their vocabulary. Suzette similarly used shorter drives to strengthen her daughter's creative thinking skills by creating ongoing stories together.

Raising children who will grow up to have the ability and the will to make change in the world isn't easy. But it is crucial, if we're going to successfully take on the problems we face as a society—global political conflicts, looming water shortages, farming crises, and other challenges that the achievers in the book are now confronting in their careers.

It's important to remember that strategic parenting has broader consequences than we might ever expect. When we toss a stone into a still pond, we create a circular ripple that spreads across the water. When a master parent sends a high achiever into the world, the effect of their parenting has a broader reach than they can know.

We want to close with a story about just how widely these ripples can reach. Marissa Diggs, a high school student who transcribed a few interviews for this book, including the one about Myrna Malveaux's ALS, was paying close attention as she typed up the stories about how high achievers like herself were raised, the colleges they went to, and what they had achieved. She was especially moved by how Suzette stepped up to learn medical procedures in order to care for her mother, and how Suzanne used her position at CNN to teach the world about ALS.

Inspired by what she'd learned, Marissa decided to apply to Harvard, was accepted, and is now part of the Harvard class of 2022. Who says she won't one day lead a team that discovers an ALS cure, as a ripple effect of the Malveauxes' parenting?

Just think of the potential benefits if future generations were filled with people reared with the Formula. Life can present many competing priorities, but no parent should second-guess the strategic time they invest in raising a fully realized human being.

ACKNOWLEDGMENTS

This book could not have been completed without all the many people who spoke to us, including the sixty people Tatsha began talking to in 2003 and all the students from Ron's project at Harvard (most of whom were not mentioned in the book), as well as the many strangers (including all those new Millennial parents), colleagues, students, and interns who became so very excited every time we discussed the Formula.

Most important, we'd like to thank the achievers who allowed us to tell their amazing stories: Kyoung, Ryan, Sangu, Maggie, Jarell, Rob, Lisa, Esther, David, Daniel, Suzette and Suzanne, Bree and Gina, Maya, Sarah, Chuck, Pam, Alfonso, Gabby, and N'Gai, Aida, and Nneka, plus Nailah and Troy.

We are particularly thankful for the master parents who discussed in detail how they raised exceptional human beings: Elizabeth Lee; Roger Quarles; Lou and Lee Peters; Yvonne and James Croal; Floyd Malveaux; Michelle Moye Martin; Dr. Edmund Nminyem Delle; Esther Wojcicki; Bob Humble Sr.; Sara Vargas; Reynaldo Hernandez; Elaine Badger; Lynne and Clarence Newsome; Elizabeth, Anny, and Mary Rosario; and Mahru Ghashghaei.

Special thanks to our hardworking transcribers: Destiny Perez in Miami, Allison T. McFarlane in New York City, and Marissa Diggs in Oakes, North Dakota. Interns Aphya Sade Verna, Autumn C. McMillian, and Camila Fang were invaluable. We owe our appreciation to photographer Andrew Prise, who hit the streets of New York City with Tatsha and traveled to Harvard to meet Ron, in order to help us document our journey.

We talked to so many people for this book that it would be simply impossible to name all of them here. Although many of their names did not appear in the final draft, their insights were present. Some brilliant people, like a handyman named Kevin, explained what they thought went wrong in their childhoods that prevented them from becoming what they believe they should have been. Others spoke in detail about how high achievement happens. Among those, there were several standouts: Michelle and Austin Harton and their daughters, Marie and Renee; Mario Baeza (Ron's college classmate); Wayne Washington; Marsha Denise Gadsen (a participant in the How I Was Parented Project at Harvard); Janna Diggs; Tau Murapa; Lasaundra Jeter-Caldwell; Lisa Gressinger; and Crystal and Craig Clarkin and Carmen, their Yale-attending daughter (Tatsha's niece).

Maxine Roel's long conversations helped us understand the master parent's thoughtfulness. Ann Marie Thomas spent many cookouts politely answering probing questions about how her daughter, former *Essence* magazine editor Vanessa Deluca, turned out to be an academic star. Dr. Melissa Clarke offered insight into her fascinating experience of being a high school–age teenager at Harvard. Paula Penn-Nabrit, whose book *Morning by Morning* provided great understanding into how she and her late husband, Charles, homeschooled three high-achieving African American boys, answered every question asked or emailed to her. Her sons Charles, Damon, and Evans, too, took the time to sit and talk very candidly about their childhoods.

We must thank the participants of the Saturday Write Workshop in New York City, who for three years served as an unofficial focus group, loud critics, and fans: Maxine Roel, Anne Rourke, Jeremy Goldstein, Greg Basham, Ann Harson, Ashley Williams,

Roslyn Karpel, Dawn Rebecky, Payal Kaur, and one of Tatsha's oldest, dearest friends, Aliah Dorene Wright.

A loving thanks to our agent, Jeff Ourvan, who also happens to run the Write Workshops. That day you said the idea of the Formula was definitely a book, you set us on a long and magnificent journey. Thank you for your expert guidance.

We owe a special word of appreciation to Leah, our extremely patient editor. We can't thank you enough for your sharp skill, flexibility, your smiley emojis :), and kindness. How lucky were we that you were raising a very young and smart little boy while working on this project. To Glenn Yeffeth and everyone at BenBella, thank you for believing in this project—and in us.

From Tatsha:

First, I'd like to thank my coauthor, Ron Ferguson. I secretly wished to write a book with Ron, so it was a special surprise when he proposed that he should join me in writing *The Formula*. Logical in thought but with a big, beautiful, poetic voice and heart, Ron made this very long journey unforgettable—and divine.

I also want to thank all the people I dub my board of directors: my talented mother, Marcia Robertson (a strong writer and my first early-learning partner); my sister Carla (my second early-learning partner); my other sisters, Francine and Kyla (my two biggest fans) and Crystal and Kiara; my brothers, Victor and Tommy; and my sweet stepmom, Dottie, and father, Tony Upshaw. Others on the board: Kristal Brent-Zook, who gave me constant words of support; the talented Rosalind Bentley; Tamika Simmons; Toya Stewart; Joelle Williams; Ross Ellis; Jessica Jiji; Sebastian Rozec at A.O.C. in Manhattan; Jacqueline Flynn; and my niece, Mahalia Otshudy (you are a writer). I owe special thanks to Jill Smolowe; her husband, Robert F. Schwartz; and Jill's daughter, Becky Treen, for those thought-provoking dinners. Many thanks to my supportive comrades Carol Kelly, Kemba Dunham, Duchesne Drew, Bryan Denis, Francie Latour, Nina Malkin, Dee Depass, and the members of my large Kilgore family (I promise I'll make the next reunion). And a word of appreciation to my supporters on Facebook and Instagram, and to everyone at my writing haunts: Starbucks and Panera Bread, both on River Road in northern New Jersey; iSpresso at Park and Merge Café, both in Union City, New Jersey; the Wiawaka Holiday House at Lake George; WeWork in Brooklyn Heights; and green desk in DUMBO, Brooklyn.

Most important for me is my deeply supportive husband, Nico, who sparked the kernel of the Formula when he asked me to come watch an episode of *60 Minutes* back in 2003, and who kept encouraging me on the book even when I was overwhelmingly tired from sixteen-hour days of researching and writing. For three years, Nico allowed me to take over his home office. He cooked delicious Blue Apron meals, and did all the grocery shopping, laundry, and cleaning while also working long hours himself building his own business. Despite the occasional challenges, Nico stayed positive and did everything he could to ensure my passion for this book could burn bright.

From Ron:

Coauthoring this book has been the deepest collaboration of my life. With Tatsha in New York and me in Massachusetts, we have become alter egos. If asked which of us conceived a particular thought or wrote a particular paragraph, there's a good chance we wouldn't remember. Thanks, Tatsha, for being a brilliant partner!

To my dear colleagues Rob Ramsdell, Sara Phillips, Alka Pateriya, Jake Rowley, Jocelyn Friedlander, Mari Barrera, Haji Shearer, Jeff Howard, and Wendell Knox at Tripod Education Partners (tripoded.com), the Achievement Gap Initiative (agi.harvard.edu), and Boston Basics (bostonbasics.org), thanks for your understanding and patience over the past three years, during all those times I kept you waiting because I was working on this book. Thanks also for the thoughtful reviews you provided as Tatsha and I were finishing the book and thinking of reordering some chapters. My new friends Edyson Julio and Ruth Summers responded to that same request, providing similarly helpful feedback.

Finally, there is my family, who has taught me not just what it means to be loved, but also about the everyday complexities of family life that convinced me writing this book could be important. To my mother, Gloria; my sons, Danny and Darren, and nephew Marcus, whom we raised as their brother; my brothers, Kenny, Homer, and Steven; and all my other nieces, nephews, and in-laws, I say thank you. And to my wife, Helen, there is nothing I could say or write to capture what you mean to me or how helpful you've been not just lately, but throughout my life. With the book complete and our fortieth wedding anniversary coming one week from the day I write these words, let's go have some fun!

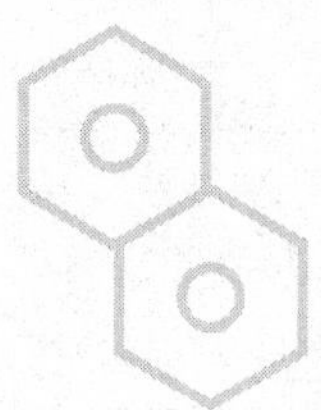

NOTES

Introduction

To see the way one Kentucky newspaper, the *Lexington Herald Leader*, announced Ryan Quarles's GOP win, visit: https://www.kentucky.com/news/politics-government/article44600505.html.

Time magazine's recognition of fourteen-year-old Sangu Delle was in the May 2005 issue.

The 2014 *Forbes* listing of "30 Most Promising Young African Entrepreneurs" is at https://www.forbes.com/sites/mfonobongnsehe/2014/02/04/30-most-promising-young-entrepreneurs-in-africa-2014/#10de964fdfe4.

Find Sangu Delle's TED Talk, titled "In Praise of Macro—Yes, Macro—Finance in Africa," at https://www.ted.com/talks/sangu_delle_in_praise_of_macro_yes_macro_finance_in_africa/discussion?quote=1725.

A May 2008 article in the *Harvard Crimson* featured Sangu Delle, "Learning to Aid a Continent: Some African Students Study with an Eye Toward Bettering Their Homelands": https://www.thecrimson.com/article/2008/5/1/learning-to-aid-a-continent-when/.

This chapter mentions a review in the *New York Times* that praised Maggie Young following her performance at Carnegie Hall. We have chosen not to include a link, as we changed her name and the reviewer's comments because Maggie worried her family might receive unwanted attention.

Chapter 1. The Mystery of Success

For one of the most famous scientific studies on twins raised apart, see: Bernard Devlin, Michael Daniels, and Kathryn Roeder (1997). "The Heritability of IQ." *Nature* 388:468–471. The authors conduct a meta-analysis of 212 previous twin studies and conclude that only about half of IQ is inherited, leaving the other half to be explained by parenting and other environmental conditions.

For a researcher who has studied twins and adoptees and concludes that adoptive parents contribute "a great deal" to how much education a child gets and how much income they earn, see: Bryce Sacerdote (2011). "Nature and Nurture Effects on Children's Outcomes: What Have We Learned from Studies of Twins and Adoptees?" *Handbook of Social Economics* (1):1–30.

For a widely cited study on how parenting and environment affect the expression of genetic potential, see: Michael J. Meaney (2001). "Maternal Care, Gene Expression, and the Transmission of Individual Differences in Stress Reactivity across Generations." *Annual Review of Neuroscience* 24:1161–1192.

On the development of differences in language processing abilities, see: Anne Fernald, Virginia Marchman, and Adriana Weisleder (2013). "SES Differences in Language Processing Skill and Vocabulary Are Evident at 18 Months." *Developmental Science* 16(2):234–248.

For a discussion of black box methodology in medical science, see: Marcia L. Meldrum (2000). "A Brief History of the Randomized Controlled Trial: From Oranges and Lemons to the Gold Standard." *Hematology/Oncology Clinics* 14(4):745–760. She laments the fact that when an experiment yields unexpected effects there is no way to understand the reason. The approach, she writes, "leaves the problem of constructing 'a rational therapeutics' unsolved."

For an authoritative tour of the research on the impact of parenting and caregiving in early childhood, see: Daniel P. Keating, editor (2011). *Nature and Nurture in Early Child Development*. New York: Cambridge University Press.

For videos and other material on the importance of parenting in shaping infant and toddler development, visit the Center for the Developing Child at Harvard website: https://developingchild.harvard.edu/.

Chapter 2. What We Mean by Success

For a lucid review of the research on human flourishing and well-being, see: Richard M. Ryan and Edward L. Deci (2001). "On Happiness and Human Potentials: A Review of Research on Hedonic and Eudaimonic Well-Being." *Annual Review of Psychology* 52:141–166.

References to Albert Einstein are based on:

Denis Brian (1996). *Einstein: A Life.* New York: John Wiley & Sons.

Jürgen Neffe (2005). *Einstein: A Biography* (translated into English in 2007 by Shelley Frisch). Baltimore: Johns Hopkins University Press.

Howard Gardner (1997). *Extraordinary Minds: Portraits of Exceptional Individuals and an Examination of Extraordinariness.* New York: Basic Books.

Walter Isaacson (2008). *Einstein: His Life and Universe.* New York: Simon & Schuster.

On the topic of *purpose*, see: William Damon (2009). *The Path to Purpose: How Young People Find Their Calling in Life.* New York: Simon & Schuster. Also on the role of purpose in youth development, see: William Damon, Jenni Menon, and Kendall Cotton Bronk (2003). "The Development of Purpose during Adolescence." *Applied Developmental Science* 7(3):119–128.

On the topic of *agency*, see:

Steven Hitlin and Glen H. Elder (2007). "Time, Self, and the Curiously Abstract Concept of Agency." *Sociological Theory* 25(2):17–191.

Albert Bandura (2001). "Social Cognitive Theory: An Agentic Perspective." *Annual Review of Psychology* 51:1–26.

Johnmarshall Reeve and Ching-Mei Tseng (2011). "Agency as a Fourth Aspect of Students' Engagement during Learning Activities." *Contemporary Educational Psychology* 36(2011):257–267.

Ronald F. Ferguson, with Sarah F. Phillips, Jacob F. S. Rowley, and Jocelyn W. Friedlander (2015). *The Influence of Teaching Beyond Standardized Test Scores: Engagement, Mindsets, and Agency.* Monograph from the Achievement Gap Initiative at Harvard University. Available at: http://agi.harvard.edu/projects/TeachingandAgency.pdf.

W. Joel Schneider's ideas on what smart is come from a blog post on the *Scientific American* website titled, "What Do IQ Tests Test?: Interview with Psychologist W. Joel Schneider." February 3, 2014. https://blogs.scientificamerican.com/beautiful-minds/what-do-iq-tests-test-interview-with-psychologist-w-joel-schneider/.

The quote from Howard Gardner regarding prodigies, "Even if one refused to believe in miracles . . . ," is from page 128 of his 1997 book *Extraordinary Minds: Portraits of Exceptional Individuals and an Examination of Extraordinariness.* New York: Basic Books.

On taxi drivers' memories and brain structure, see: Katherine Woollett and Eleanor Maguire (2011). "Acquiring 'the Knowledge' of London's Layout Drives Structural Brain Changes." *Current Biology* 21(24):2109–2114. For an earlier study of the topic by the same authors published in 2006, see: "London Taxi Drivers and Bus Drivers: A Structural MRI and Neuropsychological Analysis." *Hippocampus* 16(12):1091–1101.

Chapter 3. The Formula

The books Elizabeth Lee mentions in this chapter are:

Ezra Jack Keats (1967). *Peter's Chair.* New York: Scholastic.

P. D. Eastman (1960). *Are You My Mother?* New York: Penguin Random House.

Dr. Seuss (1960). *One Fish, Two Fish, Red Fish, Blue Fish.* New York: Penguin Random House.

Annette Lareau's work on "concerted cultivation" and "natural growth" parenting styles is presented in her 2011 book *Unequal Childhoods: Class, Race, and Family Life*. Los Angeles: University of California Press.

In 2011, Jacob E. Cheadle and Paul R. Amato used quantitative data from a large national sample, the Early Childhood Longitudinal Study, to test Lareau's findings for kindergarten and third graders. They found, as Lareau suggested, that socioeconomic status was the strongest predictor of the concerted cultivation parenting style. However, contrary to Lareau, they found that, even controlling for socioeconomic status, concerted cultivation was more common among whites than among blacks, Latinos, or Asians. See: Jacob E. Cheadle and Paul R. Amato (2011). "A Quantitative Assessment of Lareau's Qualitative Conclusions About Class, Race, and Parenting." *Journal of Family Issues* 32(5):679–706.

For the origin of Ginott's metaphor of a parent as a helicopter "hovering over" their child, see: Haim Ginott (1969). *Between Parent & Teenager*. New York: Macmillan. Social science research on the topic of helicoptering is rare, but one interesting study that finds a negative association between parental helicoptering and psychological well-being for college students is: Terri Lemoyne and Tom Buchanan (2011). "Does 'Hovering' Matter? Helicopter Parenting and Its Effect on Well-Being." *Sociological Spectrum* 31(4):399–418.

For Chua's book, see: Amy Chua (2011). *Battle Hymn of the Tiger Mother*. New York: Penguin Press.

For Su Yeong Kim and colleagues' three-wave longitudinal study of 444 Chinese American families, see: Su Yeong Kim, Yijie Wang, Diana Orozco-Lapray, Yishan Shen, and Mohammed Murtuza (2013). "Does 'Tiger Parenting' Exist? Parenting Profiles of Chinese Americans and Adolescent Developmental Outcomes." *Asian American Journal of Psychology* 4(1):7–18.

For a good overview of Diana Baumrind's model of parenting, see her 1996 paper "The Discipline Controversy Revisited." *Family Relations* 45(4):405–414. Also see: Laurence Steinberg (2001). "We Know Some Things: Parent-Adolescent Relationships in Retrospect and Prospect." *Journal of Research on Adolescence* 11(1):1–19.

Chapter 4. The Strategists

For research publications that provide insight into Lisa Son's parenting methods, see: Janet Metcalfe (2017). "Learning from Errors." *Annual Review of Psychology* 68(6):1–25; and Lisa K. Son and Mate Kornell (2010). "The Virtues of Ignorance." *Behavioural Processes* 83:207–212.

On Frederick Douglass as the most photographed American during the 1800s, see: John Stauffer (2015). *Picturing Frederick Douglass: An Illustrated Biography of the Nineteenth Century's Most Photographed American.* New York: W.W. Norton.

The video clip of the panel with Chuck Badger can be seen at: https://www.c-span.org/video/?416624-3/presidents-agenda.

For *Forbes*'s list of the most powerful women in the world, on which, in 2017, Susan Wojcicki was listed sixth, see: https://www.forbes.com/power-women/#982e315e252d.

For *Time*'s list of the most important inventions of 2008, on which Anne Wojcicki's genetic testing service ranked number one, see: http://content.time.com/time/specials/packages/article/0,28804,1852747_1854493_1854113,00.html.

The Anne Wojcicki quotation "I don't think we were ever intimidated by anyone" is from: http://time.com/4468480/how-to-raise-confident-daughters/.

Chapter 5. The Early-Learning Partner (Role #1)

On block play, also see: Dimitri A. Christakis, Frederick J. Zimmerman, and Michelle M. Garrison (2007). "Effect of Block Play on Language Acquisition and Attention in Toddlers." *Archives of Pediatric and Adolescent Medicine* 161(10):697–971. And, for a summary of the benefits of block play, see: Gwen Dewar (2016). "Why Toy Blocks Rock: The Science of Building and Construction Toys." Published online at: https://www.parentingscience.com/toy-blocks.html.

Find the MIT press release about the creation of the $5 million Lego Lab at: http://news.mit.edu/1999/lego.

See a video on the MIT Lego Lab and how it helps children become young scientists at: https://vimeo.com/143620419. The video shows children integrating the use of Lego blocks with computer programing to develop their own creations.

For the 2016 study from the University of Indiana, see: Sharlene Newman, Mitchel Hansen, and Arianna Gutierrez (2016). "An fMRI Study of the Impact of Block Building and Board Games on Spatial Ability." *Frontiers in Psychology* 7:1278.

For an article showing the importance of spatial reasoning on automotive design, see: https://www.torquenews.com/1080/how-car-design-works-start-finish.

On the value of adult-child interaction during early play, see: Ivanna K. Lukie, Sheri-Lynn Skwarchuk, Jo-Anne LeFevre, and Carla Sowinski (2013). "The Role of Child Interests and Collaborative Parent–Child Interactions in Fostering Numeracy and Literacy Development in Canadian Homes." *Early Childhood Education Journal* (2014) 42:251–259. Also see: Kenneth R. Ginsburg (2007). "The Importance of Play in Promoting Healthy Child Development and Maintaining Strong Parent-Child Bonds." *Pediatrics* 119(1):182–191.

Regarding how parental care affects migration of barnacle geese, see: Rudy M. Jonker, Marije W. Kuiper, Lysanne Snijders, Sipke E. Van Wieren, Ron C. Ydenberg, and Herbert H. T. Prins (2011). "Divergence in Timing of Parental Care and Migration in Barnacle Geese." *Behavioral Ecology* 21:326–331.

For a video of the death-defying leap of the barnacle goslings, see: http://www.bbc.com/earth/story/20141020-chicks-tumble-of-terror-filmed.

For more on Konrad Lorenz's work and perspectives, see his 1966 *Evolution and Modification of Behavior.* London: Methuen Publishing.

The story that Eugenia told neuropsychiatrist Dr. Bruce Perry and journalist Maia Szalavitz in an interview can be found on page 70 of their 2010 book, *Born for Love: Why Empathy Is Essential—and Endangered.* New York: HarperCollins.

The quotation "Although people don't have conscious memories of infancy . . ." is from page 48 of *Born for Love*, *op. cit.*

For the Germany study by Wermke and her colleagues of infants' cry patterns, see: Birgit Mampe, Angela D. Friederici, Anne Christophe, and Kathleen Wermke (2009). "Newborns' Cry Melody Is Shaped by Their Native Language." *Current Biology* 19(23):1994–1997.

On the ways that hearing stories can affect children's minds, see the *Buffer Social* blog article by Leo Widrich (2016). "The Science of Storytelling: What Listening to a Story Does to Our Brains," https://blog.bufferapp.com/science-of-storytelling-why-telling-a-story-is-the-most-powerful-way-to-activate-our-brains.

Raymond Mar's ideas concerning theories of mind are explained in his 2011 paper "The Neural Bases of Social Cognition and Story Comprehension." *Annual Review of Psychology* 62:103–134.

On social patterns and the recognition of social hierarchy, see: Hernando Santamaría-García, Miguel Burgaleta, and Nuria Sebastián-Gallés (2015). "Neuroanatomical Markers of Social Hierarchy Recognition in Humans: A Combined ERP/MRI Study." *The Journal of Neuroscience* 35(30):10843–10850.

The finding that third grade tends to be when students become conscious of whether they are ahead of, equal to, or behind their classmates academically comes from: Rhonda S. Weinstein, Herman H. Marshall, Lee Sharp, and Meryl Botkin (1987). "Pygmalion and the Student: Age and Classroom Differences in Children's Awareness of Teacher Expectations." *Child Development.* 58:1079–1092.

For a review of what neurobiologists have learned about the effects of early life experiences on brain development, see: Charles A. Nelson III and Margaret A. Sheridan (2011). "Lessons from Neuroscience Research for Understanding Causal Links between Family and Neighborhood Characteristics and Educational Outcomes." In Greg J. Duncan and Richard J. Murnane, eds., *Whither Opportunity? Rising Inequality, School, and Children's Life Chances*. New York: Russell Sage Foundation.

Chapter 6. The Flight Engineer (Role #2)

The Barack Obama quotation from *Essence* magazine is from an article entitled, "Teaching Our Children," by Angela Burt-Murray, Tatsha Robertson, and Cynthia Gordy, that appeared February 8, 2010.

The quote in this chapter from Urie Bronfenbrenner comes his *New York Times* obituary: http://www.nytimes.com/2005/09/27/nyregion/urie-bronfenbrenner-88-an-authority-on-child-development-dies.html?_r=0.

Urie Bronfenbrenner's classic book on social ecology is 1979's *The Ecology of Human Development*. Cambridge, MA: Harvard University Press. This chapter refers only to microecologies, which are social settings the developing child is a part of. However, Bronfenbrenner's framework includes three other levels: the mesoecology, which is the combination of all the microecologies and their interactions; the exoecology, which comprises settings like the local school board where the child is not an actor, but where decisions are made that affect the child's well-being; and the macroecology, which is not a place, but constitutes the norms and beliefs and the general culture that pervade the entire system. A parent can work strategically to influence how the parts of this ecological system affect their child.

The quotation from astronaut Luca Parmitano about the role of a flight engineer on the space station is from the video found at https://www.youtube.com/watch?v=QrKDL6mboc0.

On redshirting, see:

> Joe "The Nerd" Ferraro, who helps explain this type of classroom to parents, who, like Bob Senior, are often caught off guard: "What Is Transitional First and Why Do We Need It?" https://

www.huffingtonpost.com/joe-the-nerd-ferraro/what-is-transitional-firs_b_816271.html.

Daphna Bassock and Sean F. Reardon (2013). "Academic Redshirting in Kindergarten." *Educational Evaluation and Policy Analysis* 35(2):283–297.

A review by Brookings Institution researcher Michael Hansen, "To Redshirt or Not to Redshirt," in *US News*, June 16, 2016. https://www.usnews.com/opinion/articles/2016-06-16/how-much-does-it-benefit-a-child-to-delay-kindergarten-entry-for-a-year.

Sandra E. Black, Paul J. Devereux, and Kjell G. Salvanes (2011). "Too Young to Leave the Nest? The Effects of School Starting Age." *Review of Economics and Statistics* 93(2):455–467.

The German study on the relationship of independence to reading and math skills of third and fourth graders: is Greta J. Warner, Doris Fay, and Nadine Sporer (2017). "Relations Among Personal Initiative and the Development of Reading Strategy Knowledge and Reading Comprehension." *Frontline Learning Research* 5(2):1–23.

Chapter 7. Siblings

To learn more about Ronnie's grandmother Nana's mentor Jane Edna Hunter, see: https://en.wikipedia.org/wiki/Jane_Edna_Hunter and http://www.blackpast.org/aah/hunter-jane-edna-1882-1971.

The 2018 study of siblings in Sweden is: Sandra E. Black, Erik Grönqvist, and Björn Öckert (2018). "Born to Lead? The Effect of Birth Order on Noncognitive Abilities." *The Review of Economics and Statistics* 100(2): 274–286.

On ways that family environments influence siblings, see: Susan M. McHale, Kimberly A. Updegraff, and Shawn D. Whiteman (2010). "Sibling Relationships and Influences in Childhood and Adolescence." *Journal of Marriage and Family* 74:913–930; and Lois Wladis Hoffman (1991). "The Influence of the Family Environment on Personality: Accounting for Sibling Differences." *Psychological Bulletin* 110(2):187–203.

On ways that siblings may influence one another, see: Judy Dunn (1988). "Sibling Influences on Childhood Development." *Journal of Child Psychology and Psychiatry* 29(2):119–127. Also on birth order, see: Shawn D. Whiteman, Susan M. McHale, and Ann C. Crouter (2007). "Competing Processes of Sibling Influence: Observational Learning and Sibling Deidentification." *Social Development* 16(4):642–661. The latter authors identified a pattern they referred to as deidentification, in which younger siblings reported not wanting to be like their older siblings. However, this was much less common than identification.

Chapter 8. The Fixer (Role #3)

Find a video clip from the referenced segment of the 1978 *Superman* movie where he saves the train during an earthquake at: https://www.youtube.com/watch?v=Z5u1xq9MJyw.

The reference for the knowing-doing gap is: Jeffrey Pfeffer and Robert Sutton (2000). *The Knowing-Doing Gap.* Cambridge, MA: Harvard Business School Press.

There is no way of knowing what might have happened to Alfonso had his father allowed him to be punished for selling marijuana, but for research-based perspectives on the risks of disciplinary practices as predictors of later outcomes, see: Daniel J. Losen and Russell J. Skiba (2010). "Suspended Education: Urban Middle Schools in Crisis." The Civil Rights Project at UCLA and the Equity Project, Center for Evaluation and Education Policy, Indiana University. https://cloudfront.escholarship.org/dist/prd/content/qt8fh0s5dv/qt8fh0s5dv.pdf. Also see: Pedro A. Noguera (2003). "Schools, Prisons, and Social Implications of Punishment: Rethinking Disciplinary Practices." *Theory into Practice* 42(4): 341–350.

Chapter 9. The Revealer (Role #4)

The section on Einstein is based on the books cited under Chapter 2.

See the chapter by Charles A. Nelson III and Margaret A. Sheridan, cited under Chapter 5, for additional references relevant to child development during the preschool years.

The achievers tended to have dedicated places at home where they could study. For a perspective on designing a study space for a child, see: Catherine Godiva's December 2013 blog post "The Importance of a Dedicated Study Space." https://www.roomtogrow.co.uk/blog/the-importance-of-a-dedicated-study-space/.

For more on the topics of purpose and agency as discussed in this chapter, see the references on purpose and agency listed under Chapter 2.

For one of the most widely cited introductions to mastery orientation and associated achievement motivations, see: Carole Ames (1992). "Classrooms: Goals, Structures, and Student Motivation." *Journal of Educational Psychology* 84(3):261–271. While the title is focused on classrooms, the article is an excellent general treatment of the topic that is quite relevant for parenting.

For a study of engagement in the types of activities that the Revealer seeks for the child—in other words, things that are voluntary, interesting, and challenging—see: Sami Abuhamdeh and Mihaly Csikszentmihalyi (2011). "The Importance of Challenge for the Enjoyment of Intrinsically Motivated, Goal-Directed Activities." *Personality and Social Psychology Bulletin* 38:317–330.

For the experiment by Daphna Oyserman, see: Daphna Oyserman, Deborah Bybee, and Kathy Terry (2006). "Possible Selves and Academic Outcomes: How and When Possible Selves Impel Action." *Journal of Personality and Social Psychology* 9(1):188–204.

Chapter 10. The Philosopher (Role #5)

There are a number of available translations of the Bhagavad Gita; for example, see: A. C. Bhaktivedanta Swami Prabhupada (1989). *Bhagavad Gita As It Is.* Los Angeles: Bhaktivedanta Book Trust International.

The authors would like to make clear that while it is certainly true that the three philosophical themes in this chapter are common in texts throughout history, we include them in this book because they emerged organically from the interviews with the achievers and their parents. We neither anticipated nor preselected them based on any particular text or our predilections.

It may be difficult to believe that Sangu's father, Dr. Delle, really spoke with his small child about sophisticated philosophy, but he had experienced it himself: "I had a maternal uncle who was a Catholic catechist and he was the only person who treated me as an adult and taught me so much. At the time, we were not Catholics or Christians—we had our own traditional religion." Dr. Delle said of his children, "My main aim was to let them have an open mind on issues, irrespective of age . . . I never forced them to follow a specific course in an argument, but to be free to explore different aspects of an issue . . . and leave them free to decide . . . I also encouraged [Sangu] to always have an opinion, irrespective of what others thought (including what I think as his father) . . . Sangu picked this up very well as a young child." Continuing, "I think it's never too early to start thinking deeply about these issues. He and I would discuss many philosophers such as Bertrand Russell, Socrates, and the Skeptics. I taught him that he needs to develop his own philosophy and be guided by that . . . I hoped philosophy would teach him to think freely and to think critically. The real leaders in the world are the philosophers; they've had the greatest influence on us."

For the *New York Times*'s coverage of Bree Newsome's removal of the Confederate flag from the South Carolina statehouse, see: Kenneth R. Rosen, "2 Charged in Confederate Flag Removal at South Carolina Capitol." *New York Times*, June 27, 2015. https://www.nytimes.com/2015/06/28/us/2-charged-in-confederate-flag-removal-at-south-carolina-capitol.html.

Chapter 11. The Model (Role #6)

Albert Bandura was the founding father of the body of research called "social learning theory." See: Albert Bandura (1971). *Social Learning*

Theory. New York: General Learning Press. On the second page of the book, Bandura writes: "Traditional theories of learning generally depict behavior as the product of directly experienced response consequences. In actuality, virtually all learning phenomena resulting from direct experiences can occur on a vicarious basis through observation of other people's behavior and its consequences for them. Man's capacity to learn by observation enables him to acquire large, integrated units of behavior by example without having to build up the patterns gradually by tedious trial and error." The simple implication most relevant for this book, specifically, is that people can learn from observing others who, purposefully or not, serve as models. This learning is more than just a matter of imitation; the child observes the positive or negative consequences of the model's actions and uses that information in making their own decisions.

The discussion of Derek Jeter and his father is based on an interview by Tim Elmore with Charles Jeter (2015). "Eight Lessons About Leading Kids from Derek Jeter's Dad Charles." See: https://growingleaders.com/blog/eight-lessons-leading-kids-derek-jeters-dad/.

There are many books and articles about the *Plessy v. Ferguson* Supreme Court case. See, for example: Williamjames Hull Hoffer (2012). *Plessy v. Ferguson: Race and Inequality in Jim Crow America*. Lawrence: University Press of Kansas.

The reference to Daphna Oyserman's notion of "negative possible selves" is developed in her article cited here under Chapter 9.

Chapter 12. The Negotiator (Role #7)

For an introduction to basic ideas about negotiation, including the "best alternative to a negotiated agreement" (BATNA), see the still-popular classic on negotiation: Roger Fisher and William L. Ury (1983). *Getting to Yes*. New York: Penguin Books.

The reference to Einstein throwing a chair at his piano teacher is from Chapter 1 of Denis Brian (1996). *Einstein: A Life*. New York: John Wiley & Sons.

The quotation by Albert Einstein's son Hans Albert is taken from page 202 of Alice Calaprice (2011). *The Ultimate Quotable Einstein*. Princeton, NJ: Princeton University Press.

References to Amy Chua and tiger parenting are based on her book *Battle Hymn of the Tiger Mother*, cited under Chapter 2. The list of things that she would not allow comes from the first two pages of Chapter 1.

The First Amendment to the United States Constitution is the following: *Congress shall make no law respecting an establishment of religion, or prohibiting the free exercise thereof; or abridging the freedom of speech, or of the press; or the right of the people peaceably to assemble, and to petition the Government for a redress of grievances.*

The quotation about imposing standards on Asian children "not to dominate the child, but rather to assure the familial and societal goals . . ." is from page 1113 of: Ruth K. Chao (1994). "Beyond Parental Control and Authoritarian Parenting Style: Understanding Chinese Parenting Through the Cultural Notion of Training." *Child Development* 65:1111–1120.

Another study by Ruth Chao found that "first-generation Chinese adolescents more consistently differed from European Americans in the effects of authoritative parenting and closeness than did second-generation Chinese adolescents. [Findings] for second-generation Chinese primarily ranked between those of first-generation Chinese and those of European Americans." From page 1842 of: Ruth K. Chao (2001). "Extending Research on the Consequences of Parenting Style for Chinese Americans and European Americans." *Child Development* 72(6):1832–1843.

Chao (2001), just cited, also quoted on page 1842 a Chinese parent explaining the incentives that Chinese children have to do well in school: "In Chinese families, the child's personal academic achievement is the value and honor of the whole family. If you fail [in] school, you bring embarrassment to the family and lose face. If you do good, you bring honor to the family and do not lose face. A lot of value is placed on the child to do well for the family." The power of this value structure appears to diminish somewhat after the first generation in the United States.

Just in case these issues seem cut and dried, it is worth noting that there is debate among scholars of Chinese culture about the proper interpretations of Confucian teachings. See, for example: David Wong (2017). *Chinese Ethics.* Stanford Encyclopedia of Philosophy, published by the Metaphysics Research Lab, Center for the Study of Language and Information, Stanford University. On page 20 of the text, Wong points out that traditional interpretations of Confucius may overstate the intended degree of obedience, and that there are higher moral values that should guide decisions, which may require disobedience to parents.

The quote about tiger parenting versus supportive parenting, "It is actually supportive parenting, not tiger parenting, which is associated with the best developmental outcomes . . ." is from page 16 of Su Yeong Kim et al. "Does 'Tiger Parenting' Exist?" cited under Chapter 3.

This chapter mentions Mahru Ghashghaei, an Iranian-Muslim woman who, along with her husband, raised her son Troy in both the United States and Iran. Mahru wrote a self-published book, called *Nine Rubies*, about her life in revolutionary Iran. For more information on *Nine Rubies* and the authors, see: http://www.ninerubiesthebook.com/. For a video of Mahru (along with her Jewish American friend and "as told to" co-author, Susan Snyder) being interviewed by a television anchor: https://www.youtube.com/watch?v=fJE4XZP6oOk.

Chapter 13. Mastering Hurdles

Friedrich Nietzsche's famous line is from *Die Götzen-Dämmerung—Twilight of the Idols,* published in 1895. A translation by Walter Kaufmann and R. J. Hollingdale is available online at http://www.handprint.co/SC/NIE/GotDamer.html.

The Carol Dweck book Rob refers to is her 2006 *Mindset: The New Psychology of Success.* New York: Ballantine Books.

The article that finds a relationship between parents' reactions to failure and the child's development of growth mindset is: Kyla Haimovitz and Carol S. Dweck (2016). "Parents' Views of Failure Predict Children's Fixed and Growth Intelligence Mind-Sets." *Psychological Science* 27(6):559–569.

Research on resilience investigates why certain people facing adversity or "risk factors" come out fine or even stronger, while others suffer setbacks they may never overcome. See: Marc A. Zimmerman, Sarah A. Stoddard, Andria B. Eisman, Cleopatra H. Caldwell, Sophie M. Aiyer, and Alison Miller (2013). "Adolescent Resilience: Promotive Factors That Inform Prevention." *Child Development Perspectives* 7(4):215–220. In Maya's example, the resilience cultivated by the way she was raised gave her what experts call "promotive resources" that helped her bounce back from debilitating despair to get her college applications completed in time.

The social science research by David Yeager and colleagues on the importance of social belonging is exemplified by: David S. Yeager, Gregory M. Walton, Shannon T. Brady, Ezgi N. Akcinar, David Paunesku, Laura Keane, Donald Kamentz, Gretchen Ritter, Angela Lee Duckworth, Robert Urstein, Eric M. Gomez, Hazel Rose Markus, Geoffrey L. Cohen, and Carol S. Dweck (2016). "Teaching a Lay Theory Before College Narrows Achievement Gaps at Scale." *Proceedings of the National Academy of Sciences* 113(24):E3341–E3348.

The book about which Jarell challenged his teacher was: Nathaniel Hawthorne (1850). *The Scarlet Letter.* Reprint editions are available from several publishers.

Angela Duckworth's 2016 book is *Grit: The Power of Passion and Perseverance.* New York: Scribner.

For more on mastery orientation, see the late Carol Midgley's edited 2002 volume that addresses mastery orientation and related goal structures: *Goals, Goal Structures, and Patterns of Adaptive Learning.* New York: Routledge. The ideas in that volume comprise foundations for current-day emphases on growth mindset and grit. For another foundational paper, see: Carol S. Dweck (1986). "Motivational Processes Affecting Learning." *American Psychologist* 41(10):1040–1048.

The emphasis on confidence in this chapter aligns with the concept of *self-efficacy* in motivational psychology. For the classic reference on the topic, see: Albert Bandura (1982). "Self-Efficacy Mechanism in Human Agency." *American Psychologist* 37(2):122–147.

For research on purpose, see: William Damon (2009), *The Path to Purpose*, and William Damon, Jenni Menon, and Kendall Cotton Bronk (2003), "The Development of Purpose During Adolescence," both cited under Chapter 2.

Note that while Maggie Young's name is disguised, her teacher's name is not.

Chapter 14. The GPS (Role #8)

The book that the Malveaux family read was: Susan Jeffers (1987). *Feel the Fear . . . and Do It Anyway*. New York: Random House.

A July 2013 CNN feature video of Myrna Malveaux and her family coping with ALS can be found at: https://www.cnn.com/2013/07/01/health/iyw-als/index.html.

To learn more about the DynaVox technologies that enabled Myrna Malveaux to continue communicating as her ALS progressed, visit: https://www.tobiidynavox.com/products/devices/.

Conclusion: The Formula's Secret

Marissa Diggs, the North Dakota honor student who was inspired to apply to Harvard while transcribing interviews for this book, was named one of 157 Presidential Scholars in the nation. The article in her local newspaper, *The Dickinson Press,* announcing the award can be found at: https://www.thedickinsonpress.com/news/education/4448446-four-nd-students-named-us-presidential-scholars.

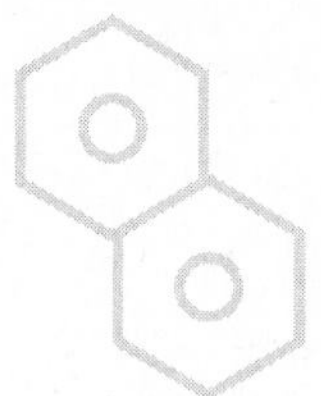

INDEX

ABOUT THE AUTHORS

Ronald F. Ferguson, PhD, is an MIT-trained economist who focuses on economic, social, and educational challenges. He has been on the faculty at Harvard's John F. Kennedy School of Government since 1983, after teaching at Brandeis and Brown Universities. In 2014, he cofounded Tripod Education Partners (tripoded.com), which provides survey research services to school systems, and shifted into an adjunct role at the Kennedy School, where he remains a faculty associate at the Malcolm Wiener Center for Social Policy and faculty director of the university-wide Achievement Gap Initiative (AGI).

During the 1980s and '90s Ron focused much of his attention on economic and community development. That work culminated in the social science synthesis volume *Urban Problems and Community Development* (1999), which remains an important text in graduate policy courses.

By the late 1980s, skill disparities were contributing to growing wage gaps between racial and ethnic groups, so his work expanded to education and youth development. In 2007, Harvard Education Press published his book *Toward Excellence with Equity: An Emerging Vision for Closing the Achievement Gap.* A February 2011 profile in the *New York Times* stated, “There is no one in America who knows more about the gap than Ronald Ferguson.”

Ron’s current focus is an early-childhood parenting initiative that grew out of the AGI. It began as the Boston Basics Campaign (bostonbasics.org), but is now a multi-city learning network with Basics campaigns in thirty cities, towns, and counties across eleven states.

Ron holds an undergraduate degree from Cornell University and a PhD from MIT, both in economics. He has been happily married for forty years and raised two adult sons and a nephew.

Tatsha Robertson is an award-winning multimedia editor and writer with more than twenty years of experience handling investigative, feature, and news stories for leading magazines, social media outlets, and newspapers. She was the first female New York City bureau chief and national rover for the *Boston Globe*. The *Boston Globe*’s Spotlight team both acknowledged Tatsha’s help the day they won the Pulitzer for their stories on church sex abuse and mentioned her in the acknowledgments of their book.

As deputy editor at *Essence* and interim managing editor of Essence.com, Tatsha pioneered *Essence* magazine’s focus on investigative and news articles. Her work there, including her interview on parenting with former president Barack Obama, led to the positioning of the magazine as a significant authority and voice on news. Most recently, she was a senior editor on the crime beat at *People*, where she led a team of veteran reporters on many major national stories. She also coauthored the true crime work *Media Circus* (BenBella, 2015) with Kim Goldman.

The founder of The Ordinary Genius Project blog, Tatsha holds a master's degree in journalism from The Ohio State University and has been an adjunct professor of journalism at New York University since 2005. Along with other writing and social media projects, Tatsha has nearly completed a speculative medical/religious thriller she's been writing since 2012 at the Write Workshop in New York City.

She lives in Weehawken, New Jersey, with her husband, Nico.